Praise for *Agile Estimating and Planning*

"Traditional, deterministic approaches to planning and estimating simply don't cut it on the slippery slopes of today's dynamic, change-driven projects. Mike Cohn's breakthrough book gives us not only the philosophy, but also the guidelines and a proven set of tools that we need to succeed in planning, estimating, and scheduling projects with a high uncertainty factor. At the same time, the author never loses sight of the need to deliver business value to the customer each step of the way."

—Doug DeCarlo, author of *eXtreme Project Management: Using Leadership, Principles and Tools to Deliver Value in the Face of Volatility* (Jossey-Bass, 2004)

"We know how to build predictive plans and manage them. But building plans that only estimate the future and then embrace change, challenge most of our training and skills. In *Agile Estimating and Planning*, Mike Cohn once again fills a hole in the Agile practices, this time by showing us a workable approach to Agile estimating and planning. Mike delves into the nooks and crannies of the subject and anticipates many of the questions and nuances of this topic. Students of Agile processes will recognize that this book is truly about agility, bridging many of the practices between Scrum and ExtremeProgramming."

—Ken Schwaber, Scrum evangelist, Agile Alliance cofounder, and signatory to the Agile Manifesto

"In *Agile Estimating and Planning*, Mike Cohn has, for the first time, brought together most everything that the Agile community has learned about the subject. The book is clear, well organized, and a pleasant and valuable read. It goes into all the necessary detail, and at the same time keeps the reader's burden low. We can dig in as deeply as we need to, without too much detail before we need it. The book really brings together everything we have learned about Agile estimation and planning over the past decade. It will serve its readers well."

—Ron Jeffries, www.XProgramming.com, author of *Extreme Programming Installed* (Addison-Wesley, 2001) and *Extreme Programming Adventures in C#* (Microsoft Press, 2004)

"*Agile Estimating and Planning* provides a view of planning that's balanced between theory and practice, and it is supported by enough concrete experiences to lend it credibility. I particularly like the quote 'planning is a quest for value.' It points to a new, more positive attitude toward planning that goes beyond the 'necessary evil' view that I sometimes hold."

—Kent Beck, author of *Extreme Programming Explained, Second Edition* (Addison-Wesley, 2005)

"Up-front planning is still the most critical part of software development. Agile software development requires Agile planning techniques. This book shows you how to employ Agile planning in a succinct, practical, and easy-to-follow manner."

—Adam Rogers, Ultimate Software

"We are true believers in the Agile methods described in this book, and have experienced a substantially positive impact from their implementation and continued use. I would highly recommend this book to anyone interested in making their software development more practical and effective."

—Mark M. Gutrich, President and CEO, Fast 401k, Inc.

study so the reader can relate the information to their own situation. Unless you are already an expert Agile planner and estimator, this book is for you."

—Alan Shalloway, CEO, Senior Consultant, Net Objectives, and coauthor of *Design Patterns Explained, Second Edition* (Addison-Wesley, 2005)

"Although I had plenty of XP experience before trying out Mike Cohn's Agile planning practices, the effectiveness of the practical and proven techniques in this book blew me away! The book recognizes that people, not tools or processes, produce great software, and that teams benefit most by learning about their project and their product as they go. The examples in the book are concrete, easily grasped, and simply reek of common sense. This book will help teams (whether Agile or not) deliver more value, more often, and have fun doing it! Whether you're a manager or a programmer, a tester or a CEO, part of an Agile team, or just looking for a way to stamp out chaos and death marches, this book will guide you."

—Lisa Crispin, coauthor of *Testing Extreme Programming* (Addison-Wesley, 2003)

"Mike Cohn does an excellent job demonstrating how an Agile approach can address issues of risk and uncertainty in order to provide more meaningful estimates and plans for software projects."

—Todd Little, Senior Development Manager, Landmark Graphics

"Mike Cohn explains his approach to Agile planning, and shows how 'critical chain' thinking can be used to effectively buffer both schedule and features. As with *User Stories Applied*, this book is easy to read and grounded in real-world experience."

—Bill Wake, author of *Refactoring Workbook* (Addison-Wesley, 2003)

"Mike brings this book to life with real-world examples that help reveal how and why an Agile approach works for planning software development projects. This book has great breadth, ranging from the fundamentals of release planning to advanced topics such as financial aspects of prioritization. I can see this book becoming an invaluable aid to Agile project managers, as it provides a wealth of practical tips such as how to set iteration length and boot-strap velocity, and communicate progress."

—Rachel Davies, Independent Consultant

"There has been a need for a solid, pragmatic book on the long-term vision of an Agile Project for project managers. *Agile Estimating and Planning* addresses this need. It's not theory—this book contains project-tested practices that have been used on Agile projects. As Mike's test subjects, we applied these practices to the development of video games (one of the most unpredictable project environments you can imagine) with success."

—Clinton Keith, Chief Technical Officer, High Moon Studios

"When I first heard Mike Cohn speak, I was impressed by a rare combination of qualities: deep experience and understanding in modern iterative and Agile methods; a drive to find and validate easy, high-impact solutions beyond the status quo of traditional (usually ineffective) methods; and the passion and clarity of a natural coach. These qualities are evident in this wonderful, practical guide. I estimate you won't be disappointed in studying and applying his advice."

—Craig Larman, Chief Scientist, Valtech, and author of *Applying UML and Patterns, Third Edition* (Prentice Hall, 2005) and *Agile and Iterative Development* (Addison-Wesley, 2004)

Agile Estimating and Planning

The Robert C. Martin Series

Visit **informit.com/martinseries** for a complete list of available publications.

The Robert C. Martin Series is directed at software developers, team-leaders, business analysts, and managers who want to increase their skills and proficiency to the level of a Master Craftsman. The series contains books that guide software professionals in the principles, patterns, and practices of programming, software project management, requirements gathering, design, analysis, testing and others.

Agile Estimating and Planning

Mike Cohn

Prentice Hall Professional Technical Reference

Upper Saddle River, NJ • Boston • Indianapolis • San Francisco
New York • Toronto • Montreal • London • Munich • Paris • Madrid
Capetown • Sydney • Tokyo • Singapore • Mexico City

The publisher offers excellent discounts on this book when ordered in quantity for bulk purchases or special sales, which may include electronic versions and/or custom covers and content particular to your business, training goals, marketing focus, and branding interests. For more information, please contact:

    U. S. Corporate and Government Sales, (800) 382-3419
    corpsales@pearsontechgroup.com

For sales outside the U. S., please contact:

    International Sales
    international@pearsoned.com

Visit us on the Web: www.phptr.com

Library of Congress Cataloging-in-Publication Data

Cohn, Mike, 1962-
    Agile estimating and planning / Mike Cohn.
        p.   cm.
    Includes bibliographical references and index.
    ISBN 0-13-147941-5 (pbk. : alk. paper)
     1. Computer software—Development. I. Title.
    QA76.76.D47C6427 2005
    005.1—dc22   2005023257

ISBN 0-13-147941-5
Text printed in the United States on recycled paper at Donnelley in Crawfordsville, In.
15   16

For Laura, with no room for doubt.

Contents

Part VII: A Case Study   259

About the Author

Mike Cohn is the founder of Mountain Goat Software, a process and project management consultancy and training firm. Mike specializes in helping companies adopt and improve their use of agile processes and techniques in order to build extremely high performance development organizations. In addition to this book, he is the author of *User Stories Applied for Agile Software Development* as well as books on Java and C++ programming. With more than twenty years of experience, Mike has previously been a technology executive in companies of various sizes, from start-up to Fortune 40. He has also written articles for *Better Software, IEEE Computer, Cutter IT Journal, Software Test and Quality Engineering, Agile Times,* and the *C/C++ Users Journal.* Mike is a frequent speaker at industry conferences, is a founding member of the Agile Alliance, and serves on its board of directors. He is a Certified ScrumMaster Trainer and a member of the IEEE Computer Society and the ACM.

For more information, visit www.mountaingoatsoftware.com or email him at mike@mountaingoatsoftware.com.

Foreword

Everywhere in the agile world I hear the same questions:

◆ How do I plan for large teams?

◆ What size iteration should we use?

◆ How should I report progress to management?

◆ How do I prioritize stories?

◆ How do I get the big picture of the project?

These questions, and many others, are skillfully addressed in this book. If you are a project manager, project lead, developer, or director, this book gives you the tools you need to estimate, plan, and manage agile projects of virtually any size.

I have known Mike Cohn for five years. I met him shortly after the Agile Manifesto was signed. Mike joined the Agile Alliance with a unique enthusiasm and energy. Any project he took on, he completed, and completed well. He was visible, and he was helpful. He very quickly became indispensable to the fledgling organization.

Now he has put the same level of competence, thoroughness, and energy into this book. And it shows. It shows big time.

It shows, because this book gives advice that is innately practical. This is not a book of theoretical abstractions. As a reader, you will not be spending your time in the clouds, looking at the problems at the 30,000 foot level. Instead, Mike provides concrete practices, techniques, tools, charts, formulae, and—best of all —cogent advice. This book is a how-to manual for estimating and planning.

Laced throughout the book are anecdotes that expose Mike's experience in using the techniques and tools he is describing. He tells you when they have worked for him, and when they haven't. He tells you what can go wrong, and what can go right. He makes no promises, offers no silver bullet, provides no guarantee. Yet at the same time he leaves you with little doubt that he is offering a large measure of his own hard-won experience.

There have been many books that have touched upon the topics of agile estimation and planning. Indeed, there have been a few that have made it their primary topic. But none have matched the depth and utility of this book, which covers the topic so completely, and so usefully, that I think it is bound to be regarded as the definitive work.

OK, I know I'm gushing, but I'm excited. I'm excited that so many long-standing questions have finally been answered with sufficient competence. I'm excited that I now have a tool I can give to my clients when they ask the hard questions. I'm excited that this book is ready, and that you are about to read it.

I am pleased and honored to have this book in my series. I think it's a winner.

Robert C. Martin
Series Editor

Foreword

In reading a book or manuscript for the first time I always ask myself the same question, "What is the author adding to the state of the art on this subject?" In Mike's case the answer is twofold: His book adds to our knowledge of "how" to do estimating and planning, and it adds to our knowledge of "why" certain practices are important.

Agile planning is deceptive. At one level, it's pretty easy—create a few story cards, prioritize them, allocate them to release iterations, then add additional detail to get a next iteration plan. You can show a team the basics of planning in a couple of hours, and they can actually turn out a tolerable plan (for a small project) in a few more hours. Mike's book will greatly help teams move from producing tolerable plans to producing very good plans. I'm using my words carefully here—I didn't say a great plan, because as Mike points out in this book, the difference between a good (enough) plan and a great plan probably isn't worth the extra effort.

My early thoughts about Mike's book have to do with the concept of agile planning itself. I'm always amused, and sometimes saddened, by the lack of understanding about agile planning. We hear criticisms like "agile project teams don't plan," or "agile teams won't commit to dates and features." Even Barry Boehm and Richard Turner got it wrong in *Balancing Agility and Discipline: A Guide for the Perplexed* (Addison-Wesley, 2004) when they talk about plan-driven versus agile methods. Actually, Boehm and Turner got the idea right, but the terms wrong. By plan-driven they actually mean "greatly weighting the balance of anticipation versus adaptation toward anticipation," while in agile methods the weighting is the opposite. The problem with the words "plan-driven" versus "agile" is that it sends entirely the wrong message—that agile teams don't plan. Nothing could be further from the state of the practice. Mike's book sends the right message—planning is an integral part of any agile project. The book contains a wealth of ideas about why planning is so important and how to plan effectively.

First, agile teams do a lot of planning, but it is spread out much more evenly over the entire project. Second, agile teams squarely face the critical factor that many non-agile teams ignore—uncertainty. Is planning important?—absolutely. Is adjusting the plan as knowledge is gained and uncertainty reduced important?—absolutely. I've gone into too many organizations where making outlandish early commitments, and then failing to meet those commitments, was acceptable, while those who tried to be realistic (and understanding uncertainty) were branded as "not getting with the program," or "not being team players." In these companies failure to deliver seems to be acceptable, whereas failure to commit (even to outlandish objectives) is unacceptable. The agile approach, as Mike so ably describes, is focused on actually delivering value and not on making outrageous and unachievable plans and commitments. Agile developers essentially say: We will give you a plan based on what we know today; we will adapt the plan to meet your most critical objective; we will adapt the project and our plans as we both move forward and learn new information; we expect you to understand what you are asking for—that flexibility to adapt to changing business conditions and absolute conformance to original plans are incompatible objectives. *Agile Estimating and Planning* addresses each of those statements.

Returning to the critical issue of managing uncertainty, Mike does a great job of looking at how an agile development process works to reduce ends uncertainty (what do we really want to build) and means uncertainty (how are we going to build it), concurrently. Many traditional planners don't understand a key concept—you can't "plan" away uncertainty. Plans are based on what we know at a given point in time. Uncertainty is another way of expressing what we don't know—about the ends or the means. For most uncertainties (lack of knowledge) the only way to reduce the uncertainty and gain knowledge is to execute—to do something, to build something, to simulate something—and then get feedback. Many project management approaches appear to be "plan, plan, plan-do." Agile approaches are "plan-do-adapt," "plan-do-adapt." The higher a project's uncertainties, the more critical an agile approach is to success.

I'd like to illustrate the "how's" and "why's" of Mike's book by looking at Chapters 4 and 5, which detail how to estimate story points or ideal days and provide an explanation of the pros and cons of each. While I have used both approaches with clients, Mike's words crystallized my thinking about the bene-fits of story-point estimation, and I realized that story points are part of an evo-lution, an evolution toward simplicity. Software development organizations have long looked for an answer to the question, "How big is this piece of software." A home builder can do some reasonable estimating based on square footage. While estimates from builders may vary, the size is fixed (although finish work, mate-rial specifications, and more will also impact the estimates) and remains a con-stant. Software developers have long searched for such a measurement.

In software development we first utilized lines-of-code to size the product (this measure still has its uses today). For much day-to-day planning, lines-of-code proved to be of limited use for a variety of reasons, including the amount of up-front work required to estimate them. Next on the scene came function points (and several similar ideas). Function points eliminated a number of the problems with lines-of-code, but still required a significant amount of up-front work to calculate (you had to estimate inputs, outputs, files, and so on). But what dooms function points from widespread use is their complexity. My guess is that as the complexity of counting has gone up—a quick perusal of the Interna-tional Function Point User Group (IFPUG) website indicates the degree of that complexity—the usage in the general population has gone down.

However, the need to estimate the "size" of a software project has not dimin-ished. The problem with both historical measures is twofold—they are complex to calculate and they are based on a waterfall approach to development. We still need a size measure, we just need one that is simple to calculate and applicable without going through the entire requirements and design phases.

The two critical differences between story points and either lines-of-code or function points are that they are simpler to calculate and they can be calculated much earlier. Why are they simpler? Because they are based on relative size more than absolute size. Why can they be calculated earlier? Because they are based on relative size more than absolute size. As Mike points out, story-point estimating is about sitting around discussing stories (gaining shared knowledge) and guestimating the relative story size. Relative sizing, as opposed to absolute sizing, goes remarkably quickly. Furthermore, after a few iterations of sizing and delivering, the accuracy of a team's guestimates improves significantly. Mike's description of both the "how" and the "why" of story-point versus ideal days esti-mating provides keen insight into this critical topic.

Another example of Mike's thoroughness shows up in Chapters 9 to 11, on the prioritization of stories. Mike isn't content with telling us to do the highest value stories first, he actually delves into the key aspects of value: financial benefits, cost, innovation/knowledge, and risk. He carefully defines each of these aspects of value (including a primer on Net Present Value, Internal Rate of Return, and other financial analysis tools), and then provides several schemes (with varying levels of simplicity) for weighting decisions using these different aspects of value.

Often, people new to agile development think that if you are doing the twelve or nineteen or eight practices of a particular methodology that you are therefore Agile, or Extreme, or Crystal Clear, or whatever. But in reality, you are Agile, Extreme, or otherwise when you know enough about the practices to adapt them to the reality of your own specific situation. Continuous learning and adaptation are core to agile development. What Mike does so well in this book is provide us with the ideas and experience that help take our agile estimating and planning practices to this next level of sophistication. Mike tells us "how" in depth—for example, the material on estimating in story points and ideal days. Mike tells us "why" in depth—for example the pros and cons of both story points and ideal days. While he usually gives us his personal recommendation (he prefers story points), he provides enough information so we feel confident in tailoring practices to specific situations ourselves.

So, this, in the end, identifies Mike's significant contribution to the state of the art—he helps us think through estimating and planning practices at a new depth of knowledge and experience (the how) and then helps us frame decisions about using this new knowledge in adapting these practices to new, unique, or merely specific situations (the why). Of the half-dozen books I regularly recommend to clients, Mike has written two of them. *Agile Estimating and Planning* goes on my "must read" list for those wanting to understand the state of the art in this aspect of agile project management.

Jim Highsmith
Agile Practice Director, Cutter Consortium
Flagstaff, Arizona
August 2005

Foreword

"Agile development won't work at Yahoo! except maybe on small tactical projects, because teams don't do any planning and team members can't estimate their own work. They need to be told what to do."

This is a real quote and something I've heard more than once since I began guiding the rollout of agile at Yahoo! People who don't understand the concepts of agile development think that it's simply a case of eliminating all documentation and planning, giving teams a license to hack. The reality could not be further from the truth.

"Teams don't do any planning." Those who say this forget that an agile team spends half a day every other week coming up with a list of tasks they'll perform in order to deliver some user-valued functionality at the end of the two weeks. That teams spread planning out across a project, rather than doing it all up front, is seen as a lack of planning. It's not, and agile teams at Yahoo! are creating products that please our product managers far more than traditional teams ever did.

"Team members can't estimate their own work and need to be told what to do." This is a classic misperception. Giving a product or project manager sage-like qualities to be able to foresee what others, who are experts in their own work, can really deliver is business suicide. Often this approach is really a way of saying yes to the business when asked to deliver on unrealistic goals. Team members are then forced to work around the clock and cut corners. And we wonder why people are burnt out and morale is so low in our industry.

Estimating and planning are among the topics I get the most questions about, especially from new teams. Having a simple approach to planning, not only for an iteration but for an entire project is invaluable. Product managers have to be concerned with meeting revenue goals and having a predictable release plan. Teams can still be flexible and change course as desired, but it's important to have a roadmap to follow. It's not enough to go fast if you are heading in the wrong direction. Learning how to estimate and plan are some of the most important ingredients for success if you hope to successfully implement agile in your organization.

Mike's estimating and planning class is the most popular of the agile classes we run at Yahoo! It gives teams the skills and tools they need to do just the right amount of planning to optimize results. If you follow Mike's advice, does it really work? Yes. The success of agile in Yahoo! has been incredible. I've had teams return from Mike's class and immediately put his advice into action. We are getting products to market faster and teams genuinely love the agile approach.

Why are agile estimating and planning methods more effective than traditional methods? They concentrate on delivering value and establishing trust between the business and the project teams. Keeping everything highly transparent, and letting the business know of any changes as they come up, means that the business can adapt quickly to make the best decisions. At my last company I saw us go from a state of permanent chaos, where we had an extremely ambitious roadmap but couldn't deliver products, to a predictable state where we could genuinely sign up for projects that we could deliver. The business said they might not always like the answers (they always want things tomorrow, after all), but at least they believed our answers and were not frustrated from feeling that they were being consistently lied to.

This books keeps it real. It doesn't tell you how to become 100% accurate with your estimates. That would be a waste of effort and impossible to achieve. Mike's book doesn't attempt to give you pretty templates to be filled out, instead he makes you think and learn how to approach and solve problems. No project, product, or organization is the same, so learning the thinking and principles are far more important. Mike brings his vast real-world experiences and personality to life in this book. It's real and it's honest. This book definitely belongs at the top of your reading list.

Gabrielle Benefield
Director, Agile Product Development
Yahoo!

Acknowledgments

I owe an even greater debt of gratitude than usual to the formal reviewers of this book. Tom Poppendieck, Steve Tockey, Paul Hodgetts, Mike Searfos, and Preston Smith all provided me with helpful comments and suggestions. This book is immensely improved because of their efforts. In particular, I wish to thank Steve and Tom for going beyond the call of duty. Steve pointed out numerous ideas and concepts I'd overlooked and pointed me toward a few references I hadn't discovered. Most importantly, he led me to what has since become my mantra when I teach classes on estimating and planning: estimate size, derive duration. Tom may have spent more effort on this book than I did. Tom was tireless in stressing to me the importance of writing this book for the whole team, not just for the project manager. It was through discussions with Tom that I realized that a book on planning needed to be broader than just answering the question, "When will we be done?" In the grand scheme of providing value to our organizations, that question is easy.

Thank you to John Goodsen of RADSoft. John and I originally planned to write this book together. Our schedules didn't mesh so that wasn't possible, but I thank John for the early discussions about the book.

One of the greatest things about the Internet is the ability to share a book with others while you are writing it. This book has been in process for twenty months on my website, and it is greatly improved because of the comments and suggestions sent to me by readers of those early drafts. In particular I would like to thank Bryan Ambrogiano, Ken Auer, Simon Baker, Ray Boehm, Leslie Borrell, Clarke Ching, Lisa Crispin, Rachel Davies, Mike Dwyer, Hakan Erdogmus, John

Favaro, Chris Gardner, John Gilman, Sven Gorts, Paul Grew, Sridhar Jayaraman, Angelo Kastroulis, Lisa Katzenmeier, Lasse Koskela, Mitch Lacey, Patrick Logan, Kent McDonald, Erik Petersen, Kert Peterson, Mike Polen, J. B. Rainsberger, Bill Ramos, Matt Read, George Reilly, Chris Rimmer, Owen Rogers, Kevin Rutherford, Dick Scheel, James Schiel, Ken Scott, Karl Scotland, Alan Shalloway, Jagadish Shrinivasavadhani, Michele Sliger, Karen Smiley, Hubert Smits, Victor Szalvay, Charlie Trainor, Raj Waghray, Rüdiger Wolf, Scott Worley, and Jason Yip.

I would also like to thank everyone who has participated in one of my agile estimating and planning classes over the past two years, whether internally at their company or at a conference. Thank you as well to each of my clients, but especially to those where I've taught classes on estimating and planning and who are using the ideas in this book, including Farm Credit Systems of America, Fast401k, High Moon Studios, Nielsen Media Research, Sun Microsystems, Ultimate Software, VisionPace, Webroot, Yahoo!, and others.

As always, the staff at Prentice Hall was wonderful to work with. Paul Petralia and Michelle Housley got the project started and were there through the finish. Tyrrell Albaugh helped with some difficult FrameMaker questions. I asked to be hit with a tough copy editor so that the book could be as good as possible. I was hit with Kathy Simpson, who was exactly what I'd asked for. Finally, Lara Wysong did a great job of overseeing the transition from manuscript to the book you have in your hands. She was also tireless in responding to my hundreds of questions and emails.

I thank Bob Martin for including this book among the other wonderful books in his series. Uncle Bob has been one of my favorite writers since back in his days as the editor of the *C++ Report*. Bob has done so much to spread agile ideas throughout the software development community that it is an honor to have this book in his series. I would also like to thank Jim Highsmith of the Cutter Consortium and Gabrielle Benefield of Yahoo! for contributing forewords. Working with each of them is always a pleasure.

I cannot thank my family enough for allowing me the time to work on this book. Much of it was supposed to be written on the road to minimize time away from them. That didn't happen. Laura, my wife and partner in everything I do, has been tireless in her devotion to me, our business, and this book. She read and re-read every chapter, and then she read them again. Without her help, I wouldn't be able to accomplish a tenth of what we do together. My beautiful daughters, Savannah and Delaney, have become so accustomed to seeing me locked in my home office typing away that it would seem odd to them if I weren't. I thank them for their hugs, kisses, and for being who they are.

Introduction

This book could have been called *Estimating and Planning Agile Projects*. Instead, it's called *Agile Estimating and Planning*. The difference may appear subtle, but it's not. The title makes it clear that the estimating and planning processes must themselves be agile. Without agile estimating and planning, we cannot have agile projects.

The book is mostly about planning, which I view as answering the question of "What should we build and by when?" However, to answer questions about planning we must also address questions of estimating ("How big is this?") and scheduling ("When will this be done?" and "How much can I have by then?").

This book is organized in seven parts and twenty-three chapters. Each chapter ends with a summary of key points and with a set of discussion questions. Because estimating and planning are meant to be whole-team activities, one of the ways I hope this book will be read is by teams who meet perhaps weekly to discuss what they've read and the questions at the end of each chapter. Because agile software development is popular worldwide, I have tried to avoid writing an overly United States–centric book. To that end, I have used the universal currency symbol, writing amounts such as ¤500 instead of perhaps $500 or €500 and so on.

Part I describes why planning is important, the problems we often encounter, and the goals of an agile approach. Chapter 1 begins the book by describing the purpose of planning, what makes a good plan, and what makes planning agile. The most important reasons why traditional approaches to estimating and planning lead to unsatisfactory results are described in Chapter 2. Finally,

Chapter 3 begins with a brief recap of what agility means and then describes the high-level approach to agile estimating and planning taken by the rest of this book.

The second part introduces a main tenet of estimating, that estimates of size and duration should be kept separate. Chapters 4 and 5 introduce story points and ideal days, two units appropriate for estimating the size of the features to be developed. Chapter 6 describes techniques for estimating in story points and ideal days, and includes a description of planning poker. Chapter 7 describes when and how to re-estimate, and Chapter 8 offers advice on choosing between story points and ideal days.

Part III, "Planning for Value," offers advice on how a project team can make sure they are building the best possible product. Chapter 9 describes the mix of factors that need to be considered when prioritizing features. Chapter 10 presents an approach for modeling the financial return from a feature or feature set and how to compare financial returns so that the team works on the most valuable items first. Chapter 11 includes advice on how to assess and then prioritize the desirability of features to a product's users. Chapter 12 concludes this part with advice on how to split large features into smaller, more manageable ones.

In Part IV, we shift our attention and focus on questions around scheduling a project. Chapter 13 begins by looking at the steps involved in scheduling a relatively simple, single-team project. Next, Chapter 14 looks at how to plan an iteration. Chapters 15 and 16 look at how to select an appropriate iteration length for the project and how to estimate a team's initial rate of progress. Chapter 17 looks in detail at how to schedule a project with either a high amount of uncertainty or a greater implication to being wrong about the schedule. This part concludes with Chapter 18, which describes the additional steps necessary in estimating and planning a project being worked on by multiple teams.

Once a plan has been established, it must be communicated to the rest of the organization and the team's progress against it monitored. These are the topics of the three chapters of Part V. Chapter 19 looks specifically at monitoring the release plan, while Chapter 20 looks at monitoring the iteration plan. The final chapter in this part, Chapter 21, deals specifically with communicating about the plan and progress toward it.

Chapter 22 is the lone chapter in Part VI. This chapter argues the case for why agile estimating and planning work and stands as a counterpart to Chapter 2, which describes why traditional approaches fail so often.

Part VII, the final part, includes only one chapter. Chapter 23 is an extended case study that reasserts the main points of this book but does so in a fictional setting.

Part I

The Problem and the Goal

To present an agile approach to estimating and planning, it is important first to understand the purpose of planning. This is the topic of the first chapter in this part. Chapter 2 presents some of the most common reasons why traditionally planned projects frequently fail to result in on-time products that wow their customers. The final chapter in this part then presents a high-level view of the agile approach that is described throughout the remainder of the book.

Chapter 1

The Purpose of Planning

> *"Planning is everything. Plans are nothing."*
> —Field Marshal Helmuth Graf von Moltke

Estimating and planning are critical to the success of any software development project of any size or consequence. Plans guide our investment decisions: We might initiate a specific project if we estimate it to take six months and ¤1 million[1] but would reject the same project if we thought it would take two years and ¤4 million. Plans help us know who needs to be available to work on a project during a given period. Plans help us know if a project is on track to deliver the functionality that users need and expect. Without plans we open our projects to any number of problems.

Yet planning is difficult, and plans are often wrong. Teams often respond to this by going to one of two extremes: They either do no planning at all, or they put so much effort into their plans that they become convinced that the plans must be right. The team that does no planning cannot answer the most basic questions, such as "When will you be done?" and "Can we schedule the product release for June?" The team that overplans deludes themselves into thinking that any plan can be "right." Their plan may be more thorough, but that does not necessarily mean it will be more accurate or useful.

That estimating and planning are difficult is not news. We've known it for a long time. In 1981, Barry Boehm drew the first version of what Steve McConnell

---

1. Remember that ¤ is the universal, generic currency symbol.

(1998) later called the "cone of uncertainty." Figure 1.1 shows Boehm's initial ranges of uncertainty at different points in a sequential development ("waterfall") process. The cone of uncertainty shows that during the feasibility phase of a project a schedule estimate is typically as far off as 60% to 160%. That is, a project expected to take 20 weeks could take anywhere from 12 to 32 weeks. After the requirements are written, the estimate might still be off +/- 15% in either direction. So an estimate of 20 weeks means work that takes 17 to 23 weeks.

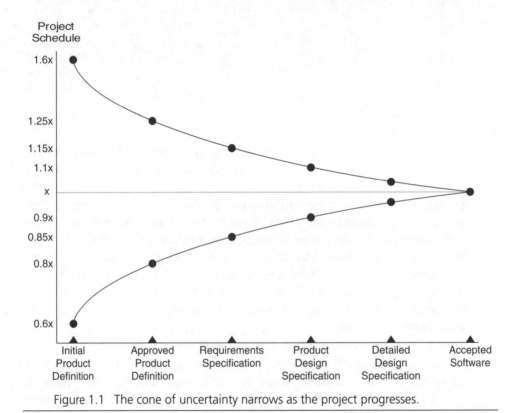

Figure 1.1   The cone of uncertainty narrows as the project progresses.

The Project Management Institute (PMI) presents a similar view on the progressive accuracy of estimates. However, rather than viewing the cone of uncertainty as symmetric, PMI views it as asymmetric. PMI suggests the creation of an initial *order of magnitude estimate*, which ranges from +75% to –25%. The next estimate to be created is the *budgetary estimate*, with a range of +25% to –10%, followed by the final *definitive estimate*, with a range of +10% to –5%.

Why Do It?

If estimating and planning are difficult, and if it's impossible to get an accurate estimate until so late in a project, why do it at all? Clearly, there is the obvious reason that the organizations in which we work often demand that we provide estimates. Plans and schedules may be needed for a variety of legitimate reasons, such as planning marketing campaigns, scheduling product release activities, training internal users, and so on. These are important needs, and the difficulty of estimating a project does not excuse us from providing a plan or schedule that the organization can use for these purposes. However, beyond these perfunctory needs, there is a much more fundamental reason to take on the hard work of estimating and planning.

Estimating and planning are not just about determining an appropriate deadline or schedule. Planning—especially an ongoing iterative approach to planning—is a quest for value. Planning is an attempt to find an optimal solution to the overall product development question: What should we build? To answer this question, the team considers features, resources, and schedule. The question cannot be answered all at once. It must be answered iteratively and incrementally. At the start of a project we may decide that a product should contain a specific set of features and be released on August 31. But in June we may decide that a slightly later date with slightly more features will be better. Or we may decide that slightly sooner with slightly fewer features will be better.

A good planning process supports this by

- Reducing risk
- Reducing uncertainty
- Supporting better decision making
- Establishing trust
- Conveying information

Reducing Risk

Planning increases the likelihood of project success by providing insights into the project's risks. Some projects are so risky that we may choose not to start once we've learned about the risks. Other projects may contain features whose risks can be contained by early attention.

The discussions that occur while estimating raise questions that expose potential dark corners of a project. Suppose you are asked to estimate how long it will take to integrate the new project with an existing mainframe legacy system that you know nothing about. This will expose the integration features as a potential risk. The project team can opt to eliminate the risk right then by spending time learning about the legacy system. Or the risk can be noted and the estimate for the work either made larger or expressed as a range to account for the greater uncertainty and risk.

Reducing Uncertainty

Throughout a project, the team is generating new capabilities in the product. They are also generating new knowledge—about the product, the technologies in use, and themselves as a team. It is critical that this new knowledge be acknowledged and factored into an iterative planning process that is designed to help a team refine their vision of the product. The most critical risk facing most projects is the risk of developing the wrong product. Yet this risk is entirely ignored on most projects. An agile approach to planning can dramatically reduce (and ideally eliminate) this risk.

The often-cited CHAOS studies (Standish 2001) define a successful project as on time, on budget, and with all features as initially specified. This is a dangerous definition because it fails to acknowledge that a feature that looked good when the project was started may not be worth its development cost once the team begins on the project. If I were to define a failed project, one of my criteria would certainly be "a project on which no one came up with any better ideas than what was on the initial list of requirements." We want to encourage projects on which investment, schedule, and feature decisions are periodically reassessed. A project that delivers all features on the initial plan is not necessarily a success. The product's users and customer would probably not be satisfied if wonderful new feature ideas had been rejected in favor of mediocre ones simply because the mediocre features were in the initial plan.

Supporting Better Decision Making

Estimates and plans help us make decisions. How does an organization decide whether a particular project is worth doing if it does not have estimates of the value and the cost of the project? Beyond decisions about whether or not to start a project, estimates help us make sure we are working on the most valuable projects possible. Suppose an organization is considering two projects; one is estimated to make ¤1 million, and the second is estimated to make ¤2 million. First, the organization needs schedule and cost estimates to determine whether these projects are worth pursuing. Will the projects take so long that they miss a market window? Will the projects cost more than they'll make? Second, the organization needs estimates and a plan so that it can decide which to pursue. The organization may be able to pursue one project, both projects, or neither if the costs are too high.

Organizations need estimates in order to make decisions beyond whether or not to start a project. Sometimes the staffing profile of a project can be more important than its schedule. For example, a project may not be worth starting if it will involve the time of the organization's chief architect, who is already fully committed on another project. However, if a plan can be developed that shows how to complete the new project without the involvement of this architect, the project may be worth starting.

Many of the decisions made while planning a project are trade-off decisions. For example, on every project we make trade-off decisions between development time and cost. Often the cheapest way to develop a system would be to hire one good programmer and allow her ten or twenty years to write the system, allowing her years of detouring to perhaps master the domain, become an expert in database administration, and so on. Obviously, though, we can rarely wait twenty years for a system, and so we engage teams. A team of thirty may spend a year (thirty person-years) developing what a lone programmer could have done in twenty. The development cost goes up, but the value of having the application nineteen years earlier justifies the increased cost.

We are constantly making similar trade-off decisions between functionality and effort, cost, and time. Is a particular feature worth delaying the release? Should we hire one more developer so that a particular feature can be included in the upcoming release? Should we release in June or hold off until August and have more features? Should we buy this development tool? To make these decisions we need estimates of both the costs and benefits.

Establishing Trust

Frequent reliable delivery of promised features builds trust between the developers of a product and the customers of that product. Reliable estimates enable reliable delivery. A customer needs estimates to make important prioritization and trade-off decisions. Estimates also help a customer decide how much of a feature to develop. Rather than investing twenty days and getting everything, perhaps investing ten days of effort will yield 80% of the benefit. Customers are reluctant to make these types of trade-off decisions early in a project unless the developers' estimates have proved trustworthy.

Reliable estimates benefit developers by allowing them to work at a sustainable pace. This leads to higher-quality code and fewer bugs. These, in turn, lead back to more reliable estimates because less time is spent on highly unpredictable work such as bug fixing.

Conveying Information

A plan conveys expectations and describes one possibility of what may come to pass over the course of a project. A plan does not guarantee an exact set of features on an exact date at a specified cost. A plan does, however, communicate and establish a set of baseline expectations. Far too often a plan is reduced to a single date, and all of the assumptions and expectations that led to that date are forgotten.

Suppose you ask me when a project will be done. I tell you seven months but provide no explanation of how I arrived at that duration. You should be skeptical of my estimate. Without additional information you have no way of determining whether I've thought about the question sufficiently or whether my estimate is realistic.

Suppose, instead, that I provide you a plan that estimates completion in seven to nine months, shows what work will be completed in the first one or two months, documents key assumptions, and establishes an approach for how we'll collaboratively measure progress. In this case you can look at my plan and draw conclusions about the confidence you should have in it.

What Makes a Good Plan?

A good plan is one that stakeholders find sufficiently reliable that they can use it as the basis for making decisions. Early in a project, this may mean that the plan says that the product can be released in the third quarter, rather than the second, and that it will contain approximately a described set of features. Later in the project, to remain useful for decision making, this plan will need to be more precise.

Suppose you are estimating and planning a new release of the company's flagship product. You determine that the new version will be ready for release in six months. You create a plan that describes a set of features that are certain to be in the new version and another set of features that may or may not be included, depending on how well things progress.

Others in the company can use this plan to make decisions. They can prepare marketing materials, schedule an advertising campaign, allocate resources to assist with upgrading key customers, and so on. This plan is useful—as long as it is somewhat predictive of what actually happens on the project. If development takes twelve months instead of the planned six, this was not a good plan.

However, if the project takes seven months instead of six, the plan was probably still useful. Yes, the plan was incorrect, and yes, it may have led to some slightly mistimed decisions. But a seven-month delivery of an estimated six-month project is generally not the end of the world and is certainly within the PMI's margin of error for a budgetary estimate. The plan, although inaccurate, was even more likely useful if we consider that it should have been updated regularly throughout the course of the project. In that case, the one-month late delivery should not have been a last-minute surprise to anyone.

What Makes Planning Agile?

This book is about agile planning, not agile plans. Plans are documents or figures; they are snapshots of how we believe a project might unfold over an uncertain future. Planning is an activity. Agile planning shifts the emphasis from the plan to the planning.

Agile planning balances the effort and investment in planning with the knowledge that we will revise the plan through the course of the project. An agile plan is one that we are not only willing, but also eager to change. We don't want to change the plan just for the sake of changing, but we want to change because change means we've learned something or that we've avoided a mistake. We may have learned that users want more of this feature or that they want less of that feature or that usability is more important than we'd believed or that programming in this new language takes longer than we'd expected. The financial impact of each of these changes can be assessed and, if worthy, can alter the plan and schedule.

As we discover these things, they affect our plans. This means we need plans that are easily changed. This is why the planning becomes more important than the plan. The knowledge and insight we gain from planning persists long after one plan is torn up and a revised one put in its place. So an agile plan is one that is easy to change.

Just because we're changing the plan does not mean we change the dates. We may or may not do that. But if we learn we were wrong about some aspect of the target product and need to do something about it, the plan needs to change. There are many ways we can change the plan without changing the date. We can drop a feature, we can reduce the scope of a feature, we can possibly add people to the project, and so on.

Because we acknowledge that we cannot totally define a project at its outset, it is important that we do not perform all of a project's planning at the outset. Agile planning is spread more or less evenly across the duration of a project. Release planning sets the stage and is followed by a number of rounds of iteration planning, after which the entire process is repeated perhaps a handful of times on a project.

So in defining agile planning we find that it

- Is focused more on the planning than on the plan
- Encourages change
- Results in plans that are easily changed
- Is spread throughout the project

Summary

Estimating and planning are critical, yet are difficult and error prone. We cannot excuse ourselves from these activities just because they are hard. Estimates given early in a project are far less accurate than those given later. This progressive refinement is shown in the *cone of uncertainty*.

The purpose of planning is to find an optimal answer to the overall product development question of what to build. The answer incorporates features, resources, and schedule. Answering this question is supported by a planning process that reduces risk, reduces uncertainty, supports reliable decision making, establishes trust, and conveys information.

A good plan is one that is sufficiently reliable that it can be used as the basis for making decisions about the product and the project. Agile planning is focused more on the planning than on the creation of a plan, encourages change, results in plans that are easily changed, and is spread throughout the project.

Discussion Questions

1. This chapter started by making the claim that overplanning and doing no planning are equally dangerous. What is the right amount of planning on your current project?

2. What other reasons can you think of for planning?

3. Think of one or two of the most successful projects in which you have been involved. What role did planning play in those projects?

Chapter 2

Why Planning Fails

> *"No plan survives contact with the enemy."*
> —Field Marshal Helmuth Graf von Moltke

The previous chapter made the argument that the purpose of planning is to arrive iteratively at an optimized answer to the ultimate new product development question of what should be developed. That is, what capabilities should the product exhibit, in what timeframe, and with which and how many resources? We learned that planning supports this by reducing risk, by reducing uncertainty about what the product should be, by supporting better decision making, by establishing trust, and by conveying information.

Unfortunately, the traditional ways in which we plan projects often let us down. In answering the combined scope/schedule/resources question for a new product, our traditional planning processes do not always lead to very satisfactory answers and products. As support of this, consider that:

- Nearly two-thirds of projects significantly overrun their cost estimates (Lederer and Prasad 1992)
- Sixty-four percent of the features included in products are rarely or never used (Johnson 2002)
- The average project exceeds its schedule by 100% (Standish 2001)

In this chapter, we look at five causes of planning failure.

Planning Is by Activity Rather Than Feature

A critical problem with traditional approaches to planning is that they focus on the completion of activities rather than on the delivery of features. A traditionally managed project's Gantt chart or work breakdown structure identifies the activities that will be performed. This becomes how we measure the progress of the team. A first problem with activity-based planning is that customers get no value from the completion of activities. Features are the unit of customer value. Planning should, therefore, be at the level of features, not activities.

A second problem occurs after a traditional schedule has been created and is being reviewed. When we review a schedule showing activities, we do so looking for forgotten activities rather than for missing features.

Further problems occur because activity-based plans often lead to projects that overrun their schedules. When faced with overrunning a schedule, some teams attempt to save time by inappropriately reducing quality. Other teams institute change-control policies designed to constrain product changes, even highly valuable changes. Some of the reasons why activity-based planning leads to schedule overruns include

- Activities don't finish early.
- Lateness is passed down the schedule.
- Activities are not independent.

Each of these problems is described in the following sections.

Activities Don't Finish Early

A few years ago I had two main projects that needed my time. I was programming some interesting new features for a product. I also needed to prepare documentation for an ISO 9001 compliance audit. The programming was fun. Writing documents for the compliance audit wasn't. Not surprisingly, I managed to expand the scope of the programming work so that it filled almost all my time and left me the bare minimum of time to prepare for the audit.

I'm not the only one who does this. In fact, this behavior is so common that it has a name, Parkinson's Law (1993), which states:

Work expands so as to fill the time available for its completion.

Parkinson is saying that we take as much time to complete an activity as we think we'll be allowed. If there's a Gantt chart hanging on the wall that says an activity is expected to take five days, the programmer assigned to that activity will generally make sure the activity takes the full five days. She may do this by adding a few bells and whistles if it looks like she'll finish early (a practice known as *gold-plating*). Or she may split time between the activity and researching some hot new technology she thinks may be useful. What she will not do very often is finish the activity early. In many organizations, if she finishes early, her boss may accuse her of having given a padded estimate. Or her boss may expect her to finish more activities early. Why risk either of these scenarios when a little web surfing can make the activity come in on schedule instead?

When a Gantt chart shows that an activity is expected to take five days, it gives implicit permission to the developer to take up to that long to complete. It is human nature when ahead of that schedule to fill the extra time with other work that we, but perhaps not others, value.

Lateness Is Passed Down the Schedule

Because traditional plans are activity based, in large measure they focus on the dependencies between activities. Consider the Gantt chart shown in Figure 2.1, which shows four activities and their dependencies. An early start for testing requires the fortuitous confluence of these events:

- ◆ Coding of the middle tier finishes early, which is influenced by when adding tables to the database is finished.
- ◆ Coding of the user interface finishes early.
- ◆ The tester is available early.

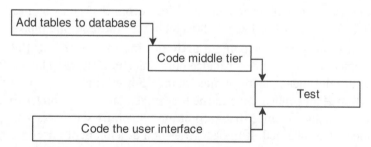

Figure 2.1 Testing will start late if anything goes worse than planned; it will start early only if everything goes better than planned.

The key here is that even in this simple case there are three things that all must occur for an early start on testing. Although multiple things must occur for testing to start early, any one of the following can cause testing to start late:

- Coding the user interface finishes late.
- Coding the middle tier takes longer than planned to complete and finishes late.
- Coding the middle tier takes the time planned but starts late because adding tables to the database finishes late.
- The tester is unavailable.

In other words, an early start requires a combination of things to go well; a late start can be caused by one thing going wrong.

The problem is compounded because we've already established that activities will rarely finish early. This means that activities will start late and that the lateness will get passed down the schedule. Because early completion is rare, it is even more rare that an activity such as testing in Figure 2.1 gets to start early.

Activities Are Not Independent

Activities are said to be independent if the duration of one activity does not influence the duration of another activity. In building a house, the amount of time it takes to excavate the basement is independent of the amount of time it will take to paint the walls. When activities are independent, a late finish on one activity can be offset by an early finish on another. Flipping a coin multiple times is another example of independent activities. A coin that lands on heads on the first flip is no more or less likely to land on heads on the second flip.

Are software development activities independent? Will the variations in completion times tend to balance out? Unfortunately, no. Many software activities are not independent of one another. For example, if I'm writing the client portion of an application and the first screen takes 50% longer than scheduled, there is a good chance that each of the remaining screens is also going to take longer than planned. If the activities of a development effort are not independent, variations in completion time will not balance out.

Many activities in a typical project plan are not independent, yet we continually forget this. When someone is late on the first of a handful of similar items we've all heard or given the answer, "Yes, I was late this time, but I'll make it up on the rest." This stems from the belief that the knowledge gained from completing the first activity will allow the remaining similar activities to be completed more quickly than called for in the plan. The real knowledge we should gain in a situation like this is that when an activity takes longer than planned, all similar activities are also likely to take longer than planned.

Multitasking Causes Further Delays

A second reason why traditional approaches to planning often fail is multitasking, which is defined as simultaneously working on multiple tasks. Multitasking exacts a horrible toll on productivity. Clark and Wheelwright (1993) studied the effects of multitasking and found that the time an individual spends on value-adding work drops rapidly when the individual is working on more than two tasks. This is illustrated in Figure 2.2, which is based on their results.

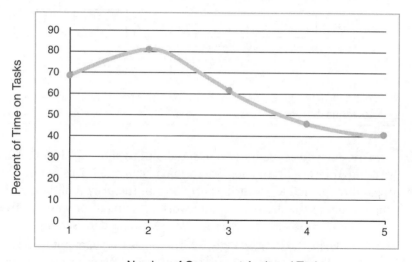

Figure 2.2   Effect of multitasking on productivity.

Logically, it makes sense that multitasking helps when you have two things to work on; if you become blocked on one, you can switch to the other. It is also logical that Figure 2.2 shows a rapid decline in time spent on value-adding tasks after a second task. We're rarely blocked on more than one task at a time; and if we're working on three or more concurrent tasks, the time spent switching among them becomes a much more tangible cost and burden.

Multitasking often becomes an issue once a project starts to have some activities finish late. At that point dependencies between activities become critical.

A developer waiting on the work of another developer will ask that developer to deliver just a subset of work so that he may continue. Suppose I am to spend ten days working on some database changes, then ten days implementing an application programming interface (API) for accessing the database, and then ten days developing a user interface. This is illustrated in the top half of Figure 2.3. Your work is held up until you get the API from me. You ask me to do just enough of the API work so that you can get started. Similarly, the tester asks me to do just enough of the user interface so that she can begin automating tests. I agree, and my schedule becomes as shown in the bottom of Figure 2.3.

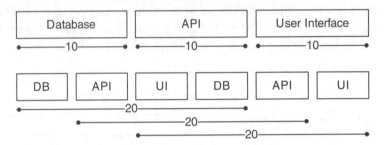

Figure 2.3 Multitasking extends the completion date of work and leaves work in process longer.

This often gives the illusion of speed; but as shown in Figure 2.3, my database and API work finish later than originally planned. This is almost certain to ripple through and affect further activities in the plan. Additionally, in this example, each of the desired units of work remains in process for twenty days rather than ten, as was the case when the work was done serially.

To make matters worse, Figure 2.3 assumes that I am not slowed by switching among these activities more frequently. The Clark and Wheelwright study indicates that a loss in productivity will occur.

Multitasking becomes a problem on a traditionally planned project for two primary reasons. First, work is typically assigned well in advance of when the work will begin, and it is impossible to allocate work efficiently in advance. Assigning work to individuals rather than to groups exacerbates the problem. Second, it encourages focusing on achieving a high level of utilization of all individuals on the project rather than on maintaining sufficient slack to cope with the inherent variability in typical project tasks. Loading everyone to 100% of capacity has the same effect as loading a highway to 100% of capacity: No one can make any progress.

Features Are Not Developed by Priority

A third reason why traditional planning fails to lead consistently to high-value products is because the work described by the plan is not prioritized by its value to the users and customer. Many traditional plans are created with the assumption that all identified activities will be completed. This means that work is typically prioritized and sequenced for the convenience of the development team.

Traditional thinking says that if all work will be completed, project customers have no preference about the sequence in which that work is done. This leads to the development team's working on features in what appears to the customer to be a relatively haphazard order. Then, with the end of the project approaching, the team scrambles to meet the schedule by dropping features. Because there was no attempt to work on features in order of priority, some of the features dropped are of greater value than those that are delivered.

We Ignore Uncertainty

A fourth shortcoming with traditional approaches to planning is the failure to acknowledge uncertainty. We ignore uncertainty about the product and assume that the initial requirements analysis led to a complete and perfect specification of the product. We assume that users will not change their minds, refine their opinions, or come up with new needs during the period covered by the plan.

Similarly, we ignore uncertainty about how we will build the product and pretend we can assign precise estimates ("two weeks") to imprecise work. We cannot hope to identify every activity that will be needed in the course of a project. Yet we often fail to acknowledge this in the plans we create.

Even with all this uncertainty, schedules are often expressed as a single, unqualified date: "We will ship on June 30," for example. During the earliest part of a project we are the most uncertain. The estimates we give should reflect our uncertainty. One way of doing this is by expressing the end date as a range: "We'll ship sometime between June and August," for example. As the project progresses and as uncertainty and risk are removed from the project, estimates can be refined and made more precise. This was the point of the cone of uncertainty in Chapter 1, "The Purpose of Planning."

The best way of dealing with uncertainty is to iterate. To reduce uncertainty about what the product should be, work in short iterations, and show (or, ideally, give) working software to users every few weeks. Uncertainty about how to develop the product is similarly reduced by iterating. For example, missing tasks can be added to plans, bad estimates can be corrected, and so on. In this way, the focus shifts from the plan to the planning.

Estimates Become Commitments

Embedded within every estimate is a probability that the work will be completed in the estimated time. Suppose your team has been asked to develop a new high-end word processor. The probability of finishing this by the end of the week is 0%. The probability of finishing it in ten years is 100%. If I ask you for an estimate, and you tell me the end of the week, that estimate comes with a probability of 0%. If the estimate you give me is ten years, that estimate comes with a probability of 100%. Each estimate between the end of the week and ten years from now comes with its own probability between 0% and 100% (Armour 2002).

A problem with traditional planning can arise if the project team or its stakeholders equate estimating with committing. As Phillip Armour (2002) points out, an estimate is a probability, and a commitment cannot be made to a probability. Commitments are made to dates. Normally the date that a team is asked (or told) to commit to is one to which they would assign a less-than-100% probability. Before making such a commitment, the team needs to assess a variety of business factors and risks. It is important that they be given this opportunity, and that every estimate does not become an implicit commitment.

Summary

After looking through this list of problems with traditional approaches to planning, it's no wonder so many projects are disappointing. Activity-based planning distracts our attention from features, which are the true unit of customer value. A variety of problems then leads to the likelihood of delivering late against a schedule derived from an activity-based plan. With good intentions, project participants view multitasking as a possible cure but are eventually forced even further behind schedule because of the hidden costs of multitasking. When the project schedule runs out of time, features are inevitably dropped. Because features are developed in the order deemed most efficient by the developers, the dropped features are not necessarily those with the lowest value to users.

Ignoring uncertainty about exactly what users will eventually want can lead to completing a project on schedule but without including important capabilities that were identified after the plan was created. Also ignoring uncertainty about how the product will be developed leads to missed activities in the project plan. This in turn increases the likelihood that the project will be late, that features will be dropped at the end, or that inappropriate quality trade-offs may be made.

Many organizations confuse estimates with commitments. As soon as a team expresses an estimate, they are forced to commit to it.

Discussion Questions

1. What problems result from plans being based on activities rather than deliverable features?

2. In your current environment, is an estimate the same as a commitment? What problems does this cause? What could you do to change this misperception?

3. In what ways does multitasking affect your current project? How could you reduce that impact?

Chapter 3

An Agile Approach

*"A good plan violently executed now is better
than a perfect plan executed next week."*
—General George S. Patton

Although it started years before, the agile movement officially began with the creation of the Agile Manifesto in February 2001 (Beck et al.). This manifesto was written and signed by seventeen "lightweight methodologists," as they were called at the time. Their document both gave a name to how they were developing software and provided a list of value statements. The authors of the Agile Manifesto wrote that they value

- Individuals and interactions over processes and tools
- Working software over comprehensive documentation
- Customer collaboration over contract negotiation
- Responding to change over following a plan

Agile teams value individuals and interactions over processes and tools because they know that a well-functioning team of great individuals with mediocre tools will always outperform a dysfunctional team of mediocre individuals with great tools and processes. Great software is made by great individuals, and as an industry we have tried too long with too little success to define a development process that relegates individuals to replaceable cogs in the machinery. Agile processes acknowledge the unique strengths (and weaknesses) of individuals and capitalize on these rather than attempting to make everyone homogeneous.

Agile teams value working software over comprehensive documentation because it leads them to have a stable, incrementally enhanced version of the product at the end of each iteration. This makes it possible to collect early, frequent feedback on both the product and the process. As the developed software grows each iteration, it can be shown to likely or actual users. Feedback from these users is fed back into the development process to make sure that the team is always working on the highest-valued features and that those features will satisfy user expectations.

Customer collaboration is valued over contract negotiation because agile teams would like all parties to the project to be working toward the same set of goals. Contract negotiation sometimes sets the development team and the project customer at odds right from the start. I enjoy playing most games, and when my oldest daughter was four, I bought her a "cooperative game" because it looked like a game she'd enjoy and because I had no idea how a cooperative game could be fun. In the game I bought her, a princess is placed under a spell, and players need to remove obstacles (a moat, a locked door, and so on) that are between them and the princess. Players take turns, as in most games, but the goal is to remove obstacles collaboratively and save the princess. All players win, or all players lose. The game is surprisingly fun, and we'd like software teams and customers to approach projects with this same attitude of collaboration and shared goals. Yes, contracts are often necessary but the terms and details in a contract can exert great influence on whether the different parties are set on a collaborative or a competitive effort.

Agile teams value responding to change over following a plan because their ultimate focus is on delivering as much value as possible to the project's customer and users. For all but the simplest projects, it is impossible for users to know every detail of every feature they want. It is inevitable that users will come up with new ideas, and almost as inevitable that they will decide that some features desired today will become lower priorities tomorrow. To an agile team, a plan is one view of the future, but many views are possible. As a team gains knowledge and experience, they will factor these into the plan. Perhaps the team is progressing faster or slower than initially expected; perhaps users like one set of features more than expected but don't like another feature that was initially considered critical.

With the four value statements of the Agile Manifesto in mind, in this chapter we consider what it means to have an agile approach to a project, as well as what it means to have an agile approach to estimating and planning.

An Agile Approach to Projects

With an understanding of the four primary agile value statements, we can turn our attention to what an agile team looks like in practice. Taken collectively, the four value statements lead to software development processes that are highly iterative and incremental and that deliver coded and tested software at the end of each iteration. The following sections cover some of the main ways in which agile teams work, including that they:

- Work as one team
- Work in short iterations
- Deliver something each iteration
- Focus on business priorities
- Inspect and adapt

An Agile Team Works As One

Critical to the success of a project is that all project participants view themselves as one team aimed at a common goal. There is no room for a "throw it over the wall" mentality on an agile project. Analysts do not throw requirements over the wall to designers. Designers and architects do not throw designs over a wall to coders; coders do not throw half-tested code over a wall to testers. A successful agile team must have a we're-all-in-this-together mindset. Although an agile team should work together as one whole team, there are a number of specific roles on the team. It is worth identifying and clarifying those roles that play a part in agile estimating and planning.

The first role is the *product owner*. The primary duties of the product owner include making sure that all team members are pursuing a common vision for the project, establishing priorities so that the highest-valued functionality is always being worked on, and making decisions that lead to a good return on the investment in the project. In commercial software development, the product owner is often someone from the marketing or product management side of the company. When developing software for internal use, the product owner may instead be a user, the users' manager, an analyst, or the person funding the project.

A second role is that of *customer*. The customer is the person who has made the decision to fund the project or to buy the software. On a project developing software for internal use, the customer is usually a representative from another group or division. On such projects, the product owner and customer roles are often combined. For a commercially distributed product, the customer will be the person who buys the software. In either case, the customer may or may not be a *user* of the software, which is, of course, another important role.

Another role worth highlighting is that of *developer*. I use *developer* very generally to refer to anyone developing software. That includes programmers, testers, analysts, database engineers, usability experts, technical writers, architects, designers, and so on. Using this definition, even the product owner may be thought of as a developer on many projects.

A final role is the *project manager*. As described by Highsmith (2004a), the role of the project manager changes on agile projects. Agile project managers focus more on leadership than on management. On some agile projects, the person fulfilling the role of project manager will also act in another role, often as a developer but occasionally as a product owner.

An Agile Team Works in Short Iterations

On an agile project there is no grand delineation of phases—no up-front requirements phase followed by analysis followed by architectural design and so on. Depending upon the actual agile process you select or define, you may put a very short design, modeling, or other phase at the front end of the project. But once the project has begun in earnest, all work (analysis, design, coding, testing, and so on) happens concurrently within each iteration.

Iterations are *timeboxed*, meaning they finish on time even if functionality is dropped. Timeboxes are often very short. Most agile teams work in iterations two to four weeks long, but some teams maintain their agility with iterations of up to three months. Most teams settle upon a relatively consistent iteration length. Some, however, choose the appropriate length for an iteration at the start of each iteration.

An Agile Team Delivers Something Each Iteration

More crucial than the specific iteration length chosen by a team is that during the iteration they transform one or more imprecise requirements statements into coded, tested, and potentially shippable software. Of course, many teams will not deliver the results of every iteration to their users; the goal is simply that they could. This means that teams make progress by adding one or more small features in each iteration but that each added feature is coded, tested, and of releasable quality.

It is essential that the product be brought to this potentially shippable state by the end of each iteration. Practically, this does not mean a team must do absolutely everything necessary to release, because they often won't release each iteration. For example, I work with one team that requires two months of mean time between failure (MTBF) testing before releasing their product, which includes both hardware and software. They cannot shorten those two months, as it is contractually required by their client, and that amount of time is often necessary to check for hardware failures. This team works in four-week iterations, and apart from running this two-month MTBF test, their product is at a truly releasable state at the end of each iteration.

Because a single iteration does not usually provide sufficient time to complete enough new functionality to satisfy user or customer desires, the broader concept of a *release* is introduced. A release comprises one or more (usually more) iterations that build upon one another to complete a set of related functionality. Although iterations are most commonly two to four weeks, a release is typically two to six months. For example, in an investment management system, one release may include all of the functionality related to buying and selling mutual funds and money market funds. This may take six two-week iterations to complete (roughly three months). A second release may add stock and bond trading and take four additional two-week iterations. Releases may occur at varying intervals. A first release may take six months to be developed. It may be followed by another release three months later, and so on.

An Agile Team Focuses on Business Priorities

Agile teams demonstrate a commitment to business priorities in two ways. First, they deliver features in the order specified by the product owner, who is expected to prioritize and combine features into a release that optimizes the return on the organization's investment in the project. To achieve this, a release plan is created based on the team's capabilities and a prioritized list of desired new features. For the product owner to have the most flexibility in prioritizing, features must be written so as to minimize the technical dependencies among them. It is difficult for a product owner to prioritize features into a release plan if the selection of one feature requires the prior development of three others. A team is unlikely to achieve a goal of absolutely no dependencies; however, keeping dependencies at a minimum is often quite feasible.

Second, agile teams focus on completing and delivering user-valued features rather than on completing isolated tasks (that eventually combine into a user-valued feature). One of the best ways to do this is to work with user stories, which are a lightweight technique for expressing software requirements (Cohn 2004). A *user story* is a brief description of functionality as viewed by a user or customer of the system. User stories are free-form, and there is no mandatory syntax. However, it can be useful to think of a story generally fitting this form: "As a <type of user>, I want <capability> so that <business value>." With this template as an example, you may have the story "As a book buyer, I want to search for a book by ISBN so that I can find the right book quickly."

User stories are lightweight because the work to gather and document them is not all done up front. Rather than writing a lengthy requirements specification, agile teams have found it better to pursue a just-in-time requirements approach. Typically this begins with a short description of a user story being handwritten on a note card or perhaps typed into a computer for larger or distributed teams. The story card is just the beginning, though, and each user story is accompanied by as many conversations between the developers and the product owner as needed. These conversations happen as often as needed and include whoever is necessary. Written documentation may continue to exist when a story-based requirements approach is used. However, the focus is shifted dramatically from written to verbal communication.

An Agile Team Inspects and Adapts

The plan created at the start of any project is not a guarantee of what will occur. In fact, it is only a point-in-time guess. Many things will conspire to invalidate the plan—project personnel may come or go, technologies will work better or worse than expected, users will change their minds, competitors may force us to respond differently or more rapidly, and so on. Agile teams view every such change as presenting both the opportunity and need to update the plan to better reflect the reality of the current situation.

At the start of each new iteration, an agile team incorporates all new knowledge gained in the preceding iteration and adapts accordingly. If a team has learned something that is likely to affect the accuracy or value of the plan, they adjust the plan. The accuracy of the plan may be affected by the team's discovering they have over- or underestimated their rate of progress. Or they may discover that a certain type of work is more time consuming than previously thought.

The value of the plan may be altered by knowledge the product owner has gained about the desires of likely users. Perhaps, based on feedback from seeing the software from an earlier iteration, the product owner has learned that users would like to see more of one type of feature and that they don't value another feature as much as was previously thought. The value of the plan could be increased in this case by moving more of the desired features into the release at the expense of some of the lesser-valued features.

None of this is to say that agile teams take an ad hoc view of changing priorities. Priorities do tend to be relatively stable from one iteration to the next. However, the opportunity to alter priorities between iterations is a powerful contributor to the ability to maximize the return on the project investment.

An Agile Approach to Planning

Estimating and planning the development of a new product is a daunting task made more difficult by our misconceptions about projects. Macomber (2004) points out that we should not view a project solely as the execution of a series of steps. Instead, it is important that we view a project as rapidly and reliably generating a flow of useful new capabilities and new knowledge. The new capabilities are delivered in the product; the new knowledge is used to make the product the best that it can be.

On an agile project, we use this flow of new capabilities and knowledge to guide the ongoing work. The new knowledge generated by the project may be about the product or the project. New *product knowledge* helps us know more about what the product should be. New *project knowledge* is information about the team, the technologies in use, the risks, and so on.

We frequently fail to acknowledge and plan for this new knowledge. Failing to plan to acquire new knowledge leads to plans built on the assumption that we know everything necessary to create an accurate plan. In the world of software development, that is rarely, if ever, the case. Ward Cunningham has said that "it's more planning what you want to learn, not what it [the product] will be in the end" (Van Schooenderwoert 2004).

I often equate the traditional view of a project as running a 10-kilometer race. You know exactly how far away the finish line is, and your goal is to reach it as quickly as possible. On an agile project, we don't know exactly where the finish line is, but we often know we need to get to it or as close as we can by a known date. An agile project is more like a timed race than a 10-kilometer race: run as far as possible in sixty minutes. In this way, the agile project team knows when they will finish but not what they will deliver. When we acknowledge that the result is both somewhat unknown as well as unknowable in advance, planning becomes a process of setting and revising goals that lead to a longer-term objective.

Multiple Levels of Planning

When setting and revising goals, it is important to remember that we cannot see past the horizon and that the accuracy of a plan decreases rapidly the further we attempt to plan beyond where we can see. Suppose you are standing on a small boat and that your eyes are nine feet above the water. The distance to the horizon in this case is slightly over four miles.[1] If you are planning a twenty-mile trip, you should plan on looking ahead at least five times, once every four miles. Because you cannot see past the horizon, you need to look up occasionally and adjust your plan.

A project is at risk if its planning extends well beyond the planner's horizon and does not include time for the planner to raise her head, look at the new horizon, and make adjustments. A progressive elaboration of the plan is needed. Agile teams achieve this by planning at three distinct horizons. The three horizons are the release, the iteration, and the current day. The relationships among these (and other) planning horizons are illustrated in the planning onion of Figure 3.1.

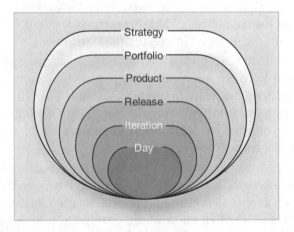

Figure 3.1   The planning onion. Agile teams plan at least at the release, iteration, and day levels.

Most agile teams are concerned only with the three innermost levels of the planning onion. Release planning considers the user stories or themes that will be developed for a new release of a product or system. The goal of release

---

1. To calculate the distance to the horizon in miles, multiply the square root of the height of your eyes by 1.35.

planning is to determine an appropriate answer to the questions of scope, schedule, and resources for a project. Release planning occurs at the start of a project but is not an isolated effort. A good release plan is updated throughout the project (usually at the start of each iteration) so that it always reflects the current expectations about what will be included in the release.

At the next level is iteration planning, which is conducted at the start of each iteration. Based on the work accomplished in the just-finished iteration, the product owner identifies high-priority work the team should address in the new iteration. Because we are looking at a closer horizon than with release planning, the components of the iteration plan can be smaller. During iteration planning, we talk about the tasks that will be needed to transform a feature request into working and tested software.

Finally, there is daily planning. Most agile teams use some form of daily stand-up meeting to coordinate work and synchronize daily efforts. Although it may seem excessive to consider this planning in the formal sense, teams definitely make, assess, and revise their plans during these meetings. During their daily meetings, teams constrain the planning horizon to be no further away than the next day, when they will meet again. Because of this, they focus on the planning of tasks and on coordinating the individual activities that lead up to the completion of a task.

By planning across these three time horizons—release, iteration, and day—agile teams focus on what is visible and important to the plan they are creating.

Outside the concern of most individual agile teams (and this book) are product, portfolio, and strategic planning. Product planning involves a product owner's looking further ahead than the immediate release and planning for the evolution of the released product or system. Portfolio planning involves the selection of the products that will best implement a vision established through an organization's strategic planning.

Conditions of Satisfaction

Every project is initiated with a set of objectives. Your current project may be to create the world's best word processor. Creating the world's best word processor, however, will typically be only one objective for this project. There will almost certainly be additional objectives regarding schedule, budget, and quality. These objectives can be thought of as the customer or product owner's *conditions of satisfaction*—that is, the criteria that will be used to gauge the success of the project.

Way back when I was in high school and assigned to write a paper about a book such as *Moby Dick*, I would always ask the teacher how long the paper had to be. She'd respond something like "Five pages," and then I knew her primary condition of satisfaction. There were, of course, a number of additional, unwritten conditions of satisfaction, such as that the paper would be well written, my own work, in English, and so on.

At the start of release planning, the team and product owner collaboratively explore the product owner's conditions of satisfaction. These include the usual items—scope, schedule, budget, and quality—although agile teams typically prefer to treat quality as non-negotiable. The team and product owner look for ways to meet all of the conditions of satisfaction. The product owner may, for example, be equally satisfied with a release in five months that includes one set of user stories as with a release a month later that includes additional user stories.

Sometimes, however, all of the product owner's conditions of satisfaction cannot be met. The team can build the world's best word processor, but they cannot build it by next month. When no feasible solution can be found, the conditions of satisfaction must change. Because of this, release planning and exploration of the product owner's conditions of satisfaction are highly iterative, as illustrated in Figure 3.2.

Once a release plan covering approximately the next three to six months is established, it is used as input into the planning of the first iteration. Just as release planning began with consideration of the product owner's conditions of satisfaction, so does iteration planning. For an iteration, the product owner's conditions of satisfaction are typically the features she'd like developed next and some high-level tests about each feature.

As an example, consider a travel site that includes the user story "As a user, I want to be able to cancel a reservation." In discussing this story with the product owner, the developers learn that her conditions of satisfaction for this story include

- A user who cancels more than twenty-four hours in advance gets a complete refund.
- A user who cancels less than twenty-four hours in advance is refunded all but a ¤25 cancellation fee.
- A cancellation code is displayed on the site and is emailed to the user.

Like release planning, iteration planning is iterative. The product owner and the team discuss various ways of best meeting the conditions of satisfaction for the iteration.

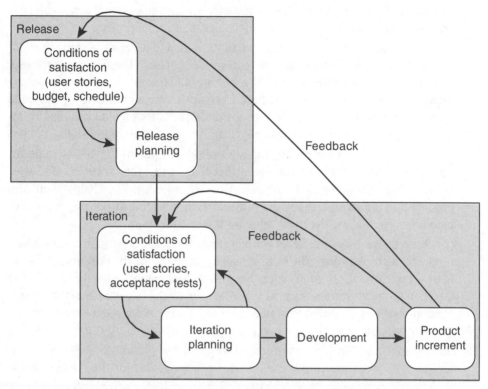

Figure 3.2   Conditions of satisfaction drive both release and iteration planning.

Feedback loops are shown in Figure 3.2 from the resulting new product increment back into the conditions-of-satisfaction boxes at the start of both release and iteration planning. Based on their experience developing the product increment during the iteration, the team may have gained knowledge or experience that affects planning at one or more of these levels. Similarly, showing the product increment to existing or likely users may generate new knowledge that would cause changes to the plans. An agile team will incorporate these changes into their plans to the extent that they lead to a higher-value product.

Summary

Agile teams work together as a team but include roles filled by specific individuals. First is the product owner, who is responsible for the product vision and for prioritizing features the team will work on. Next is the customer, who is the person paying for the project or purchasing the software once it's available. Users, developers, and managers are other roles on an agile project.

Agile teams work in short, timeboxed iterations that deliver a working product by the end of each iteration. The features developed in these iterations are selected based on the priority to the business. This ensures that the most important features are developed first. User stories are a common way for agile teams to express user needs. Agile teams understand that a plan can rapidly become out of date. Because of this, they adapt their plans as appropriate.

Projects should be viewed as rapidly and reliably generating a flow of useful new capabilities and new knowledge, rather than as just the execution of a series of steps. Projects generate two types of new knowledge: knowledge about the product and knowledge about the project. Each is useful in refining a product plan toward achieving the most value for the organization.

Agile teams use three levels of planning: release planning, iteration planning, and daily planning. The release plan looks ahead for the duration of the release—typically, three to six months. An iteration plan looks ahead only the duration of one iteration—typically, two to four weeks. A daily plan is the result of team member commitments made to each other in a daily stand-up meeting.

Understanding the product owner's conditions of satisfaction is critical in both release and iteration planning. During release planning, the whole team identifies a way of meeting the conditions of satisfaction for the release, which include scope, schedule, and resources. To achieve this, the product owner may need to relax one or more of her conditions of satisfaction. A similar process occurs during iteration planning, when the conditions of satisfaction are the new features that will be implemented and the high-level test cases that demonstrate the features were implemented correctly.

Discussion Questions

1. How would working as a unified whole team have affected your current or last project?

2. What are the conditions of satisfaction on your current project? Do all project stakeholders and participants agree on all of them? What risks are there to proceeding on a project that does not have agreement on all conditions of satisfaction?

3. Why are budget and schedule listed in Figure 3.2 as conditions of satisfaction to be considered during release planning but not during iteration planning?

Part II

Estimating Size

Agile teams separate estimates of size from estimates of duration. To understand the distinction, suppose I am tasked with moving a large pile of dirt from one corner of my yard to another. I could look at the pile of dirt, assess my tools (a shovel and a wheelbarrow), and directly estimate the job at five hours. In arriving at this estimate, I bypassed any estimate of size and went directly to an estimate of duration.

Suppose instead that I look at the pile and estimate its size. Based on its dimensions, I estimate the pile to contain about 300 cubic feet of dirt. This is my estimate of the size of this project. But an estimate of size alone is not useful in this case. We want to know how long it will take to move the dirt. We need to convert the estimate of size (300 cubic feet) into an estimate of duration.

A label on my wheelbarrow says it has a capacity of 6 cubic feet. Dividing 300 cubic feet by 6 cubic feet, I decide that moving the dirt will take 50 trips with the wheelbarrow. I estimate that each trip will take 3 minutes to load the wheelbarrow, 2 minutes to walk to the other side of the yard and dump the dirt, and 1 minute to walk back with the empty wheelbarrow. Total trip time will be 6 minutes. Because I anticipate making 50 trips, my estimate of duration is 300 minutes or 5 hours.

For a software project, the process of estimating duration is shown in Figure II.1.

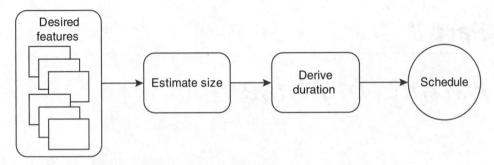

Figure II.1 Estimating the duration of a project begins with estimating its size.

In this part, we first look at two measures of size: story points and ideal time. We then look at techniques for estimating followed by advice on when to re-estimate. This part concludes with suggestions on how to choose between estimating in story points and estimating in ideal time.

Chapter 4

Estimating Size with Story Points

> *"In a good shoe, I wear a size six,*
> *but a seven feels so good, I buy a size eight."*
> —Dolly Parton in *Steel Magnolias*

Suppose a new restaurant opens nearby, and you decide to try it. For the first course, you can have either a cup or a bowl of soup. You can have the entrée as either a full or half portion. And you can have either a small or a large soda. You've probably been to many restaurants like this and can quite easily order about the right amount of food without asking how many ounces are in the cups and bowls of soup and exactly how big the entrée portions are. At most, you may ask the server something like "How big is the salad?" The server will likely respond by holding his hands apart to illustrate the size. In cases such as these, you are ordering by relative rather than measured size. You're saying, "Give me the large portion" or "I'd like the small serving." You are not ordering by exact size, such as "I'd like fourteen ounces of soda, six ounces of lasagna, and three ounces of bread."

It's possible to estimate an agile project's user stories or features in the same way. When I'm at an unfamiliar restaurant and order a large soda, I don't really know how many ounces I'll get. About all I do know is that a large soda is larger than a small or medium soda and that it's smaller than an extra-large one. I also know from experience that when I'm about as thirsty as I am now, a large soda at other restaurants has been the right size. Fortunately, this is all the knowledge I need. And on software projects it's even easier: All I need to know is whether a particular story or feature is larger or smaller than other stories and features.

Story Points Are Relative

Story points are a unit of measure for expressing the overall size of a user story, feature, or other piece of work. When we estimate with story points, we assign a point value to each item. The raw values we assign are unimportant. What matters are the relative values. A story that is assigned a two should be twice as much as a story that is assigned a one. It should also be two-thirds of a story that is estimated as three story points.

The number of story points associated with a story represents the overall size of the story. There is no set formula for defining the size of a story. Rather, a story-point estimate is an amalgamation of the amount of effort involved in developing the feature, the complexity of developing it, the risk inherent in it, and so on.

There are two common ways to get started. The first approach is to select a story that you expect to be one of the smallest stories you'll work with and say that story is estimated at one story point. The second approach is instead to select a story that seems somewhat medium and give it a number somewhere in the middle of the range you expect to use. Personally, I prefer most of my stories to be in the range of one to ten. (I'll explain why in Chapter 6, "Techniques for Estimating.") This means I'll look for a medium-size story and call it five story points. Once you've fairly arbitrarily assigned a story-point value to the first story, each additional story is estimated by comparing it with the first story or with any others that have been estimated.

The best way to see how this works is to try it. Instead of story points, let's estimate dog points for a moment. Let's define a dog point as representing the height of the dog at the shoulder. With that in mind, assign dog points to each of these breeds:

- ◆ Labrador retriever
- ◆ Terrier
- ◆ Great Dane
- ◆ Poodle
- ◆ Dachshund
- ◆ German shepherd
- ◆ Saint Bernard
- ◆ Bulldog

Before reading on, really spend a moment thinking about how many dog points you would assign to each breed. The discussion that follows will be much more clear if you do.

My estimates are shown in Table 4.1. I determined these values by starting with Labrador retriever. This breed seems medium-size to me, so I gave it a five. Great Danes seem about twice as tall, so I gave them a ten. Saint Bernards seem a little less than twice as tall, so I gave them a nine. A dachshund seems about as short as a dog gets and so got a one. Bulldogs are short, so I gave them a three. However, if I had been estimating dog points based on weight, I would have given bulldogs a higher number.

Table 4.1 One Possible Assignment of Dog Points

Breed	Dog Points
Labrador retriever	5
Terrier	3
Great Dane	10
Poodle	3
Dachshund	1
German shepherd	5
Saint Bernard	9
Bulldog	3

On an agile project it is not uncommon to begin an iteration with incompletely specified requirements, the details of which will be discovered during the iteration. However, we need to associate an estimate with each story, even those that are incompletely defined. You've already seen how to do this if you assigned dog points to poodle and terrier. Without more detail, it should have been difficult to assign dog points to poodle and terrier. There are toy, miniature, and standard poodles, each of a different height. Similarly, terrier is a group of more than twenty breeds. Some terriers (West Highland, Norwich, Norfolk) are less than a foot tall; others (Airedale) are nearly two feet tall.

When you're given a loosely defined user story (or dog), you make some assumptions, take a guess, and move on. In Table 4.1, I took a guess for terrier and poodle, and assigned each three dog points. I reasoned that even the largest are smaller than Labrador retrievers and that the small terriers and poodles would be one- or two-point dogs, so on average a three seemed reasonable.

Velocity

To understand how estimating in unitless story points can possibly work, it is necessary to introduce a new concept: velocity. *Velocity* is a measure of a team's rate of progress. It is calculated by summing the number of story points assigned to each user story that the team completed during the iteration.[1] If the team completes three stories each estimated at five story points, their velocity is fifteen. If the team completes two five-point stories, their velocity is ten.

If a team completed ten story points of work last iteration, our best guess is that they will complete ten story points this iteration. Because story points are estimates of relative size, this will be true whether they work on two five-point stories or five two-point stories.

In the introduction to this part of the book, the model in Figure 4.1 was used to show how an estimate of size could be turned into an estimate of duration and a schedule. It should be possible now to see how story points and velocity fit into this model.

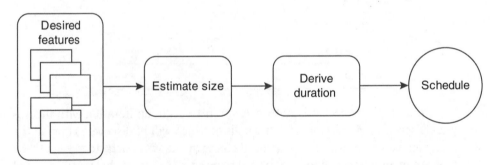

Figure 4.1 Estimating the duration of a project begins with estimating its size.

If we sum the story-point estimates for all desired features we come up with a total size estimate for the project. If we know the team's velocity we can divide

---

1. This definition will suffice for now. The next chapter will introduce the idea of estimating in ideal time as an alternative to story points. A team that estimates in ideal time will calculate velocity as the sum of the ideal time estimates of the stories completed.

size by velocity to arrive at an estimated number of iterations. We can turn this duration into a schedule by mapping it onto a calendar.

A key tenet of agile estimating and planning is that we estimate size but derive duration. Suppose all of the user stories are estimated and the sum of those estimates is 100 story points. This is the estimated size of the system. Suppose further that we know from past experience that the team's velocity has been ten points per two-week iteration, and that they will continue at the same velocity for this project. From our estimate of size and our known velocity value, we can derive a duration of ten iterations or twenty weeks. We can count forward twenty weeks on the calendar, and that becomes our schedule.

This very simplistic explanation of release planning works for now. It will be extended in Part IV, "Scheduling." Additionally, this example was made very simple because we used the team's past velocity. That is not always the case; velocity must sometimes be estimated instead. This can be difficult, but there are ways of doing it, which will be covered in Chapter 16, "Estimating Velocity."

Velocity Corrects Estimation Errors

Fortunately, as a team begins making progress through the user stories of a project, their velocity becomes apparent over the first few iterations. The beauty of a points-based approach to estimating is that planning errors are self-correcting because of the application of velocity. Suppose a team estimates a project to include 200 points of work. They initially believe they will be able to complete twenty-five points per iteration, which means they will finish in eight iterations. However, once the project begins, their observed velocity is only twenty. Without re-estimating any work they will have correctly identified that the project will take ten iterations rather than eight.

To see how this works, suppose you are hired to paint an unfamiliar house. You are shown the floor plan in Figure 4.2 and are told that all materials will be provided, including a brush, roller, and paint. For your own purposes, you want to know how long this job will take you, so you estimate it. Because all you have is the floor plan, and you cannot see the actual house yet, you estimate based on what you can infer from the floor plan. Suppose that you estimate the effort to paint each of the smaller bedrooms to be five points. The five doesn't mean anything. It does indicate, however, that the effort will be about the same for each bedroom. Because the master bedroom is about twice the size of the other bedrooms, you estimate it as ten points.

However, look more closely at Figure 4.2 and notice that there are no dimensions given. Are the two bedrooms 8' x 10' or 16' x 20'? It's impossible to tell from the floor plan. Are the estimates you've given completely worthless at this point? No. In fact, your estimates remain useful because they are estimates of the relative effort of painting each room. If you find that the bedrooms are twice the size you thought, the master bedroom is also twice the size you thought. The estimates remain the same, but because the rooms have four times the area you expected, your rate of progress through them will be slower.

The beauty of this is that estimating in story points completely separates the *estimation of effort* from the *estimation of duration*. Of course, effort and schedule are related, but separating them allows each to be estimated independently. In fact, you are no longer even estimating the duration of a project; you are computing it or deriving it. The distinction is subtle but important.

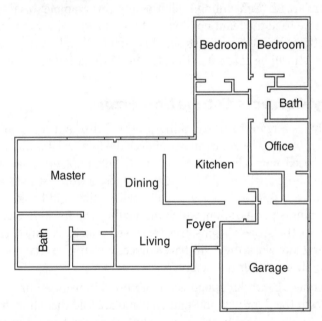

Figure 4.2 How long will it take to paint this house?

Summary

Story points are a relative measure of the size of a user story. A user story estimated as ten story points is twice as big, complex, or risky as a story estimated as five story points. A ten-point story is similarly half as big, complex, or risky as a twenty-point story. What matters are the relative values assigned to different stories.

Velocity is a measure of a team's rate of progress per iteration. At the end of each iteration, a team can look at the stories they have completed and calculate their velocity by summing the story-point estimates for each completed story.

Story points are purely an estimate of the size of the work to be performed. The duration of a project is not estimated as much as it is derived by taking the total number of story points and dividing it by the velocity of the team.

Discussion Questions

1. What story-point values would you put on some features of your current project?

2. After having assigned dog points to the dogs in this chapter, what estimate would you assign to an elephant if, as your project customer, I told you I misspoke and meant to give you a list of mammals not dogs?

3. It's fairly easy to estimate that two things of very similar size are the same. Over what range (from the smallest item to the largest) do you think you can reliably estimate? Five times the smallest item? Ten times? A hundred times? A thousand times?

Chapter 5

Estimating in Ideal Days

"To achieve great things, two things are needed:
a plan, and not quite enough time."
—Leonard Bernstein

How long is a game of American football?

You could answer that it has four fifteen-minute quarters and is therefore sixty minutes long. Or you could answer that it is somewhere around three hours long. Either answer would be correct in its own way. The difference highlights the distinction between ideal time and elapsed time. *Ideal time* is the amount of time that something takes when stripped of all peripheral activities. In that sense, a football game takes sixty minutes. *Elapsed time*, on the other hand, is the amount of time that passes on a clock (or perhaps a calendar). A football game requires around three hours of elapsed time.

Each way of measuring duration serves its own purpose. In a football game, ideal time is used by the officials to know when the quarters and game are complete. Certainly, that is a necessary function. On the other hand, if you're going to the game, and your spouse asks how long you'll be gone, it does you no good to say you'll be gone sixty minutes. Rather, you'll be gone for three hours (plus whatever travel time is needed).

It is almost always far easier and more accurate to predict the duration of an event in ideal time than in elapsed time. Suppose you are asked to estimate the duration of a specific football game this weekend. If you choose to give your estimate in ideal time, you can give a quick, off-the-cuff answer of sixty minutes. If you want to give a more precise estimate, you might look up the number of over-time games last year, crunch some numbers, and announce that, based on historical averages, this weekend's game will last 62.3 minutes.

On the other hand, suppose you choose to express your estimate in elapsed time. Some games last year took two-and-a-half hours; other games took over four hours. Some of the difference is based on random events such as injuries, but another part of the difference can be attributed to the playing styles of the teams, how many penalties each receives, and so on. Televised games take longer because of extra timeouts for commercials. Weather can either prolong or shorten games, depending on the teams involved. To come up with an estimate that will be as accurate as your off-the-cuff ideal time estimate, you would need to consider each of these factors.

Of course, if I look at the programming guide on my television, it tells me that the game starts at 1:00 and ends at 4:00. Clearly, someone at the network has made a prediction in elapsed time. What do they know that we don't know? A number of things. First, they plan to add or remove a few commercials based on how quickly the game is progressing. Second, most games are somewhere close to three hours. If the game finishes earlier, the network will run extra commercials, interviews, or other filler. If the game goes long, so what? Viewers interested in the game are likely to continue watching for another fifteen or thirty minutes. They won't turn the game off simply because the program guide said it should be over at 4:00. Viewers who aren't interested in the game but have tuned to the channel to watch a different show at 4:00 will also likely wait if the delay isn't too long. Finally, after decades of televising football games, the networks have accustomed us not to expect a precise finish time.

This last difference is an important one. After years of this, most football fans know that when a football game is scheduled to end at 4:00, that is only an estimate. No one is surprised when the game goes till 4:15 (an overrun of 8%). They may be frustrated or annoyed but not surprised. Why, then, are we surprised when a software project estimated at twelve months takes thirteen (an equivalent 8% overrun)? Which duration seems harder to estimate?

Ideal Time and Software Development

On a software project, ideal time differs from elapsed time not because of time-outs, incomplete passes, and injuries, but because of the natural overhead we experience every day. On any given day, in addition to working on the planned activities of a project, a team member may spend time answering email, making a support call to a vendor, interviewing a candidate for the open analyst position, and attending two meetings. More examples of why ideal time does not equal elapsed time are

- Supporting the current release
- Sick time
- Meetings
- Demonstrations
- Personnel issues
- Phone calls
- Special projects
- Training
- Email
- Reviews and walk-throughs
- Interviewing candidates
- Task switching
- Bug fixing in current releases
- Management reviews

Additionally, in looking at why ideal time does not equal elapsed time, consider that managers are able to work an average of only five minutes between interruptions (Hobbs 1987). Even if the typical developer is interrupted only one-third as often, that is still an interruption every fifteen minutes.

Problems can arise when a manager asks a team member the inevitable question: "How long will this take?" The team member responds, "Five days," so the manager counts off five days on her calendar and marks the day with a big red X. The team member, however, really meant to say, "Five days if that's all I do, but I do a lot of other things, so probably two weeks."

On a software project, multitasking also broadens the gap between ideal time and elapsed time. A football player is never told by his coach, "Since you're not busy on every play, I want you to play in this high-priority hockey game at the same time." A software developer who is told to multitask loses a great deal of efficiency while switching between two (or more) tasks.

On a software project, we may choose to estimate user stories or other work in *ideal days*. When estimating in ideal days, you assume

- The story being estimated is the only thing you'll work on.

◆ Everything you need will be on hand when you start.
◆ There will be no interruptions.

Ideal Days as a Measure of Size

When we estimate the number of ideal days that a user story will take to develop, test, and accept, it is not necessary to consider the impact of the overhead of the environment in which the team works. If developing a particular screen will take me one ideal day, it will take me one ideal day regardless of whether I'm employed by a start-up with no overhead or other demands on my time or by a huge bureaucracy. The amount of time that elapses on a clock (or calendar) will differ, of course. I may be able to achieve close to an ideal day of work at a low-overhead start-up. As additional demands are placed on my time, I have less time to work on deliverables for the project, and the amount of elapsed time to complete one ideal day of work will increase.

When considerations of organizational overhead are ignored, ideal days can be thought of as another estimate of size, just as story points are. Then an estimate of size expressed as a number of ideal days can be converted into an estimate of duration using velocity in exactly the same way as with story points.

One Estimate, Not Many

If you choose to estimate in ideal days, assign one aggregate estimate to each user story. Some teams are tempted to estimate a number of ideal days for each individual or group who will work on a story. For example, such a team might estimate that a particular user story will take two ideal days from a programmer, one ideal day from a database engineer, one ideal day from a user interaction designer, and two ideal days from a tester. I've seen teams then write the estimate on the story card with a different-colored marker for each role or on a different-colored sticky piece of paper for each role that is affixed to the story card.

In the vast majority of cases, my advice is not to do this. This level of focus on the individual roles on a team shifts team thinking away from the "we're all in this together" mentality we'd like to exist on an agile team. Further, it vastly increases the amount of work necessary to plan a release. If each story is assigned an estimate for each role that will work on the story, the release plan should realistically take each role into account. This means we'd have to track velocity and remaining work for each role as well.

While this is rarely worth the additional effort, it may sometimes be necessary. I was with one client recently who is working on three versions of a product—one for the Macintosh, one for Windows, and one for handheld computers. In this case, it is absolutely critical that each version be released with exactly the same functionality. Further, the individuals on this team do not currently have the skills to switch among Mac, Windows, and handheld development. A team in this situation may want to estimate the ideal time for each role on each story. They should, however, be aware of the extra administrative burden this will require.

Summary

Ideal time and elapsed time are different. The ideal time of a game of American football is sixty minutes (four fifteen-minute quarters). However, three or more hours will typically pass on a clock before a sixty-minute game is finished. The reason for the difference, of course, is all the interruptions that may occur during the game.

The amount of time a user story will take to develop can be more easily estimated in ideal days than in elapsed days. Estimating in elapsed days requires us to consider all of the interruptions that might occur while working on the story. If we instead estimate in ideal days, we consider only the amount of time the story will take. In this way, ideal days are an estimate of size, although less strictly so than story points.

When estimating in ideal days, it is best to associate a single estimate with each user story. Rather than estimating that a user story will take four programmer days, two tester days, and three product owner days, it is better to sum those and say the story as a whole will take nine ideal days.

Discussion Questions

1. If an ideal day is eight hours of uninterrupted, focused work, how many hours of elapsed time in your environment equates to one ideal day?
2. What might you be able to do to improve this?

Chapter 6

Techniques for Estimating

"Prediction is very difficult,
especially about the future."
—Niels Bohr, Danish physicist

The more effort we put into something, the better the result. Right? Perhaps, but we often need to expend just a fraction of that effort to get *adequate* results. For example, my car is dirty, and I need to wash it. If I wash it myself, I'll spend about an hour on it, which will be enough to wash the exterior, vacuum the interior, and clean the windows. For a one-hour investment, I'll have a fairly clean car.

On the other hand, I could call a car-detailing service and have them wash my car. They'll spend four hours on it. They do everything I do but much more thoroughly. They'll also wax the car, shine the dashboard, and so on. I watched one time, and they used tiny cotton swabs to clean out the little places too small to reach with a rag. That's a lot of effort for slightly better results. For me, the law of diminishing returns kicks in well before I'll use a cotton swab on my car.

We want to remain aware, too, of the diminishing return on time spent estimating. We can often spend a little time thinking about an estimate and come up with a number that is nearly as good as if we had spent a lot of time thinking about it. The relationship between estimate accuracy and effort is shown in Figure 6.1. The curve in this graph is placed according to my experience, corroborated in discussions with others. It is not based on empirical measurement.

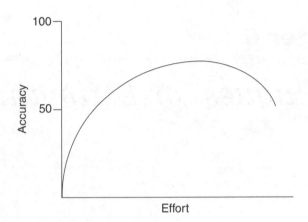

Figure 6.1 Additional estimation effort yields very little value beyond a certain point.

To understand this relationship better, suppose you decide to estimate how many cookies I've eaten in the past year. You could put no effort into the estimate and just take a random guess. Mapping this onto Figure 6.1, you'd be completely to the left on the effort axis, and your estimate would be unlikely to be accurate. You could move to the right on the effort axis by spending a half-hour or so researching national averages for cookie consumption. This would improve your accuracy over the pure guess. If you felt the need to be more accurate, you could do some research—call my friends and family, subpoena my past cookie orders from the Girl Scouts, and so on. You could even follow me around for a day—or, better yet, a month—and then extrapolate your observations into how many cookies you think I eat in a year.

Vary the effort you put into estimating according to purpose of the estimate. If you are trying to decide whether or not to send me a box of cookies as a gift, you do not need a very accurate estimate. If the estimate will be used to make a software build versus buy decision, it is likely enough to determine that the project will take six to twelve months. It may be unnecessary to refine that to the point where you can say it will take seven or eight months.

Look carefully at Figure 6.1, and notice a couple of things. First, no matter how much effort is invested, the estimate is never at the top of the accuracy axis. No matter how much effort you put into an estimate, an estimate is still an estimate. No amount of additional effort will make an estimate perfect. Next, notice how little effort is required to move the accuracy up dramatically from the baseline. As drawn in Figure 6.1, about 10% of the effort gets 50% of the potential accuracy. Finally, notice that eventually, the accuracy of the estimate declines. It is possible to put too much effort into estimating, with the result being a less accurate estimate.

When starting to plan a project, it is useful to think about where on the curve of Figure 6.1 we wish to be. Many projects try to be very high up the accuracy axis, forcing teams far out on the effort axis even though the benefits diminish rapidly. Often, this is the result of the simplistic view that we can lock down budgets, schedules, and scope and that project success equates to on-time, on-budget delivery of an up-front, precisely planned set of features. This type of thinking leads to a desire for extensive signed requirements documents, lots of up-front analysis work, and detailed project plans that show every task a team can think of. Then, even after all this additional up-front work, the estimates still aren't perfect.

Agile teams, however, choose to be closer to the left in a figure like Figure 6.1. They acknowledge that we cannot eliminate uncertainty from estimates, but they embrace the idea that small efforts are rewarded with big gains. Even though they are less far up the accuracy/effort scale, agile teams can produce more reliable plans because they frequently deliver small increments of fully working, tested, integrated code.

Estimates Are Shared

Estimates are not created by a single individual on the team. Agile teams do not rely on a single expert to estimate. Despite well-known evidence that estimates prepared by those who will do the work are better than estimates prepared by anyone else (Lederer and Prasad 1992), estimates are best derived collaboratively by the team, which includes those who will do the work. There are two reasons for this.

First, on an agile project we tend not to know specifically who will perform a given task. Yes, we may all suspect that the team's database guru will be the one to do the complex stored procedure task that has been identified. However, there's no guarantee that this will be the case. She may be busy when the time comes, and someone else will work on it. So because anyone may work on anything, it is important that everyone have input into the estimate.

Second, even though we may expect the database guru to do the work, others may have something to say about her estimate. Suppose that the team's database guru, Kristy, estimates a particular user story as three ideal days. Someone else on the project may not know enough to program the feature himself, but he may know enough to say, "Kristy, you're nuts; the last time you worked on a feature like that, it took a lot longer. I think you're forgetting how hard it was last time." At that point Kristy may offer a good explanation of why it's different this time. However, more often than not in my experience, she will acknowledge that she was indeed underestimating the feature.

The Estimation Scale

Studies have shown that we are best at estimating things that fall within one order of magnitude (Miranda 2001; Saaty 1996). Within your town, you should be able to estimate reasonably well the relative distances to things like the nearest grocery store, the nearest restaurant, and the nearest library. The library may be twice as far as the restaurant, for example. Your estimates will be far less accurate if you are asked also to estimate the relative distance to the moon or a neighboring country's capital. Because we are best within a single order of magnitude, we would like to have most of our estimates in such a range.

Two estimation scales I've had good success with are

◆ 1, 2, 3, 5, and 8

◆ 1, 2, 4, and 8

There's a logic behind each of these sequences. The first is the Fibonacci sequence.[1] I've found this to be a very useful estimation sequence because the gaps in the sequence become appropriately larger as the numbers increase. A one-point gap from 1 to 2 and from 2 to 3 seems appropriate, just as the gaps from 3 to 5 and from 5 to 8 do. The second sequence is spaced such that each number is twice the number that precedes it. These nonlinear sequences work well because they reflect the greater uncertainty associated with estimates for larger units of work. Either sequence works well, although my slight personal preference is for the first.

Each of these numbers should be thought of as a bucket into which items of the appropriate size are poured. Rather than thinking of work as water being poured into the buckets, think of the work as sand. If you are estimating using 1, 2, 3, 5, and 8, and have a story that you think is just the slightest bit bigger than the other five-point stories you've estimated, it would be OK to put it into the five-point bucket. A story you think is a 7, however, clearly would not fit in the five-point bucket.

---

1. A number in the Fibonacci sequence is generated by taking the sum of the previous two numbers.

You may want to consider including 0 as a valid number within your estimation range. Although it's unlikely that a team will encounter many user stories or features that truly take no work, including 0 is often useful. There are two reasons for this. First, if we want to keep all features within a 10x range, assigning nonzero values to tiny features will limit the size of largest features. Second, if the work truly is closer to 0 than 1, the team may not want the completion of the feature to contribute to its velocity calculations. If the team earns one point in this iteration for something truly trivial, in the next iteration their velocity will either drop by one or they'll have to earn that point by doing work that may not be as trivial.

If the team does elect to include 0 in their estimation scale, everyone involved in the project (especially the product owner) needs to understand that $13 \times 0 \neq 0$. I've never had the slightest problem explaining this to product owners, who realize that a 0-point story is the equivalent of a free lunch. However, they also realize there's a limit to the number of free lunches they can get in a single iteration. An alternative to using 0 is to group very small stories and estimate them as a single unit.

Some teams prefer to work with larger numbers, such as 10, 20, 30, 50, and 100. This is fine, because these are also within a single order of magnitude. However, if you go with larger numbers, such as 10 to 100, I still recommend that you pre-identify the numbers you will use within that range. Do not, for example, allow one story to be estimated at 66 story points or ideal days and another story to be estimated at 67. That is a false level of precision, and we cannot discern a 1.5% difference in size. It's acceptable to have one-point differences between values such as 1, 2, and 3. As percentages, those differences are much larger than between 66 and 67.

User Stories, Epics, and Themes

Although in general, we want to estimate user stories whose sizes are within one order of magnitude, this cannot always be the case. If we are to estimate everything within one order of magnitude, it would mean writing all stories at a fairly fine-grained level. For features that we're not sure we want (a preliminary cost estimate is desired before too much investment is put into them) or for features that may not happen in the near future, it is often desirable to write one much larger user story. A large user story is sometimes called an *epic*.

Additionally, a set of related user stories may be combined (usually by a paper clip if working with note cards) and treated as a single entity for either estimating or release planning. Such a set of user stories is referred to as a *theme*. An epic, by its very size alone, is often a theme on its own.

By aggregating some stories into themes and writing some stories as epics, a team is able to reduce the effort they'll spend on estimating. However, it's important that they realize that estimates of themes and epics will be more uncertain than estimates of the more specific, smaller user stories.

User stories that will be worked on in the near future (the next few iterations) need to be small enough that they can be completed in a single iteration. These items should be estimated within one order of magnitude. I use the sequence 1, 2, 3, 5, and 8 for this.

User stories or other items that are likely to be more distant than a few iterations can be left as epics or themes. These items can be estimated in units beyond the 1 to 8 range I recommend. To accommodate estimating these larger items I add 13, 20, 40, and 100 to my preferred sequence of 1, 2, 3, 5, and 8.

Deriving an Estimate

The three most common techniques for estimating are

- Expert opinion
- Analogy
- Disaggregation

Each of these techniques may be used on its own, but the techniques should be combined for best results.

Expert Opinion

If you want to know how long something is likely to take, ask an expert. At least, that's one approach. In an expert opinion-based approach to estimating, an expert is asked how long something will take or how big it will be. The expert relies on her intuition or gut feel and provides an estimate.

This approach is less useful on agile projects than on traditional projects. On an agile project, estimates are assigned to user stories or other user-valued functionality. Developing this functionality is likely to require a variety of skills normally performed by more than one person. This makes it difficult to find suitable experts who can assess the effort across all disciplines. On a traditional project for which estimates are associated with tasks, this is not as significant of a problem, because each task is likely performed by one person.

A nice benefit of estimating by expert opinion is that it usually doesn't take very long. Typically, a developer reads a user story, perhaps asks a clarifying question or two, and then provides an estimate based on her intuition. There is even evidence that says this type of estimating is more accurate than other, more analytical approaches (Johnson et al. 2000).

Analogy

An alternative to expert opinion comes in the form of estimating by analogy, which is what we're doing when we say, "This story is a little bigger than that story." When estimating by analogy, the estimator compares the story being estimated with one or more other stories. If the story is twice the size, it is given an estimate twice as large. There is evidence that we are better at estimating relative size than we are at estimating absolute size (Lederer and Prasad 1998; Vicinanza et al. 1991).

When estimating this way, you do not compare all stories against a single baseline or universal reference. Instead, you want to estimate each new story against an assortment of those that have already been estimated. This is referred to as triangulation. To triangulate, compare the story being estimated against a couple of other stories. To decide if a story should be estimated at five story points, see if it seems a little bigger than a story you estimated at three and a little smaller than a story you estimated at eight.

Disaggregation

Disaggregation refers to splitting a story or feature into smaller, easier-to-estimate pieces. If most of the user stories to be included in a project are in the range of two to five days to develop, it will be very difficult to estimate a single story that may be 100 days. Not only are large things notoriously more difficult to estimate, but also in this case there will be very few similar stories to compare. Asking "Is this story fifty times as hard as that story" is a very different question from "Is this story about one-and-a-half times that one?"

The solution to this, of course, is to break the large story or feature into multiple smaller items and estimate those. However, you need to be careful not to go too far with this approach. The easiest way to illustrate the problem is with a nonsoftware example. Let's use disaggregation to estimate my golf score this weekend. Assume the course I am playing has eighteen holes each with a par of four. (If you're unfamiliar with golf scoring, the par score is the number of shots it should take a decent player to shoot his ball into the cup at the end of the hole.)

To estimate by disaggregation, we need to estimate my score for each hole. There's the first hole, and that's pretty easy, so let's give me a three on that. But then I usually hit into the lake on the next hole, so that's a seven. Then there's the hole with the sandtraps; let's say a five. And so on. However, if I'm mentally re-creating an entire golf course it is very likely I'll forget one of the holes. Of course, in this case I have an easy check for that, as I know there must be eighteen individual estimates. But when disaggregating a story, there is no such safety check.

Not only does the likelihood of forgetting a task increase if we disaggregate too far, but summing estimates of lots of small tasks also leads to problems. For example, for each of the 18 holes, I may estimate my score for that hole to be in the range 3 to 8. Multiplying those by 18 gives me a full round range of 54 to 144. There's no chance that I'll do that well or that poorly. If asked for an estimate of my overall score for a full round, I'm likely to say anywhere from 80 to 120, which is a much smaller range and a much more useful estimate.

Specific advice on splitting user stories is provided in Chapter 12, "Splitting User Stories."

Planning Poker

The best way I've found for agile teams to estimate is by playing planning poker (Grenning 2002). Planning poker combines expert opinion, analogy, and disaggregation into an enjoyable approach to estimating that results in quick but reliable estimates.

Participants in planning poker include all of the developers on the team. Remember that *developers* refers to all programmers, testers, database engineers, analysts, user interaction designers, and so on. On an agile project, this will typically not exceed ten people. If it does, it is usually best to split into two teams. Each team can then estimate independently, which will keep the size down. The product owner participates in planning poker but does not estimate.

At the start of planning poker, each estimator is given a deck of cards. Each card has written on it one of the valid estimates. Each estimator may, for example, be given a deck of cards that reads 0, 1, 2, 3, 5, 8, 13, 20, 40, and 100. The cards should be prepared prior to the planning poker meeting, and the numbers should be large enough to see across a table. Cards can be saved and used for the next planning poker session.

For each user story or theme to be estimated, a moderator reads the description. The moderator is usually the product owner or an analyst. However, the moderator can be anyone, as there is no special privilege associated with the role. The product owner answers any questions that the estimators have. However, everyone is asked to remain aware of the effort/accuracy curve (Figure 6.1). The goal in planning poker is not to derive an estimate that will withstand all future scrutiny. Rather, the goal is to be somewhere well on the left of the effort line, where a valuable estimate can be arrived at cheaply.

After all questions are answered, each estimator privately selects a card representing his or her estimate. Cards are not shown until each estimator has made a selection. At that time, all cards are simultaneously turned over and shown so that all participants can see each estimate.

It is very likely at this point that the estimates will differ significantly. This is actually good news. If estimates differ, the high and low estimators explain their estimates. It's important that this does not come across as attacking those estimators. Instead, you want to learn what they were thinking about.

As an example, the high estimator may say, "Well, to test this story, we need to create a mock database object. That might take us a day. Also, I'm not sure if our standard compression algorithm will work, and we may need to write one that is more memory efficient." The low estimator may respond, "I was thinking we'd store that information in an XML file—that would be easier than a database for us. Also, I didn't think about having more data—maybe that will be a problem."

The group can discuss the story and their estimates for a few more minutes. The moderator can take any notes she thinks will be helpful when this story is being programmed and tested. After the discussion, each estimator re-estimates by selecting a card. Cards are once again kept private until everyone has estimated, at which point they are turned over at the same time.

In many cases, the estimates will already converge by the second round. But if they have not, continue to repeat the process. The goal is for the estimators to converge on a single estimate that can be used for the story. It rarely takes more than three rounds, but continue the process as long as estimates are moving closer together. It isn't necessary that everyone in the room turns over a card with exactly the same estimate written down. If I'm moderating an estimation meeting, and on the second round four estimators tell me 5, 5, 5, and 3, I will ask the low estimator if she is OK with an estimate of 5. Again, the point is not absolute precision but reasonableness.

The Right Amount of Discussion

Some amount of preliminary design discussion is necessary and appropriate when estimating. However, spending too much time on design discussions sends a team too far up the effort/accuracy curve of Figure 6.1. Here's an effective way to encourage some amount of discussion but make sure that it doesn't go on too long.

Buy a two-minute sand timer, and place it in the middle of the table where planning poker is being played. Anyone in the meeting can turn the timer over at any time. When the sand runs out (in two minutes), the next round of cards is played. If agreement isn't reached, the discussion can continue. But someone can immediately turn the timer over, again limiting the discussion to two minutes. The timer rarely needs to be turned over more than twice. Over time this helps teams learn to estimate more rapidly.

Smaller Sessions

It is possible to play planning poker with a subset of the team, rather than involving everyone. This isn't ideal but may be a reasonable option, especially if there are many, many items to be estimated, as can happen at the start of a new project.

The best way to do this is to split the larger team into two or three smaller teams, each of which must have at least three estimators. It is important that each of the teams estimates consistently. What your team calls three story points or ideal days had better be consistent with what my team calls the same. To achieve this, start all teams together in a joint planning poker session for an hour or so. Have them estimate ten to twenty stories. Then make sure each team has a copy of these stories and their estimates and that they use them as baselines for estimating the stories they are given to estimate.

When to Play Planning Poker

Teams will need to play planning poker at two different times. First, there will usually be an effort to estimate a large number of items before the project officially begins or during its first iterations. Estimating an initial set of user stories may take a team two or three meetings of from one to three hours each. Naturally, this will depend on how many items there are to estimate, the size of the team, and the product owner's ability to clarify the requirements succinctly.

Second, teams will need to put forth some ongoing effort to estimate any new stories that are identified during an iteration. One way to do this is to plan to hold a very short estimation meeting near the end of each iteration. Normally, this is quite sufficient for estimating any work that came in during the iteration, and it allows new work to be considered in the prioritization of the coming iteration.

Alternatively, Kent Beck suggests hanging an envelope on the wall with all new stories placed in the envelope. As individuals have a few spare minutes, they will grab a story or two from the envelope and estimate them. Teams will establish a rule for themselves, typically that all stories must be estimated by the end of the day or by the end of the iteration. I like the idea of hanging an envelope on the wall to contain unestimated stories. However, I'd prefer that when someone has a few spare minutes to devote to estimating, he find at least one other person and that they estimate jointly.

Why Planning Poker Works

Now that I've described planning poker, it's worth spending a moment on some of the reasons why it works so well.

First, planning poker brings together multiple expert opinions to do the estimating. Because these experts form a cross-functional team from all disciplines on a software project, they are better suited to the estimation task than anyone else. After completing a thorough review of the literature on software estimation, Jørgensen (2004) concluded that "the people most competent in solving the task should estimate it."

Second, a lively dialogue ensues during planning poker, and estimators are called upon by their peers to justify their estimates. This has been found to improve the accuracy of the estimate, especially on items with large amounts of uncertainty (Hagafors and Brehmer 1983). Being asked to justify estimates has also been shown to result in estimates that better compensate for missing information (Brenner et al. 1996). This is important on an agile project because the user stories being estimated are often intentionally vague.

Third, studies have shown that averaging individual estimates leads to better results (Hoest and Wohlin 1998) as do group discussions of estimates (Jørgensen and Moløkken 2002). Group discussion is the basis of planning poker, and those discussions lead to an averaging of sorts of the individual estimates.

Finally, planning poker works because it's fun.

Summary

Expending more time and effort to arrive at an estimate does not necessarily increase the accuracy of the estimate. The amount of effort put into an estimate should be determined by the purpose of that estimate. Although it is well known that the best estimates are given by those who will do the work, on an agile team we do not know in advance who will do the work. Therefore, estimating should be a collaborative activity for the team.

Estimates should be on a predefined scale. Features that will be worked on in the near future and that need fairly reliable estimates should be made small enough that they can be estimated on a nonlinear scale from 1 to 10 such as 1, 2, 3, 5, and 8 or 1, 2, 4, and 8. Larger features that will most likely not be implemented in the next few iterations can be left larger and estimated in units such as 13, 20, 40, and 100. Some teams choose to include 0 in their estimation scale.

To arrive at an estimate, we rely on expert opinion, analogy, and disaggregation. A fun and effective way of combining these is planning poker. In planning poker, each estimator is given a deck of cards with a valid estimate shown on each card. A feature is discussed, and each estimator selects the card that represents his or her estimate. All cards are shown at the same time. The estimates are discussed and the process repeated until agreement on the estimate is reached.

Discussion Questions

1. How good are your estimates today? Which techniques do you primarily rely on: expert opinion, analogy, or disaggregation?
2. Which estimation scale do you prefer? Why?
3. Who should participate in planning poker on your project?

Chapter 7

Re-Estimating

"There's no sense in being precise
when you don't even know what you're talking about."
—John von Neumann

One of the most common questions about estimating with story points or ideal days is "When do we re-estimate?" To arrive at an answer it is critical to remember that story points and ideal days are estimates of the overall size and complexity of the feature being implemented. Story points in particular are not an estimate of the amount of time it takes to implement a feature, even though we often fall into the trap of thinking of them as such. The amount of time that implementing a feature will take is a function of its size (estimated in either ideal days or story points) *and* the team's rate of progress (as reflected by its velocity).

If we keep in mind that story points and ideal time estimate size, it's easier to see that we should re-estimate only when we believe a story's relative size has changed. When working with story points or ideal time, we do not re-estimate solely because a story took longer to implement than we thought. The best way to see this is through some examples.

Introducing the SwimStats Website

Throughout the rest of this chapter and some of the upcoming chapters, we will be working on SwimStats, a hypothetical website for swimmers and swim coaches. SwimStats will be sold as a service to competitive age-group, school, and college swim teams. Coaches will use it to keep track of their roster of swim-mers, organize workouts, and prepare for meets; swimmers will use the site to see meet results, check their personal records, and track improvements over time. Officials at swim meets will enter results into the system. A sample screen from SwimStats is shown in Figure 7.1.

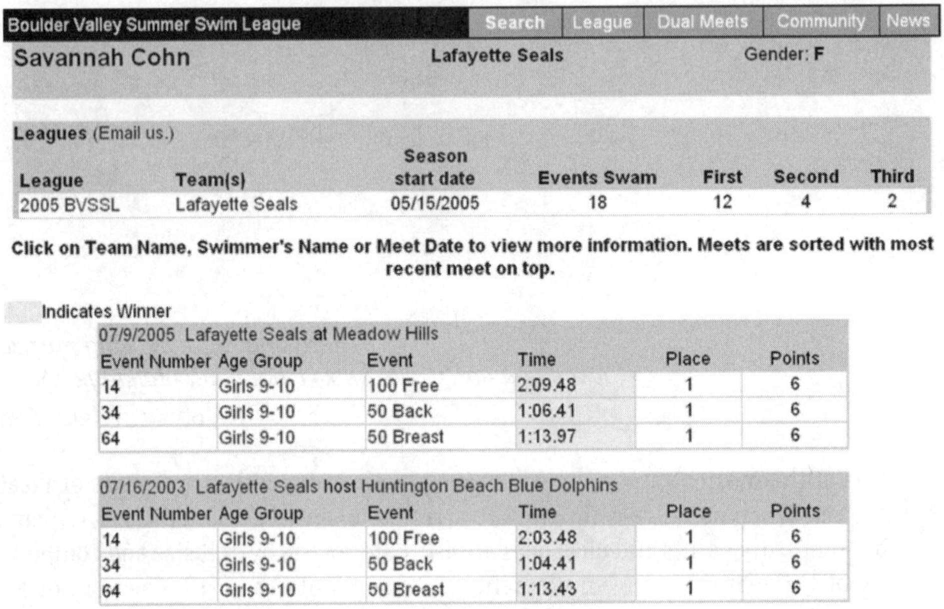

Boulder Valley Summer Swim League			Search	League	Dual Meets	Community	News
Savannah Cohn		**Lafayette Seals**				**Gender: F**	

Leagues (Email us.)

League	Team(s)	Season start date	Events Swam	First	Second	Third
2005 BVSSL	Lafayette Seals	05/15/2005	18	12	4	2

Click on Team Name, Swimmer's Name or Meet Date to view more information. Meets are sorted with most recent meet on top.

Indicates Winner

07/9/2005 Lafayette Seals at Meadow Hills

Event Number	Age Group	Event	Time	Place	Points
14	Girls 9-10	100 Free	2:09.48	1	6
34	Girls 9-10	50 Back	1:06.41	1	6
64	Girls 9-10	50 Breast	1:13.97	1	6

07/16/2003 Lafayette Seals host Huntington Beach Blue Dolphins

Event Number	Age Group	Event	Time	Place	Points
14	Girls 9-10	100 Free	2:03.48	1	6
34	Girls 9-10	50 Back	1:04.41	1	6
64	Girls 9-10	50 Breast	1:13.43	1	6

Figure 7.1   One screen from the SwimStats website.

When Not to Re-Estimate

Using SwimStats as an example, let's first look briefly at a case when we should not re-estimate. Suppose we have the stories shown in Table 7.1. At the conclu-sion of the first iteration, the first two stories are complete. The team doesn't feel good about this because they thought they would complete twice as many points (twelve rather than six) per iteration. They decide that each of those stories was twice as big or complex as initially thought, which is why they took twice as long as expected to complete. The team decides to double the number of story points associated with each. This means that their velocity was twelve (two six-point stories), which they feel better about.

However, before the project started, the team considered all four stories of Table 7.1 to be of equivalent size and complexity, so each was estimated at three story points. Because they still believe these stories are equivalent, the estimates for Stories 3 and 4 must now also be doubled. The team has given themselves more points for the stories they completed, which doubled their velocity. But, because they also doubled the amount of work remaining in the project, their situation is the same as if they'd left all the estimates at three and velocity at six.

Table 7.1 Some Stories and Estimates for the SwimStats Website

Story ID	Story	Estimate
1	As a coach, I can enter the names and demographic information for all swimmers on my team.	3
2	As a coach, I can define practice sessions.	3
3	As a swimmer, I can see all of my times for a specific event.	3
4	As a swimmer, I can update my demographics information.	3

Velocity Is the Great Equalizer

What's happened here is that velocity is the great equalizer. Because the estimate for each feature is made relative to the estimates for other features, it does not matter if our estimates are correct, a little incorrect, or a lot incorrect. What matters is that they are consistent. We cannot simply roll a die and assign that number as the estimate to a feature. However, as long as we are consistent with our estimates, measuring velocity over the first few iterations will allow us to hone in on a reliable schedule.

Let's look at another example. Suppose a project consists of fifty user stories, each of which is estimated as one story point. For simplicity, suppose that I am the only person working on this project and that I expect I can complete one story point per work day. So on a two-week iteration, I expect to finish ten stories and have a velocity of ten. Further, I expect to finish the project in five iterations (ten weeks). However, after the first iteration, rather than having completed ten stories, I've completed only five. If I let velocity take care of correcting my misperceptions, I will realize that the project will take ten iterations, because my velocity is half of what I'd planned.

What happens, though, if I re-estimate? Suppose I re-estimate the five completed stories, assigning each an estimate of two. My velocity is now ten (five completed stories, each re-estimated at two), and forty-five points of work remain. With a velocity of ten and with forty-five points remaining, I expect to finish the project in 4.5 iterations. The problem with this is that I am mixing revised and original estimates. Using hindsight, I have re-estimated the completed stories at two points each. Unfortunately, when still looking forward at the remaining forty-five stories, I cannot predict which of those one-point stories I will want to say were worth two points in hindsight.

When to Re-Estimate

Let's continue working on the SwimStats website, this time with the user stories and estimates shown in Table 7.2.

Table 7.2 Initial Estimates for Some SwimStats Stories

Story ID	Story	Estimate
1	As a swimmer, I can see a line chart of my times for a particular event.	3
2	As a coach, I can see a line chart showing the progress over the season of all of my swimmers in a particular event.	5
3	As a swimmer, I can see a pie chart showing how many first, second, third, and lower places I've finished in.	3
4	As a coach, I can see a text report showing each swimmer's best time in each event.	3
5	As a coach, I can upload meet results from a file exported from the timing system used at the meet.	3
6	As a coach, I can have the system recommend who should swim in each event subject to restrictions about how many events a swimmer can participate in.	5

The first three of these stories each has to do with displaying a chart for the user. Suppose the team has planned the first iteration to include Stories 1, 2, and 6 from Table 7.2. Their planned velocity is thirteen. However, at the end of the iteration they have finished only Stories 1 and 6. They say they got less done than expected because Story 1 was much harder than expected and that it should have been "at least a six." Suppose that rather than one difficult story, the team has completely underestimated the general difficulty of displaying charts. In that case, if Story 1 turned out to be twice as big as expected, we can expect the same of Stories 2 and 3.

Let's see how this plays out across three scenarios.

Scenario 1: No Re-Estimating

In this scenario, we will leave all estimates alone. The team achieved a velocity of eight points in the last iteration. That leads us to the expectation that they'll average eight points in the upcoming iterations. However, the team knows they cannot complete Stories 2 and 3 in a single iteration, even though they represent only eight points. Because each of those stories involves charting, and because the team expects each charting story to be twice as big as its current estimate (just like Story 1 was), the team concludes that they cannot do Stories 2 and 3 in one iteration. It's eight points, but it's too much.

Scenario 2: Re-Estimating the Finished Story

In this scenario, let's see if adjusting only the estimate of Story 1 fixes this problem. After finishing the iteration, the team felt that Story 1 was twice as big as had been expected. So they decide to re-estimate it at six instead of three. That means that velocity for the prior iteration was eleven—six points for Story 1 and five points for Story 6.

Because no other stories are re-estimated, the team plans its next iteration to comprise Stories 2, 3, and 4. These stories are worth eleven points, the same amount of work completed in the prior iteration. However, they run into the same problem as in the first scenario: Stories 2 and 3 will probably take twice as long as expected, and the team will not be able to average eleven points per iteration, as expected.

Scenario 3: Re-Estimating When Relative Size Changes

In this scenario, the team re-estimates each of the charting stories. The estimates for Stories 1, 2, and 3 are double what is shown in Table 7.2. As in the second scenario, velocity for the first iteration is eleven—six points for Story 1 and five points for Story 6. Because velocity was eleven in the first iteration, the team expects approximately that velocity in the next iteration. However, when they plan their next iteration, only Story 2 will be selected. This story, initially estimated as five, was doubled to ten and is so big there is no room for an additional story.

Re-estimating was helpful only in this third scenario. This means that you should re-estimate a story only when its relative size has changed.

Re-Estimating Partially Completed Stories

You may also wish to re-estimate when the team finishes only a portion of a story during an iteration. Suppose the team has been working on a story that says, "As a coach, I can have the system recommend who should swim in each event." This story is initially estimated as five points, but it is deceptively complex.

Teams in a swim meet receive points based on the finishing places of the swimmers. However, planning for a swim meet is not as easy as putting the team's fastest swimmer for each event into that event. Each swimmer is limited in the number of events he or she can swim. This means we may not elect to have Savannah swim the 100-meter backstroke because we need her more in the 100-meter breaststroke. So suppose the team reaches the end of the iteration, and the system can optimize the assignment of swimmers to individual events. However, the team has not begun to think about how to assign swimmers to relay events. How many points should the team count toward the velocity of the current iteration? How many points should they assign to the remaining work?

First, let me point out that I'm generally in favor of an all-or-nothing stance toward counting velocity: if a story is done (coded, tested, and accepted by the product owner), the team earns all the points, but if anything on the story isn't done, they earn nothing. At the end of an iteration, this is the easiest case to assess: If everything is done, they get all the points; if anything is missing, they get no points. If the team is likely to take on the remaining portion of the story in the next iteration, this works well. Their velocity in the first iteration is a bit lower than expected because they got no credit for partially completing a story. In the second iteration, however, their velocity will be higher than expected because they'll get all of the points, even though some work had been completed prior to the start of the iteration. This works well as long as everyone remembers that we're mostly interested in the team's average velocity over time, not in whether velocity jumped up or down in a given iteration.

However, in some cases the unfinished portion of a story may not be done in the next iteration. In these cases it can be appropriate to allow the team to take partial credit for the completed portion of the story. The remaining story (which is a subset of the initial story) is re-estimated based on the team's current knowledge. In this case, the original story was estimated at five points. If the team feels that the subset they completed (scheduling individual events) is equivalent to three points or ideal days, they will give themselves that much credit. The unfinished portion of the original story in this case could be rewritten to be "As a coach, I can have the system recommend who should swim in each relay." The team could then estimate that smaller story relative to all other stories. The combined estimates would not need to equal the original estimate of five.

However, the two best solutions to allocating points for incomplete stories are not to have any incomplete stories and to use sufficiently small stories that partial credit isn't an issue.

The Purpose of Re-Estimating

Do not become overly concerned with the need to re-estimate. Whenever the team feels one or more stories are misestimated relative to other stories, re-estimate as few stories as possible to bring the relative estimates back in line. Use re-estimating as a learning experience for estimating future user stories. As Tom Poppendieck has taught me, "Failure to learn is the only true failure." Learn from each re-estimated story, and turn the experience into a success.

Summary

Remembering that story points and ideal days are estimates of the size of a feature helps you know when to re-estimate. You should re-estimate only when your opinion of the relative size of one or more stories has changed. Do not re-estimate solely because progress is not coming as rapidly as you'd expected. Let velocity, the great equalizer, take care of most estimation inaccuracies.

At the end of an iteration, I do not recommend giving partial credit for partially finished user stories. My preference is for a team to count the entire estimate toward their velocity (if they completely finished and the feature has been accepted by the product owner) or for them to count nothing toward their story otherwise. However, the team may choose to re-estimate partially complete user stories. Typically, this will mean estimating a user story representing the work that was completed during the iteration and one or more user stories that describe the remaining work. The sum of these estimates does not need to equal the initial estimate.

Discussion Questions

1. How does velocity correct bad estimates?
2. Why should you re-estimate only when the relative size has changed? Identify some examples on a current or recent project when the relative size of one or more features changed.

Chapter 8

Choosing between Story
Points and Ideal Days

"If you tell people where to go,
but not how to get there,
you'll be amazed at the results."
—General George S. Patton

As measures of size, story points and ideal days each have their advantages. To
help you decide which one to use, this chapter outlines the key considerations in
favor of each approach.

Considerations Favoring Story Points

This section outlines the key points in favor of estimating in story points. These
include

 ◆ Story points help drive cross-functional behavior.
 ◆ Story-point estimates do not decay.
 ◆ Story points are a pure measure of size.
 ◆ Estimating in story points typically is faster.
 ◆ My ideal days are not your ideal days.

Story Points Help Drive Cross-Functional Behavior

One of the reasons why agile teams are successful is that the teams are cross-functional. That is, agile teams include members from all disciplines necessary to build the product, including programmers, testers, product managers, usability designers, analysts, database engineers, and so on. Often, when we first assemble a cross-functional team, some members have a hard time letting go of their departmental identity. The product will benefit to the extent that the project participants view themselves as team members first and as specialist contributors second—that is, "I am on the Napa project and am a tester" rather than "I am a tester assigned to the Napa project." The distinction may be subtle, but the change in mindset is not.

Estimating in story points can help teams learn to work cross-functionally. Because a story-point estimate needs to be a single number that represents all of the work for the whole team, estimating story points initiates high-level discussions about everything that will be involved. Estimating ideal days, on the other hand, often involves specialty groups estimating how long "their part" of a story will take and then summing these subestimates. For example, the programmers may conclude that they need three ideal days, the database engineer needs one, and the tester needs two. An estimate of six ideal days is then assigned to the story.

This small difference in how the earliest discussions about a story occur has an ongoing impact on how the story is developed.

Story-Point Estimates Do Not Decay

An estimate expressed in story points has a longer shelf life than an estimate in ideal days. An estimate in ideal days can change based on the team's experience with the technology, the domain, and themselves, among other factors. To see why, suppose a programmer is learning a new language and is asked how long it will take to program a small application. His answer may be five days. Now jump forward a few months and ask the same programmer how long it will take to develop an application that is exactly the same size and complexity. His answer may be one day because he has become more skilled in the language. We have a problem now, because the two applications are exactly the same size, yet they have been estimated differently.

We would like to think that measuring velocity over time would correct or account for this problem. It won't. Instead, we'll see a consistent velocity even though more work is being done. Suppose that this programmer is the only person on the team and that he is working in one-week iterations. The first time he develops the application, he has estimated it will take five ideal days. Let's suppose he's in an environment where a calendar day equals an ideal day. He starts this application on the first day of the iteration and finishes it on the fifth. He has a velocity of five for that iteration. Then, a few months later, because he estimates a similar application as one ideal day, he will complete five of them in an iteration. His velocity is again five, even though he did five times as much work as before. For some projects, especially those adopting new technologies or on which the team is new to the domain, this can be significant.

Note that both story-point and ideal-day estimates will need to be updated if the size of an effort changes based on the development of a framework, for example. However, only ideal-day estimates need to change when the team becomes better at something.

Story Points Are a Pure Measure of Size

As described in the introduction to this part, an important first step in estimating how long something will take is estimating how big it is or how much of it there is to do. Story points are a *pure* measure of size. Ideal days are not. Ideal days may be used as a measure of size, but with some deficiencies. As noted in the preceding section, an estimate in ideal days will change as a developer's proficiency changes. This does not happen with story points—the size is what it is and doesn't change. That is a desirable attribute of any measure of size.

That story points are a pure measure of size has a couple of advantages. First, this means that we can estimate story points by analogy only. There is credible evidence that we are better at estimating "this is like that" than we are at estimating the absolute size of things (Lederer and Prasad 1998; Vicinanza et al. 1991). When we estimate in ideal days, on the other hand, we can still estimate by analogy. But when estimating in ideal days, we also tend to think of the calendar and how long a story will take to develop.

Second, because story points are a pure measure of size and are entirely abstract, there can be no temptation to compare them with reality. Teams that estimate in ideal days almost inevitably have their ideal days compared with actual days. They then find themselves justifying why they completed "only" eight ideal days of work in a ten-day iteration.

Estimating in Story Points Typically Is Faster

Teams that estimate in story points seem to do so more quickly than teams that estimate in ideal days. To estimate many stories, it is necessary to have a very high-level design discussion about the story: Would we implement this in the database? Can we reuse the user interface? How will this affect the middle tier? All these questions come up at one time or another.

My experience is that teams estimating in ideal days have a tendency to take these discussions a little deeper than do teams estimating in story points. The difference is presumably because when estimating in ideal days, it is more tempting to think about the individual tasks necessary to develop a story than to think in terms of the size of the story relative to other stories.

My Ideal Days Are Not Your Ideal Days

Suppose two runners, one fast and one slow, are standing at the start of a trail. Each can see the whole course of the trail, and they can agree that it is one kilometer. They can compare it with another trail they've each run and agree that it is about half the length of that other trail. Their discussions of trail size (really distance, in this case) are meaningful.

Suppose instead of discussing the length of the trails, these two runners discussed the time it took to run the trails. The fast runner might say, "This is a five-minute trail," to which the slow runner would respond, "No, it's at least a eight-minute trail." Each would be right, of course, but they would have no way of settling their differences other than agreeing always to discuss trails in terms of how long one of them (or some other runner) would take to run the trail.

This same problem exists with ideal days. You may think you can completely develop a particular user story in three ideal days. I think I can do it in five days. We're probably both right. How can we come to an agreement? We might choose to put your estimate on it because we think you'll be the one to do the work. But that might be a mistake, because by the time we actually do the work, you may be too busy and I have to do it. And I'll be late, because it's estimated at three days for you, but will take me five.

What most teams do is ignore this issue. This is acceptable if all developers are of approximately the same skill or if programmers always work in pairs, which helps balance out extreme differences in productivity.

Considerations Favoring Ideal Days

This section outlines the key points in favor of estimating in ideal days. These include the following:

- ◆ Ideal days are easier to explain outside the team.

+ Ideal days are easier to estimate at first.

Ideal Days Are Easier to Explain Outside the Team

There is a very intuitive feel to ideal days—"This is the amount of time it would take me if it's all that I worked on." Because of this intuitive feel, ideal days are easy to understand, which makes them easy to explain to others outside the project team. Everyone understands that not every minute of the work day is spent programming, testing, designing, or otherwise making progress toward new features.

It is usually necessary to explain to outsiders (and the team, at first) the concept of a story point as a measure of size. However, you can often use the need to explain story points as an opportunity to describe the overall approach to estimating and planning your project will take. This is an excellent opportunity to accustom outside stakeholders to ideas such as the cone of uncertainty, the progressive refinement of plan accuracy, and how observing velocity over a number of periods will lead to greater reliability in the plans you produce.

Ideal Days Are Easier to Estimate at First

In addition to being easier to explain to others, it is often easier for the team itself to get started with ideal days. When a team chooses to estimate in story points, the first handful of stories they estimate can be difficult to estimate or have an unsettling feeling. Without a baseline such as a nine-to-five day or some previously estimated stories, the team that uses story points has to find its own baseline by estimating a few stories.

Fortunately, most teams get through this initial phase of story-point estimating very, very quickly. Usually within an hour, many teams estimate in story points as naturally as if they'd been doing it for years. However, those first few stories can feel uncomfortable.

Recommendation

My preference is for story points. I find that the benefits they offer as pure measure of size are compelling. That story points help promote cross-functional team behavior is a huge advantage. Shifting a team's thinking from "my part will take three ideal days, and your part will take two ideal days, so the total is five ideal days" is very different from "overall, this story seems about the same size as that one, so let's call it five story points also." That a story point to me can be the same as a story point to you, while the same may not be true of an ideal day, is another big benefit. Two developers of different skill or experience can agree on the size of something while disagreeing about how long it will take to do.

The shortcomings of story points are indeed short. Yes, it's easier to get started with ideal days. However, the discomfort of working with nebulous story points is short-lived. Ideal days are definitely easier to explain to those outside the team, but we probably shouldn't choose based on how hard it will be to explain to outsiders. That ideal days are so easily understandable causes problems as well. In some organizations there will be pressure to make an actual day closer to an ideal day. Pressure for more focus and concentration on our work is fine. But organizational pressure for each actual day to be close to an ideal day will also have the effect of causing us to estimate in actual time while calling it an ideal day. That is, an ideal day will become redefined as "a day where I make six hours of progress and do other things for two hours."

I occasionally start a team estimating in ideal days. I usually do this only with a team that cannot accept that it is beneficial to separate estimates of size and duration. Some individuals are so used to being asked for estimates and responding immediately with a date that the jump to story points is difficult.

In these cases, I have the team start estimating in ideal days, but as quickly as possible, I start to ask questions like "How big is this one compared with the one we estimated five minutes ago?" Or I'll ask, "So this one is a little smaller than the story we just estimated?" The purpose of these questions is to shift the conversation to be more abstract and about the relative size of the stories than about how long it will take to design a screen, code a stored procedure, and write some HTML. In this way, a team can start with estimating in ideal days but gradually separate their estimates from a number of days.

Summary

A team can choose to estimate in either story points or ideal days. Each is a viable choice with advantages to recommend it.

Story points have the advantage of helping promote cross-functional team behavior. Additionally, because story points are a more pure measure of size, they do not need to be re-estimated if the team improves in a technology or the domain. Estimating in story points is often faster than estimating ideal days. Finally, unlike ideal days, story points can be compared among team members. If one team member thinks something will take her four ideal days, and another team member thinks it will take him one ideal day, they may each be right, yet they have no basis on which to argue and establish a single estimate.

Ideal days have the advantages of being more easily explained to those outside the team and of being easier to get started with.

My preference is for story points. The advantages of estimating in story points are more compelling. If a team is struggling with the concept of estimating pure size, I will start them estimating in ideal days but will then convert them to story points. I do this by asking more questions such as "How big is this compared with the other stories we've estimated?" rather than "How many ideal days will this take?" Most teams hardly notice the gradual switch, and by the time they do, they are thinking about points rather than ideal days.

Discussion Questions

1. Which approach do you prefer—story points or ideal days? Why?
2. How might you introduce this to your organization? What obstacles do you anticipate, and how could you address them?

Part III

Planning for Value

Before planning a project, we must consider what it is that our users need. Simply generating a list of things we think they want and then scheduling the development of those features is not enough. Achieving the best combination of product features (scope), schedule, and cost requires deliberate consideration of the cost and value of the user stories and themes that will comprise the release.

The four chapters of this part begin with a description of the four specific factors that need to be considered when prioritizing user stories and themes. Next, some simple ways of modeling the financial return of a story or theme are described, including how to compare the resulting values. Next, we look at two different approaches to assessing the desirability of stories and themes. The part concludes with some advice on splitting large user stories or features into smaller ones that are ready for implementation.

Chapter 9

Prioritizing Themes

> *"The indispensable first step to getting what you want is this:*
> *Decide what you want."*
> —Ben Stein

There is rarely, if ever, enough time to do everything. So we prioritize. The responsibility for prioritizing is shared among the whole team, but the effort is led by the product owner. Unfortunately, it is generally difficult to estimate the value of small units of functionality, such as a single user story. To get around this, individual user stories or features are aggregated into *themes*. Stories and themes are then prioritized relative to one another for the purpose of creating a release plan. Themes should be selected such that each defines a discrete set of user- or customer-valued functionality. For example, in developing the SwimStats website, we would have themes such as these:

- Keep track of all personal records and let swimmers view them.
- Allow coaches to assign swimmers to events optimally and predict the team score of a meet.
- Allow coaches to enter practice activities and track practice distances swum.
- Integrate with popular handheld computers for use at the pool.
- Import and export data.
- Allow officials to track event results and score a meet.

Each of these themes has tangible value to the users of the software. And it would be possible to put a monetary value on each. With some research we could determine that support for handheld computers is likely to result in ¤150,000 of new sales. We could compare that with the expected ¤200,000 in new sales if the next version can be used for scoring a swim meet. We could then prioritize those themes. There is more to prioritizing, however, than simply considering the monetary return from each new set of features.

Factors in Prioritization

Determining the value of a theme is difficult, and product owners on agile projects are often given the vague and mostly useless advice of "prioritize on business value." This may be great advice at face value, but what is *business value?* To provide a more practical set of guidelines for prioritizing, in this chapter we will look at four factors that must be considered when prioritizing the development of new capabilities.

1. The financial value of having the features.
2. The cost of developing (and perhaps supporting) the new features.
3. The amount and significance of learning and new knowledge created by developing the features.
4. The amount of risk removed by developing the features.

Because most projects are undertaken either to save or to make money, the first two factors often dominate prioritization discussions. However, proper consideration of the influence of learning and risk on the project is critical if we are to prioritize optimally.

Value

The first factor in prioritizing work is the financial value of the theme. How much money will the organization make or save by having the new features included in the theme? This alone is often what is meant when product owners are given the advice to "prioritize on business value."

Often, an ideal way to determine the value of a theme is to estimate its financial impact over a period of time—usually the next few months, quarters, or possibly years. This can be done if the product will be sold commercially, as, for example, a new word processor or a calculator with embedded software would be. It can also be done for applications that will be used within the organization developing them. Chapter 10, "Financial Prioritization," describes various approaches to estimating the financial value of themes.

It can be difficult to estimate the financial return on a theme. Doing so usually involves estimating the number of new sales, the average value of a sale (including follow-on sales and maintenance agreements), the timing of sales increases, and so on. Because of the complexity in doing this, it is often useful to have an alternate method for estimating value. Because the value of a theme is related to the desirability of that theme to new and existing users, it is possible to use nonfinancial measures of desirability to represent value. This will be the subject of Chapter 11, "Prioritizing Desirability."

Cost

Naturally, the cost of a feature is a huge determinant in the overall priority of a feature. Many features seem wonderful until we learn their cost. An important, yet often overlooked, aspect of cost is that the cost can change over time. Adding support for internationalization today may take four weeks of effort; adding it in six months may take six weeks. So we should add it now, right? Maybe. Suppose we spend four weeks and do it now. Over the next six months, we may spend an additional three weeks changing the original implementation based on knowledge gained during that six months. In that case, we would have been better off waiting. Or what if we spend four weeks now and later discover that a simpler and faster implementation would have been adequate? The best way to reduce the cost of change is to implement a feature as late as possible—effectively when there is no more time for change.

Themes often seem worthwhile when viewed only in terms of the time they will take. As trite as it sounds, it is important to remember that time costs money. Often, the best way to do this while prioritizing is to do a rough conversion of story points or ideal days into money. Suppose you add up the salaries for everyone involved in a project over the past twelve weeks and come up with ¤150,000. This includes the product owner and the project manager, as well as all of the programmers, testers, database engineers, analysts, user interface designers, and so on. During those twelve weeks, the team completed 120 story points. We can tell that at a total cost of ¤150,000, 120 story points cost ¤1,250 each. Suppose a product owner is trying to decide whether thirty points of functionality should be included in the next release. One way for her to decide is to ask herself whether the new functionality is worth an investment of ¤37,500 $(30 \times 1,250 = 37,500)$.

Chapter 10, "Financial Prioritization," will have much more to say about cost and about prioritizing based on financial reward relative to cost.

New Knowledge

On many projects, much of the overall effort is spent in the pursuit of new knowledge. It is important that this effort be acknowledged and considered fundamental to the project. Acquiring new knowledge is important because at the start of a project, we never know everything that we'll need to know by the end of the project. The knowledge that a team develops can be classified into two areas:

- Knowledge about the product
- Knowledge about the project

Product knowledge is knowledge about *what* will be developed. It is knowledge about the features that will be included and about those that will not be included. The more product knowledge a team has, the better able they will be to make decisions about the nature and features of the product.

Project knowledge, by contrast, is knowledge about *how* the product will be created. Examples include knowledge about the technologies that will be used, about the skills of the developers, about how well the team functions together, and so on.

The flip side of acquiring knowledge is reducing uncertainty. At the start of a project there is some amount of uncertainty about what features the new product should contain. There is also uncertainty about how we'll build the product. Laufer (1996) refers to these types of uncertainty as *end uncertainty* and *means uncertainty*. End uncertainty is reduced by acquiring more knowledge about the product; means uncertainty is reduced through acquiring more knowledge about the project.

A project following a waterfall process tries to eliminate all uncertainty about what is being built before tackling the uncertainty of how it will be built. This is the origin of the common advice that analysis is about what will be built, and design is about how it will be built. Figure 9.1 shows both the waterfall and agile views of removing uncertainty.

On the waterfall side of Figure 9.1, the downward arrow shows a traditional team's attempt to eliminate all end uncertainty at the start of the project. This means that before they begin developing, there will be no remaining uncertainty about the end that is being pursued. The product is fully defined. The rightward arrow on the waterfall side of Figure 9.1 shows that means uncertainty (about how the product will be built) is reduced over time as the project progresses. Of course, the complete up-front elimination of all end uncertainty is unachievable. Customers and users are uncertain about exactly what they need until they begin to see parts of it. They can then successively elaborate their needs.

Contrast this view with the agile approach to reducing uncertainty, which is shown on the right side of Figure 9.1. Agile teams acknowledge that it is impossible at the start of a project to eliminate all uncertainty about what the product is to be. Parts of the product need to be developed and shown to customers, feedback needs to collected, opinions refined, and plans adjusted. This takes time. While this is occurring the team will also be learning more about how they will develop the system. This leads to simultaneously reducing both end and means uncertainty, as shown in the agile view in Figure 9.1.

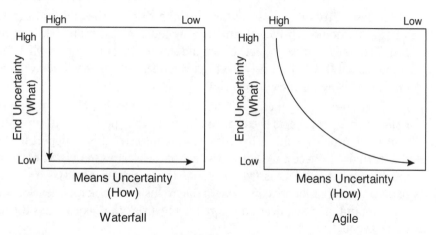

Figure 9.1 Traditional and agile views of reducing uncertainty. Adapted from Laufer (1996).

I've drawn the curve in the agile side of Figure 9.1 to show a preference toward early reduction of end uncertainty. Why didn't I draw a straight line or one that favors early reduction of means uncertainty? I drew the line as I did to reflect the importance of reducing uncertainty about what a product should be as early as possible. End uncertainty does not need to be eliminated at the outset (as hoped for in the traditional view), and it cannot be. However, one of the greatest risks to most projects is the risk of building the wrong product. This risk can be dramatically reduced by developing early those features that will best allow us to get working software in front of or in the hands of actual users.

Risk

Closely aligned with the concept of new knowledge is the final factor in prioritization: risk. Almost all projects contain tremendous amounts of risk. For our purposes, a risk is anything that has not yet happened but might and that would jeopardize or limit the success of the project. There are many different types of risk on projects, including:

◆ Schedule risk ("We might not be done by October")

◆ Cost risk ("We might not be able to buy hardware for the right price")

◆ Functionality risk ("We might not be able to get that to work")

Additionally, risks can be classified as either technological or business risks.

A classic struggle exists between the high-risk and the high-value features of a project. Should a project team start by focusing on high-risk features that could derail the entire project? Or should a project team focus on what Tom Gilb (1988) called the "juicy bits," the high-value features that will deliver the most immediate bang for the customer's buck?

To choose among them, let's consider the drawbacks of each approach. The risk-driven team accepts the chance that work they perform will turn out to be unneeded or of low value. They may develop infrastructural support for features that turn out unnecessary as the product owner refines her vision of the project based on what she learns from users as the project progresses. On the other hand, a team that focuses on value to the exclusion of risk may develop a significant amount of an application before hitting a risk that jeopardizes the delivery of the product.

The solution, of course, is to give neither risk nor value total supremacy when prioritizing. To prioritize work optimally, it is important to consider both risk and value. Consider Figure 9.2, which maps the relationship between the risk and value of a feature into four quadrants. At the top right are high-risk, high-value features. These features are highly desirable to the customer but possess significant development risk. Perhaps features in this quadrant rely on unproven technologies, integration with unproven subcontractors, technical innovation (such as the development of a new algorithm), or any of a number of similar risks. At the bottom right are features that are equally desirable but that are less risky. Whereas features in the right half of Figure 9.2 are highly desirable, features falling in the left half are of lower value.

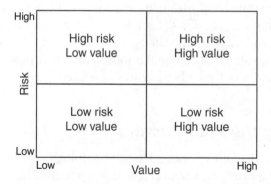

Figure 9.2 The four quadrants of the risk–value relationship.

The appropriate development sequence for the features is shown in Figure 9.3. The high-value, high-risk features should be developed first. These features deliver the most value, and working on them eliminates significant risks. Next are the high-value, low-risk features. These features offer as much value as the first set, but they are less risky. Therefore, they can be done later in the schedule. Because of this, use the guideline to work first on high-value features, but use risk as a tie-breaker.

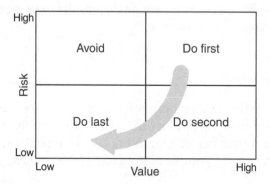

Figure 9.3 Combining risk and value in prioritizing features.

Next are the low-value, low-risk features. These are sequenced third because they will have less impact on the total value of the product if they are dropped, and because they are low risk.

Finally, features that deliver low value, but are high risk, are best avoided. Defer work on all low-value features, especially those that are also high risk. Try to defer low-value, high-risk items right out of the project. There is no reason to take on a high degree of risk for a feature of limited value. Be aware that a feature's risk and value profile changes over time. A low-value, low-risk feature in the Avoid quadrant of Figure 9.3 today could be in the Do first quadrant six months from now if all other features have been finished.

Combining the Four Factors

To combine the four prioritization factors, think first about the value of the feature relative to what it would cost to develop today. This gives you an initial priority order for the themes. Those themes with a high value-to-cost ratio are those that should be done first.

Next, think of the other prioritization factors as moving themes forward or backward. Suppose that based on its value and cost, a theme is of medium priority. Therefore, the team would tend to work on this theme midway through the current release. However, the technology needed to develop this story is very risky. This would move the theme forward in priority and on the schedule.

It's not necessary that this initial ranking followed by shifting forward and back be a formal activity. It can (and often does) take place entirely in the head of the product owner. The product owner will then typically present her priorities to the team, who may entreat the product owner to alter priorities slightly based on its assessment of the themes.

Some Examples

To make sure that these four prioritization factors are practical and useful, let's see how they can be applied to two typical prioritization challenges: infrastructure and user interface design. In the following sections, I'll consider a theme and show how these prioritization factors can be applied.

Infrastructure

One common prioritization challenge comes in the form of developing the infrastructure or architectural elements of an application. As an example, consider a security framework that will be used throughout an application. Considered solely on the merits of the value it delivers to customers, a security framework is unlikely to be prioritized into the early iterations of a project. After all, even though security is critical to many applications, most applications are not generally purchased solely because of how secure they are. The application must do something before security is relevant.

The next prioritization factor is cost. Adding a security framework to our website today will probably cost less than adding the same security framework later. This is true for many infrastructure elements, and is the basis for many arguments in favor of developing them early. However, if a feature is developed early, there is a chance that it will change by the end of the project. The cost of these changes needs to be considered in any now/later decision. Additionally, introducing the security framework early may add complexity that will be a hidden cost on all future work. This cost, too, would need to be considered.

Our next factor says that we should accelerate the development of features that generate new product or project knowledge. Depending upon the product being built, a security framework is unlikely to generate relevant new knowledge about the product. However, developing the security framework may generate new knowledge about the project. For example, I worked on a project a handful of years ago that needed to authenticate users through an LDAP server. None of the developers had done this before, so there was a lot of uncertainty about how much effort it would take. To eliminate that uncertainty, the stories about LDAP authentication were moved up to around the middle of a project rather than being left near the end.

The final prioritization factor is risk. Is there a risk to the project's success that could be reduced or eliminated by implementing security earlier rather than later? Perhaps not in this example. However, the failure of a framework, key component, or other infrastructure is often a significant risk to a project. This may be enough to warrant moving development sooner than would be justified solely on the basis of value.

User Interface Design

Common agile advice is that user interface design should be done entirely within the iteration in which the underlying feature is developed. However, this sometimes runs counter to arguments that the usability of a system is improved when designers are allowed to think about the overall user interface up front. What can we learn from applying our prioritization factors?

First, will the development of the user interface generate significant, useful new knowledge? If so, we should move some of the work forward in the schedule. Yes, in many cases developing some of the main user interface components or the navigational model will generate significant, useful new knowledge about the product. The early development of parts of the user interface allows for the system to be shown to real or likely users in an early form. Feedback from these users will result in new knowledge about the product, and this knowledge can be used to make sure the team is developing the most valuable product possible.

Second, will developing the user interface reduce risk? It probably doesn't eliminate technical risk (unless this is the team's first endeavor with this type of user interface). However, early development of features that show off the user interface often reduces the most serious risk facing most projects: the risk of developing the wrong product. A high prioritization of features that will show off significant user-facing functionality will allow for more early feedback from users. This is the best way of avoiding the risk of building the wrong product.

Finally, if the cost of developing the user interface will be significantly lower if done early, that would be another point in favor of scheduling such features early. In most cases, this is not the case.

So because of the additional learning and risk reduction that can be had, it seems reasonable to move earlier in the schedule those themes that will allow users to provide the most feedback on the usability and functionality of the system. This does not mean that we would work on the user interface in isolation or separate from the functionality that exists beneath the user interface. Rather, this means that it might be appropriate to move forward in the schedule those features with significant user interface components that would allow us to get the most useful feedback from customers and users.

Summary

Because there is rarely enough time to do everything, we need to prioritize what is worked on first. There are four primary factors to be considered when prioritizing.

1. The financial value of having the features.
2. The cost of developing (and perhaps supporting) the new features.
3. The amount and significance of learning and new knowledge created by developing the features.
4. The amount of risk removed by developing the features.

These factors are combined by thinking first of the value and cost of the theme. Doing so sorts the themes into an initial order. Themes can then be moved forward or back in this order based on the other factors.

Discussion Questions

1. A feature on the project to which you have been assigned is of fairly low priority. Right now it looks like it will make it into the current release, but it could be dropped if time runs out. The feature needs to be developed in a language no one on the team has any familiarity with. What do you do?

2. What types of product and project knowledge have your current team acquired since beginning the project? Is there additional knowledge that needs to be acquired quickly and that should be accounted for in the project's priorities?

Chapter 10

Financial Prioritization

Some projects are undertaken to generate revenue and others to cut expenses, and some strive for both. If we can estimate the amount of money that will be made or saved by each theme, we can use that to help prioritize. Forecasting the financial value of a theme is the responsibility of the product owner, but it is a responsibility shared with all other team members—programmers, testers, analysts, project managers, and so on. In most cases, the product owner will also need to draw on business knowledge and forecasts from the sales and marketing groups.

The way I like to determine the financial value of a theme is to hold a meeting attended by as many of these individuals as practical. The goal of such a theme valuation meeting is to complete a form like the one shown in Table 10.1 for each theme. Depending on the number of themes and participants, this may take more than one meeting.

Table 10.1 includes a row for each quarter in the next two years. The time horizon is up to the team. In some cases, teams may want to look at monthly returns for one or two years. In other cases, quarterly forecasts are adequate. I find that looking out two years works well on most projects. It strikes a good balance between guessing at the distant future and looking far enough ahead. Because of the high amount of uncertainty on software development projects, others concur (Bills 2004a).

Table 10.1 An Empty Theme-Return Worksheet

Quarter	New Revenue	Incremental Revenue	Retained Revenue	Operational Efficiencies
1				
2				
3				
4				
5				
6				
7				
8				

Table 10.1 also includes columns for various types of returns a theme may have. If your project has different types of returns, use different column headings. Similarly, use different column headings if a theme will benefit from more specific column headings (perhaps Increased Revenue from U.S. Customers and Increased Revenue for European Customers). It is not necessary to estimate all themes with the same set of columns.

Meeting participants complete the worksheet by estimating the value in a cell that they believe will be affected by the development of the theme. A sample completed theme-return worksheet is shown in Table 10.2. In this case, the availability of this theme will attract new customers (New Revenue) and will also lead to increased revenue from existing customers (Incremental Revenue). The new theme will have no impact on either retained revenue or on operational efficiencies.

Where do these numbers come from? Ideally from the market research that was used in the business case that initiated the project. At a minimum, whoever requested the theme should be able to quantify the reasons for developing it.

Table 10.2 A Sample Theme-Return Worksheet

Quarter	New Revenue	Incremental Revenue	Retained Revenue	Operational Efficiencies
1	¤25,000	¤20,000	0	0
2	¤35,000	¤30,000	0	0
3	¤50,000	¤40,000	0	0
4	¤70,000	¤60,000	0	0
Total	**¤180,000**	**¤150,000**	**0**	**0**

We cannot compare projects and make prioritization decisions simply by summing the total row of a worksheet like Table 10.2 for each theme. A revenue stream that delivers ¤100k in the first quarter, ¤200k the next, and ¤500k in the third quarter is far less valuable than a stream that delivers those same returns but in the opposite sequence. To compare multiple themes, we need to use one or more standard financial measures. In this chapter, we will look at

- Net present value
- Internal rate of return
- Payback period
- Discounted payback period

However, before looking at these financial measures, we must consider how projects make or save money.

Sources of Return

The return on a project can come from a variety of sources. For convenience, we can categorize these as new revenue, incremental revenue, retained revenue, and operational efficiencies. Although it is common for one category to dominate the return of a specific project, most projects will earn returns from more than one category.

New Revenue

Certainly, one of the most common contributors to the return on a project is the opportunity for *new revenue*. Very few companies are satisfied with their market share, and most companies would like new customers. Even if a software product is not sold directly, adding new features can lead to new revenue. For example, I worked at a company that developed software for our own use in serving our hospital customers. At one point, our CEO realized that with some enhancements, our software could be used to provide those same services to health insurers. We made the changes and were able to bring an entirely new source of revenue into the company because of what the new software enabled.

Incremental Revenue

It is often useful to distinguish revenue from new customers from additional, incremental revenue from existing customers. *Incremental revenue* can result because the new system or product:

- Encourages existing customers to purchase more licenses
- Includes optional, add-on modules that can be sold separately
- Includes features that allow charging a higher price
- Encourages the use of consulting services (for example, to integrate with a separate third-party application)

Retained Revenue

Separate from both new and incremental revenue is retained revenue. *Retained revenue* refers to the revenue an organization will lose if the project or theme is not developed. Suppose you've been successfully selling a patient scheduling product to solo-practitioner chiropractors. Some of your customers have been doing well and are expanding to have two or three chiropractors in the practice. Unless your software is enhanced to support scheduling patients among multiple chiropractors, you stand to lose the business of these growing practices. A project to add this capability would allow the company to retain this revenue. Interestingly, there could also be an opportunity for incremental revenue because you may be able to charge more for the version that supports more than one chiropractor.

Operational Efficiencies

No organization is ever as efficient as it could be. There's always some task that could be streamlined or eliminated. If you're developing software for use by internal customers, you are probably quite aware of the importance of operational efficiencies. However, even if you're working on commercial software that is sold to others outside your company, some tasks within your project may still contribute to improving operational efficiencies. In your case, though, most often this will refer to your own inefficiency. For example, a number of projects I've been on have chosen to develop their own object-relational mapping tool to simplify the mapping of objects in the programming language to relational database tables. Similarly, almost every project I've been on has developed some form of tool to assist in the work of developing the software.

Often, the drive to improve operational efficiencies comes from anticipated growth. An inefficiency that may not be a problem today rapidly becomes a problem when the company becomes much larger. As an example, suppose your company has developed a website for selling picture frames. You sell a huge variety of standard frames but also sell frames in custom sizes. Business is doing well, and the company anticipates strong growth over the next two years. In fact, it expects sales to increase tenfold over that period. As in any business, a certain percentage of sold items end up being sent back to the company as returned merchandise. It's never been a high priority to have a highly automated, efficient solution for processing returns, and right now it takes one person about two hours a day to process returns, including updating inventory and crediting the buyer's credit card. The two hours spent on this may not be a critical issue today. But when sales have increased 1,000%, returned items will probably increase 1,000%, and processing returns will take twenty person-hours each day. By that point, it will certainly be worth considering whether this is an operational inefficiency that should be addressed.

In looking to improve operational efficiency, some likely places include

- Anything that takes a long time or that would take a long time if the company grew
- Better integration or communication between departments
- Reduced employee turnover
- Shorter training time for new employees
- Any time-sensitive process
- Combining multiple processes
- Anything that improves accuracy and reduces rework

An Example: WebPayroll

Using these techniques, let's estimate the returns for a project. Suppose our company, WebPayroll, offers a web-based payroll system to companies too small to calculate their own payroll taxes, print checks, and so on. We're fairly successful already but are enhancing the software to improve turnaround time.

Currently, we tell customers that they need to enter payroll information on our website three days before they need checks to distribute to their employees. Our goal with the new system is to offer next-day service. If payroll information is entered on the WebPayroll site by 5:00 p.m., we can generate checks, print them, and have them delivered overnight. Checks will be in our customers' hands the next morning.

Before we can begin estimating the return on the overnight project, we need to decide when it will be available. Assume that the developers have already estimated the stories in this theme and that they came up with 150 story points. At the team's historical velocity of 20 story points per two-week iteration, developing the theme will take $150/20 = 7.5 = 8$ iterations. This means that increased revenue and operational efficiencies can begin after the eighth iteration (unless we can find a way to deliver a partial solution, which should always be a goal).

Calculating New Revenue

Offering next-day instead of three-day service will open new revenue opportunities. To quantify these opportunities, we first estimate the number of new customers we'll acquire. We don't have any solid data. But our main salesperson, Terry, says that around one-third of the customers she talks with reject WebPayroll because of our three-day requirement. Based on current sales projections, Terry believes she can attract fifty new customers per quarter this year and then one hundred customers per quarter next year. These values are added to the New Customers column of Table 10.3. Even though the overnight feature won't be available until the middle of the second quarter, Terry believes she can still sign up fifty new customers in that quarter.

Next, we estimate the revenue per customer. We can do this by thinking about likely new customers relative to our current customers. We know, for example, that the average WebPayroll customer pays us ¤400 per year in fees. However, we think that overnight delivery will be most appealing to smaller customers—those that pay us an average of ¤200 per year. We think we'll make another ¤100 per year from each of these customers. The total value of each new customer is then ¤300 per year, or ¤75 per quarter. Because overnight service will be available only for two-thirds of the second quarter, the revenue per customer is lowered appropriately in that quarter. These values are added to the Revenue per Customer column of Table 10.3, which also allows us to calculate the New Revenue column.

Table 10.3 Projected New Revenue from the WebPayroll Project

Quarter	New Customers	Revenue per Customer	New Revenue
1	0	¤0	¤0
2	50	¤50	¤2,500
3	50	¤75	¤3,750
4	50	¤75	¤3,750
5	100	¤75	¤7,500
6	100	¤75	¤7,500
7	100	¤75	¤7,500
8	100	¤75	¤7,500

Calculating Incremental Revenue

Incremental revenue refers to additional revenue we can get from existing customers. Based on what we know of our current customers, how often they are late submitting payroll information, and so on, we estimate that we'll sign up about 100 customers per quarter until 400 of our current customers are using the overnight service. As for new customers, the service will generate about ¤100 per year or ¤25 per quarter after it's available a third of the way into the second quarter. Table 10.4 is created to calculate the total incremental revenue per quarter from these estimates.

Calculating Retained Revenue

Retained revenue is what we will no longer lose because customers are dissatisfied with our product, outgrow it, or otherwise decide to switch away from WebPayroll. The company currently doesn't have any good metric for tracking this. We know it's beginning to be an issue and will become much more significant over the next few years.

Table 10.4 Projected Incremental Revenue from the WebPayroll Project

Quarter	Customers	Revenue per Customer	Incremental Revenue
1	0	¤0	¤0
2	100	¤16	¤1,600
3	200	¤25	¤5,000
4	300	¤25	¤7,500
5	400	¤25	¤10,000
6	400	¤25	¤10,000
7	400	¤25	¤10,000
8	400	¤25	¤10,000

We estimate that by having an overnight service, we'll prevent the loss of twenty customers per quarter in the first year and forty customers per quarter in the second year. Significantly, these customers will stick with WebPayroll now, even though the functionality won't be available until the second quarter. That means that the benefits of the overnight project begin in the first quarter, even though overnight delivery won't be available until the second quarter.

Because each current customer is worth ¤400 per year, that is ¤100 per quarter. With that, we can calculate retained revenue as shown in Table 10.5.

Calculating Operational Efficiencies

For the overnight project to be successful, we will need to eliminate almost all of the manual intervention our system relies on today. Currently, the system relies on a payroll clerk in the WebPayroll office to verify the correctness of the payroll information, and then submit it manually through a couple of workflow steps. We have two payroll clerks doing this today.

Without the overnight features, the staffing plan calls for adding two clerks in the middle of this year and two in the middle of next year. Because of the efficiencies planned as part of the overnight project, we expect to be able to eliminate one of these positions each year.

Table 10.5 Projected Retained Revenue from the WebPayroll Project

Quarter	Retained Customers	Revenue per Customer	Retained Revenue
1	20	¤100	¤2,000
2	20	¤100	¤2,000
3	20	¤100	¤2,000
4	20	¤100	¤2,000
5	40	¤100	¤4,000
6	40	¤100	¤4,000
7	40	¤100	¤4,000
8	40	¤100	¤4,000

Payroll clerks make an average of ¤20,000 per year. Each one, however, also takes up space in the office, is assigned some equipment and software, and is given benefits. In total, these additional, hidden expenses account for around another 50% of an employee's salary, meaning the true cost of a payroll clerk is closer to ¤30,000 annually. This is known as the *fully burdened labor cost*. The number of clerks not hired and the fully burdened labor cost for each can be multiplied each quarter to give the total operational efficiencies, as shown in Table 10.6.

Table 10.6 Projected Operational Efficiencies from the WebPayroll Project

Quarter	Payroll Clerks Not Needed	Fully Burdened Labor Cost	Operational Efficiencies
1	0	0	0
2	0	0	0
3	1	¤7,500	¤7,500
4	1	¤7,500	¤7,500
5	1	¤7,500	¤7,500
6	1	¤7,500	¤7,500
7	2	¤7,500	¤15,000
8	2	¤7,500	¤15,000

Estimating Development Cost

To complete the investment profile of the WebPayroll overnight project, we need to estimate the expected development cost of the theme. To do this, let's look at the salaries of everyone involved in the project, as shown in Table 10.7.

Table 10.7 The WebPayroll Project Team

Role	Annual Salary	Fully Burdened Labor Cost	Burdened Cost per Iteration	Time on Project	Adjusted Cost per Iteration
Product owner	¤50,000	¤75,000	¤2,900	100%	¤2,900
Programmer	¤50,000	¤75,000	¤2,900	100%	¤2,900
Programmer	¤30,000	¤45,000	¤1,700	50%	¤850
Analyst	¤40,000	¤60,000	¤2,300	100%	¤2,300
Tester	¤30,000	¤45,000	¤1,700	100%	¤1,700
Tester	¤50,000	¤75,000	¤2,900	100%	¤2,900
				Total	**¤13,550**

The fully burdened labor cost in Table 10.7 is calculated as 50% more than each person's salary alone. Because iterations are two weeks, the burdened cost per iteration is 1/26th of the fully burdened labor cost. The Time on Project column indicates the portion of time that each team member allocates to the project. Everyone is full time except one programmer. The Adjusted Cost per Iteration column shows the cost to the project of each individual based on burdened labor cost and the amount of time spent on the project. In total, the team shown in Table 10.7 costs ¤13,550 per iteration. We'll round that to ¤13,500.

It is often useful to know the cost per story point (or ideal day). To calculate this, divide the adjusted cost per iteration by the team's average or expected velocity. Because the WebPayroll team has an average velocity of 20 story points per iteration, their cost per story point is $13,500/20 = 675$. This information is useful because if the team is asked how much it will cost to develop something estimated at 100 story points, they know the answer is ¤67,500 (100×675).

The cost of the WebPayroll team can be summarized as shown in Table 10.8.

Table 10.8 Summary of Costs for the WebPayroll Team

Measure	Cost
Cost per story point	¤675
Cost per week	¤6,750
Cost per iteration	¤13,500

Putting It All Together

From this analysis of cost, new revenue, incremental revenue, and operational efficiencies, we can put together Table 10.9.

Table 10.9 Projected Returns from the WebPayroll Project

Quarter	Development Cost	New Revenue	Incremental Revenue	Retained Revenue	Operational Efficiencies	Net Cash Flow
1	−¤87,750	¤0	¤0	¤2,000	¤0	−¤85,750
2	−¤20,250	¤2,500	¤1,600	¤2,000	¤0	−¤14,150
3		¤3,750	¤5,000	¤2,000	¤7,500	¤18,250
4		¤3,750	¤7,500	¤2,000	¤7,500	¤20,750
5		¤7,500	¤10,000	¤4,000	¤7,500	¤29,000
6		¤7,500	¤10,000	¤4,000	¤7,500	¤29,000
7		¤7,500	¤10,000	¤4,000	¤15,000	¤36,500
8		¤7,500	¤10,000	¤4,000	¤15,000	¤36,500

The overnight feature is expected to be finished in the eighth iteration, or after sixteen weeks. The first quarter will be thirteen of those weeks for a cost of ¤87,750 (13 × 6,750). The second quarter will be another three weeks for a cost of ¤20,250.

Financial Measures

Having come up with a way of estimating the cash flow stream that will be generated by each theme, we next turn our attention to various ways of analyzing and evaluating those cash flow streams. In this section, we will look at net present value, internal rate of return, payback period, and discounted payback period. Each of these measures can be used for comparing the returns on a theme. But first, it's important to understand the time value of money.

The Time Value of Money

In the early Popeye comic strips, Wimpy would tell the other characters, "I'll gladly pay you on Tuesday for a hamburger today." Only a sucker would take Wimpy up on that deal, because money today is more valuable than money next Tuesday.

To determine the value today of a future amount of money, we think in terms of how much money would have to be put in the bank today for it to grow to the future amount. To buy a ¤5 hamburger next Tuesday, I might need to put ¤4.99 in the bank today. The amount I have to invest today to have a known amount in the future is called the *present value*. As a simple case, if I can earn 10% on my money and want to have ¤1.00 a year from now, I need to invest ¤0.91 today. In other words, with a 10% interest rate, ¤0.91 is the present value of ¤1.00 in a year. If I could earn 20% on my money, I would need to invest only ¤0.83 today.

The process of moving future amounts back into their present value is known as *discounting*. Clearly, the interest rate that is used for discounting future amounts is critical to determining the present value of a future amount. The rate at which organizations discount future money is known as their *opportunity cost* and reflects the percentage return that is passed up to make this investment. We all—individuals and organizations—have various opportunities for investing our money. I can put my money into a bank saving account, or I can invest in stocks. I can invest it in real estate, or I can put it under my mattress. Organizations can invest their money in these same ways, or they can invest money on various projects. If an organization has typically earned 20% on past projects, new projects should be assessed against this same 20%. The organization's opportunity cost is 20% because an investment in a new project means that the organization gave up the opportunity to invest in some other project, which would have earned 20%.

Net Present Value

The first formula we'll look at for evaluating a theme is the *net present value* (*NPV*). To determine NPV, sum the present values of each item in a stream of future values. The formula for doing so is

$$NPV(i) = \sum_{t=0}^{n} F_t(1 + i)^{-t}$$

where i is the interest rate and F_t is the net cash flow in period t.

To see how this works, let's continue with the WebPayroll example. As determined earlier, the overnight project is expected to cost ¤108,000 and to generate the revenue and savings summarized in Table 10.9, which are repeated in the Net Cash Flow column of Table 10.10. The Present Value Factor column of that table is the $(1 + i)^{-t}$ portion of the NPV calculation and represents the amount by which the future net cash flow will be discounted. The final column, Present Value, is the product of the Net Cash Flow and Present Value Factor columns. It indicates, for example, that the present value of ¤18,250 at the end of the third quarter year is ¤16,701. Summing the values in the Present Value column gives the total NPV, which is ¤46,341 in this case.

Table 10.10 Determining the NPV for WebPayroll

End of Quarter	Net Cash Flow	Present Value Factor (12% / Year)	Present Value
1	−¤85,750	0.971	−¤83,252
2	−¤14,150	0.943	−¤13,338
3	¤18,250	0.915	¤16,701
4	¤20,750	0.888	¤18,436
5	¤29,000	0.863	¤25,016
6	¤29,000	0.837	¤24,287
7	¤36,500	0.813	¤29,677
8	¤36,500	0.789	¤28,813
		NPV (12%) =	**¤46,341**

Using net present value to compare and prioritize themes has the advantages of being easy to calculate and easy to understand. The primary disadvantage to NPV is that comparing the values of two different cash flow streams can be misleading. Suppose we are trying to choose between two projects. The first project requires huge up-front investments but has an NPV of ¤100,000. The second project requires only a small up-front investment but also has an NPV of ¤100,000. Clearly, we'd prefer to make the investment in the theme that ties up less cash but that has the same NPV. What we'd really like is to express the return on a theme in percentage terms so that we can compare themes directly.

Internal Rate of Return

Internal Rate of Return (*IRR*, and sometimes called *Return on Investment* or *ROI*) provides a way of expressing the return on a project in percentage terms. Where NPV is a measure of how much money a project can be expected to return (in today's present value), IRR is a measure of how quickly the money invested in a project will increase in value. With IRR we can more readily compare projects, as shown in Table 10.11. Which project would you prefer?

Table 10.11 Comparing Two Projects across NPV and IRR

Project	Investment	NPV	IRR
Project A	¤200,000	¤98,682	27%
Project B	¤100,000	¤79,154	43%

Most people would prefer to make 43% on their money, even though the NPV is higher for Project A, which also requires the higher initial investment. Cash flows for these two projects are shown in Table 10.12.

Many organizations will specify a *minimum attractive rate of return,* or MARR. Only projects or themes with an IRR that exceeds the MARR will be funded. It is impractical to set a similar threshold for NPV, because NPV values are highly dependent on the magnitude of the project. If an NPV threshold were in place, small (but valuable) projects would never be approved.

IRR is defined as the interest rate at which the NPV of a cash flow stream is equal to 0. In other words, it is the value for i* such that

$$0 = PV(i^*) = \sum_{t=0}^{n} F_t(1+i)^{-t}$$

Table 10.12 Cash Flows for the Projects in Table 10.11

Year	Project A	Project B
0	–200,000	–100,000
1	50,000	50,000
2	75,000	75,000
3	100,000	50,000
4	170,000	50,000

The formula for calculating IRR is complex and beyond the scope of this book. Fortunately, most major spreadsheet programs include easy-to-use IRR functions. If you want to calculate IRR by hand, Steve Tockey (2004) provides the best description. However, even though you can use a spreadsheet to calculate IRR, there are a couple of preconditions for its use that you need to be aware of:

◆ The first one or more items in the cash flow stream must be expenses. (Note that there must be at least one.)

◆ Once the cash flow stream turns positive, it must remain positive.

◆ The sum of the positive items is larger than the sum of the negative items— that is, money is made overall.

Because the cash stream for the WebPayroll overnight-delivery theme satisfies these preconditions, we can calculate the IRR for the theme. To do so in Excel, enter this formula into a cell:

+IRR({0, –85750, –14150, 18250, 20750, 29000, 29000, 36500, 36500})

The numbers within the curly braces are the cash flow streams for each of the eight quarters. The initial 0 indicates that no up-front costs occurred on the first day of the project (as might if WebPayroll had to buy additional servers to initiate the project). For the WebPayroll overnight project the IRR is 12%, which means that the expected cash flow stream is equivalent to earning a 12% annual return on the company's investment.

A first advantage to using IRR is that there is no requirement to establish (or, in the worst case, guess at) an organization's discount rate, as is necessary when calculating NPV.

A second advantage to IRR is that it can be used directly in comparing projects. A project with a 45% IRR has a higher return on its investment than does a project with a 25% IRR. You cannot usually use IRR in isolation, though, for making decisions. Suppose the project returning 45% is very small, so the 45% return comes on a small investment yet the project ties up a critical developer. Further, suppose that the project returning 25% does so against a large investment but requires the same critical developer. You may choose to make more money by doing the second project, the one with the lower IRR.

As an additional example, you may prefer the project with the 45% IRR, but it requires two years of investment before it begins generating spectacular returns. The project with 25% IRR begins earning money after a year. If the organization cannot afford to make two years of investment, the project with the lower IRR may be preferable.

A first disadvantage to IRR is that because the calculation is hard to do by hand, the result may be more subject to distrust by some. A second disadvantage is that IRR cannot be calculated in all situations. As we saw previously, three preconditions must be met to calculate a meaningful IRR.

Payback Period

Through NPV, we can look at a cash flow stream as a single, present value amount. Alternatively, we can look at a cash flow stream as an interest rate through IRR. An additional way of looking at a cash flow stream is as the amount of time required to earn back the initial investment. This is known as the *payback period*. To see how it is determined, Table 10.13 shows the payback calculations for the WebPayroll overnight project.

Table 10.13 Determining the Payback Period for the WebPayroll Overnight Project

Quarter	Net Cash Flow at End of Quarter	Running Total
1	–¤85,750	–¤85,750
2	–¤14,150	–¤99,900
3	¤18,250	–¤81,650
4	¤20,750	–¤60,900
5	¤29,000	–¤31,900
6	¤29,000	–¤2,900
7	¤36,500	¤33,600
8	¤36,500	¤70,100

During the first quarter, WebPayroll invests ¤85,750 in the project. In the second quarter, it makes an additional net investment of ¤14,150. In the third quarter it starts earning back the investment by making ¤18,250. Sometime during the seventh quarter, the net investment in the project turns positive, and the project's payback period is said to be seven quarters.

There are two primary advantages to using payback period when comparing and prioritizing themes. First, the calculations and interpretation are straightforward. Second, it measures the amount and duration of financial risk taken on by the organization. The larger the payback period, the riskier the project, because anything could change during that period.

The primary disadvantage to payback period is that it fails to take into account the time value of money. Money received three years in the future is valued as highly as money paid out today. The second drawback to payback period is that it is not a measure of the profitability of a project or theme. Payback period will tell us that an organization will recover its money in seven quarters, but it doesn't address how much money will be made.

Discounted Payback Period

It is easy to remedy the first drawback of the payback-period calculation. To do so we simply apply the appropriate discount factor to each item in the cash flow stream. The way to do this is shown in Table 10.14 for the WebPayroll overnight project.

Table 10.14 Determining the WebPayroll Overnight Project's Discounted Payback Period

End of Quarter	Net Cash Flow	Present Value Factor (12%/ Year)	Discounted Cash Flow	Running Total
1	–¤85,750	0.971	–¤83,252	–¤83,252
2	–¤14,150	0.943	–¤13,338	–¤96,590
3	¤18,250	0.915	¤16,701	–¤79,889
4	¤20,750	0.888	¤18,436	–¤61,453
5	¤29,000	0.863	¤25,016	–¤36,437
6	¤29,000	0.837	¤24,287	–¤12,150
7	¤36,500	0.813	¤29,677	¤17,527
8	¤36,500	0.789	¤28,813	¤46,340

As Table 10.14 shows, the running total of discounted cash flow becomes positive in the seventh quarter (just as it did in the simple payback-period calculation).

Comparing Returns

As you assess each theme, you build up information that can be used to compare the themes and make the prioritization decisions that are driving this analysis. The results of valuing multiple themes can be presented as shown in Table 10.15. A table such as this lets an organization quickly review its options and choose to work on the highest-valued themes.

In this case, the overnight theme has the highest net present value, but it takes the longest to earn back the investment. The partner integration theme has the highest return on investment and the shortest discounted payback period, but it has the lowest NPV. Custom reporting has the lowest rate of return on investment. However, it could be combined with partner integration and done with the same cost as the overnight service theme. Making a decision is not cut and dried; the product owner and team will need to consider a variety of situationally specific factors, such as the organization's tolerance for risk, need for short payback periods, availability of resources, other options for investment money, and so on.

Table 10.15 Various Valuations for Each Theme in a Project

Theme	Story Points	Cost	NPV	ROI	Discounted Payback Period
Overnight service	150	¤101,250	¤46,341	45%	7 quarters
Custom reporting	90	¤60,750	¤34,533	15%	6 quarters
Partner integration	60	¤40,500	¤30,013	49%	3 quarters

For More on Project Economics

Although this chapter provides a basic overview of how to use and calculate four financial measures, much more could be said. For more on the subject of software project economics, Steve Tockey's *Return on Software: Maximizing the Return on Your Software Investment* (2004) is a wonderful book. The four financial measures here, including their formulas, are drawn from Tockey's book.

Summary

Financial analysis of themes helps in prioritization because for most organizations the bottom line is the amount of money earned or saved. It is usually sufficient to forecast revenue and operational efficiencies for the next two years. You can look further ahead, however, if necessary.

A good way of modeling the return from a theme is to consider the revenue it will generate from new customers, from current customers buying more copies or additional services, from customers who might have otherwise gone to a competitive product, and from any operational efficiencies it will provide.

Money earned or spent today is worth more than money earned or spent in the future. To compare a current amount with a future amount, the future amount is discounted back into a current amount. The current amount is the amount that could be deposited in a bank or into some other relatively safe investment and that would grow to the future amount by the future time.

Four good ways to evaluate a cash flow stream are net present value, internal rate or return (return on investment), payback period, and discounted payback period. By calculating these values for each theme, the product owner and team can make intelligent decisions about the relative priorities of the themes.

Discussion Questions

1. If your organization were choosing among the themes in Table 10.15, what would be the most appropriate decision? Why?

2. How would you model the return for a theme on your current project? Are the suggested categories of new revenue, incremental revenue, retained revenue, and operational efficiencies appropriate? What categories would you use instead?

Chapter 11

Prioritizing Desirability

*"If you have a choice of two things
and can't decide, take both."*
—Gregory Corso

As I write this I am sitting in a hotel room. The room has a bed, a bathroom, and a desk, and is reasonably clean. Each of these features is a basic attribute I expect of every hotel room. If any of these were absent, I would not stay at the hotel. This hotel also has a bed that is more comfortable than most, includes free wireless Internet access, is larger than most hotel rooms, and has a fitness center. I really appreciate these additional features, but they are not mandatory for me to stay at a hotel. However, the more features like this the hotel offers, the more I'm willing to pay for a room here. Finally, this hotel delighted me in two ways: Each treadmill in the fitness center has a television built into it, and a free bottle of water was left in my room each day.

I could group the features of this hotel room into the following categories:

- ◆ Must-haves: a bed, a bathroom, a desk, clean
- ◆ The more, the better: comfort of the bed, size of the room, variety and quantity of equipment in the fitness center
- ◆ Exciting: built-in televisions on the treadmills, free bottle of water in my room each day

Kano Model of Customer Satisfaction

Separating product features into the previous three categories can provide a great deal of information about how to prioritize work for a new product release. The process of doing so was originated by Noriaki Kano, whose approach gives us a way to separate features into three categories:

- Threshold, or must-have, features
- Linear features
- Exciters and delighters

Threshold features are those that must be present in the product for it to be successful. They are often referred to as *must-have* features. These are the bed, bathroom, desk, and cleanliness of my hotel room. Improving the performance or amount of a threshold feature will have little impact on customer satisfaction. For example, as long as the hotel bathroom meets my basic needs I don't care what the countertops are made from.

A linear feature is one for which "the more, the better" holds true. The bigger the hotel room is, the better. These are called linear features because customer satisfaction is correlated linearly with the quantity of the feature. The better one of these features performs (or the more of it there is), the more satisfied the customers will be. Because of this, product price is often related to linear attributes. If the hotel has dumbbells and two nice treadmills, I'll be happier than if it just has one rusty old stair climber. I'll be even happier if it also has elliptical trainers and spinning bikes. And important for the hotel, I'll be more likely to return and to pay a premium for its rooms.

Finally, exciters and delighters are those features that provide great satisfaction, often adding a price premium to a product. However, the lack of an exciter or delighter will not decrease customer satisfaction below neutral. The built-in television on the hotel's treadmill was an exciter for me. I would not have been dissatisfied if the hotel didn't offer these because I didn't know anyone had them. In fact, exciters and delighters are often called unknown needs because customers or users do not know they need these features until they see them.

The relationship among these three different feature types is shown in Figure 11.1. The arrow through the bottom right of this diagram shows that once some amount of a must-have feature has been implemented, customer satisfaction cannot be increased by adding more of that feature. Also, no matter how much of a must-have feature is added, customer satisfaction never rises above the midpoint.

On the other hand, the line in the top left shows that customer satisfaction rises dramatically based on even a partial implementation of an exciter or delighter. Finally, the line through the middle shows the direct relationship between the inclusion of linear features and customer satisfaction.

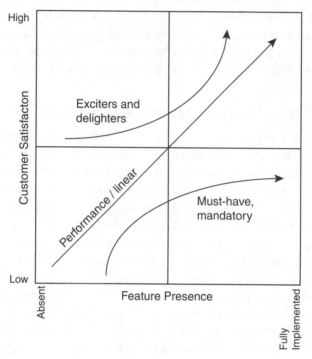

Figure 11.1   The Kano model of customer satisfaction.

Because must-have features are required for a product to play in its market segment, emphasis should be placed on prioritizing the development of all threshold features. A product's must-have features do not need to be developed in the first iterations of a release. However, because users consider these features to be mandatory, they need to be available before the product is released. Keep in mind, though, that partial implementation of must-have features may be adequate, because gains in customer satisfaction drop off quickly after a base level of support for threshold features has been established. For example, I am writing this book with Adobe FrameMaker, which pays lip service to an undo feature by allowing one level of undo. For me personally, they moved pretty far up the customer satisfaction axis with a one-level undo feature, yet I would have preferred much more.

Secondary emphasis should be placed on completing as many linear features as possible. Because each of these features leads directly to greater customer satisfaction, the more of these features that can be included, the better (excluding, of course, such situations as a product that is already bloated with too many features). Finally and with time permitting, at least a few delighters should be prioritized such that they are included in the release plan.

Keep in mind that features tend to migrate down the Kano diagram over time. A short time ago, wireless Internet access in a hotel room was a delighter. Now it's a linear feature well on its way to becoming a threshold feature.

Assessing Themes on the Kano Model

The easiest way to make use of a Kano model on an agile project is to think about each theme and make an educated guess about the type of each. A much better way, however, is to speak with customers or users to determine the type of each theme. This is surprisingly easy because it can be done with a written questionnaire and you may need to survey as few as twenty to thirty users to accurately prioritize requirements (Griffin and Hauser 1993).

Kano proposed determining the category of a feature by asking two questions: one question regarding how the user would feel if the feature were present in the product and one question about how the user would feel if it were absent. The first of these questions is known as the functional form, because it refers to the case when a function is present. The second question is known as the dysfunctional form, because it refers to when the function is not present. Each question is answered on the same five-point scale.

1. I like it that way.
2. I expect it to be that way.
3. I am neutral.
4. I can live with it that way.
5. I dislike it that way.

As an example, let's return to the SwimStats website. Suppose we are contemplating three new features:

- The ability to see a graph of a swimmer's times in an event over the past season.
- The ability for swimmers to post autobiographical profiles.

- The ability for any registered site member to upload photos.

To determine which type of feature these are, we survey prospective users, asking them:

- If you can graph a swimmer's times in an event over the past season, how do you feel?
- If you cannot graph a swimmer's times in an event over the past season, how do you feel?
- If swimmers can post autobiographical profiles, how do you feel?
- If swimmers cannot post autobiographical profiles, how do you feel?
- If you can upload photos, how do you feel?
- If you cannot upload photos, how do you feel?

The first pair of these questions and hypothetical answers from one user are shown in Figure 11.2.

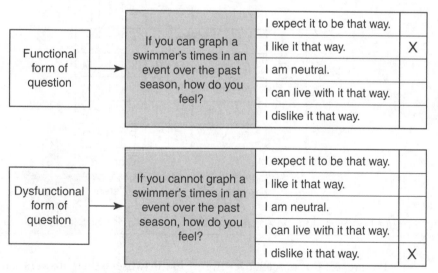

Figure 11.2 The functional and dysfunctional forms of a question.

From looking at Figure 11.2, it's apparent that it is possible for a user to give inconsistent responses. A user could, for example, say that she likes graphing a swimmer's event times and that she also likes not having the same feature. There are twenty-five possible combinations of answers to the functional and dysfunctional forms of a question. We need a way of looking at both answers simultaneously and assessing a user's opinion.

Categorizing Responses

The method for doing this is shown in Figure 11.3. By cross-referencing the answer to the functional question with the answer to the dysfunctional question, a prospective user's responses can be reduced to a single meaning. So if a user says she expects to be able to graph event times and that she would dislike it if it did not (which are the answers given in Figure 11.2), we cross-reference those answers and get that she considers the feature to be mandatory. In her mind, graphing event times is a must-have feature.

		Dysfunctional Question				
		Like	Expect	Neutral	Live with	Dislike
Functional Question	Like	Q	E	E	E	L
	Expect	R	I	I	I	M
	Neutral	R	I	I	I	M
	Live with	R	I	I	I	M
	Dislike	R	R	R	R	Q

M	Must-have	R	Reverse
L	Linear	Q	Questionable
E	Exciter	I	Indifferent

Figure 11.3 Categorizing a feature from answers to a pair of questions.

If we repeat this process over twenty to thirty users, their answers can be aggregated and their distributions determined as is shown in Table 11.1. From examining this table, we can tell that graphing event times is a one-dimensional (linear) feature and that uploading photos is a must-have feature.

Table 11.1 Distribution of Results from Surveying Users

Theme	E	L	M	I	R	Q	Category
Graph event times	18.4	**43.8**	22.8	12.8	1.7	0.5	Linear
Can upload photos	8.3	30.9	**54.3**	4.2	1.4	0.9	Must-have
Post autobiographical profile	**39.1**	14.8	**36.6**	8.2	0.2	1.1	Exciter Must-have

Occasionally you'll encounter a feature, such as posting autobiographical profiles in Table 11.1, that has high values for two responses. This indicates that different types of customers and users have different expectations. In these cases, you should consider analyzing responses based on some factor that differentiates your customer or user subpopulation. You may, for example, separate answers from users at small companies from users at large companies. Or you may choose to separate answers based on job role within a company or by industry segment.

Relative Weighting: Another Approach

Karl Wiegers (1999) has recommended an approach that is similar to Kano's in that it considers both the positive benefit of the presence of a feature and the negative impact of its absence. Rather than use questionnaires, this approach relies on expert judgment. Collaboratively, but led by the product owner, the team assesses each feature being considered for the next release. Each feature is assessed in terms of the benefits it will bring if implemented, as well as the penalty that will be incurred if it is not implemented. As with estimates of story points and ideal time, the estimates of benefits and penalties are relative. A scale of 1 to 9 is used. Table 11.2, which again uses the SwimStats features, shows how this works.

The benefit of including graphs of a swimmer's event times over a season is estimated at 8. This feature is slightly less valuable than uploading photos but is much more valuable than the ability for swimmers to post autobiographical profiles. As for the relative penalties if these features are absent, there is very little penalty if users cannot upload photos. (In Kano's terms, uploading photos is probably an exciter—users would like it but would not reject the product if it were absent.) There is more of a penalty if event times cannot be graphed or autobiographies posted.

Table 11.2 The Relative Weighting Approach to Prioritization

Feature	Relative Benefit	Relative Penalty	Total Value	Value %	Estimate	Cost %	Priority
Graph event times	8	6	14	42	32	53	0.79
Can upload photos	9	2	11	33	21	34	0.97
Post autobiographical profile	3	5	8	25	8	13	1.92
Total	**20**	**13**	**33**	**100**	**61**	**100**	

For each feature, the relative benefit and penalty are summed and entered in the Total Value column. If you wish, you could weight the benefits and penalties. For example, to weight the relative benefit as twice as important as the relative penalty, multiply the Relative Benefit by 2 before adding it to Relative Penalty to get the Total Value.

The sum of the Total Value column (in this case, 33) represents the total value of delivering all features. To calculate the relative contribution of each feature, divide its total value by the sum of the Total Value column. For example, graphing event times has a value of 14. The total value of all features is 33. Dividing 14 by 33 results in 0.42, or 42%. This means that graphing event times represents 42% of the total value of all listed features.

The next column, Estimate, holds the story-point or ideal-days estimate. Exactly as with Total Value, the Estimate column is summed (61, in this case) and the percentage of each estimate is calculated in the Cost % column. In this example, graphing event times is estimated at 32 story points or ideal days. The three combined are 61 story points or ideal days. So graphing event times represents 53% of the total cost of these three stories ($32/61 = 0.53$).

The final column, Priority, is calculated by dividing the Value % by the Cost %. Higher numbers represent higher priorities because they will create more value for the effort invested in them. You can see this in Table 11.2 by looking at the feature to post autobiographical profiles. This feature generates a little more than half the value of graphing event times (a Total Value of 8 compared with 14), but it does so at one-fourth the cost (an estimate of 8 compared with 32). Because of its high value-to-cost ratio, posting autobiographical profiles is the highest-priority feature in this analysis.

The Importance of Including Relative Penalty

You may be tempted to drop the Relative Penalty column. Don't. As with the Kano approach, it can be very useful to look at features from the perspective of how users will be affected by the presence of the feature as well as by the absence of the feature.

One of my clients in the financial services industry provides a good example of the importance of considering the relative penalty. The product owner for their team was able to prioritize most features quite easily. However, one feature she had to prioritize would bring no value to the company other than keeping the company in compliance with certain new government regulations. She joked that the only downside to not implementing the feature was that the CEO might spend some time in prison. And she (because she wasn't the CEO) was OK with that risk if it meant getting other features into the product instead.

This is a clear example of a feature with a relative benefit of 1 but a relative penalty of 9.

Summary

Let's step back for a moment and remember why we're doing this. In the previous chapter, we learned that there are four factors to consider when prioritizing features.

1. The amount and significance of learning and new knowledge created by developing the features.
2. The amount of risk removed by developing the features.
3. The financial value of having the features.
4. The cost of developing (and perhaps supporting) the new features.

The previous chapter, "Prioritizing Themes," described the importance of factoring learning and risk reduction into the overall prioritization of a feature. This chapter presented two approaches to prioritizing the desirability of features: Kano analysis and relative weighting.

In Kano analysis, features are segregated into must-have features, linear features, and exciters. This is done by asking potential users two questions about each feature: how they would feel if the feature were present and how they would feel if it were not present.

Relative weighting provides an approach to assessing the benefits of implementing a feature, the penalties of not implementing it, and the cost into a single value representing the priority of a feature.

Discussion Questions

1. What are the relative merits of Kano analysis and relative weighting in your current organization?

2. What exciters are going into your current project?

3. Does your current project have the right mix of exciters, linear features, and must-have features?

Chapter 12

Splitting User Stories

> *"These days we do not program software module by module;*
> *we program software feature by feature."*
> —Mary Poppendieck

As user stories rise to the top of the release plan, meaning that they will be implemented soon, they often need to be split. After all, if implementing a particular user story will take longer than the length of the iteration, there's no choice but to split the story into two or more stories. Learning how to see ways to split stories is not a particularly difficult skill to acquire, but it does take practice and experience. The more different user stories you've split in the past, the easier it becomes. With that in mind, this chapter offers advice on splitting stories by providing a number of examples. From these examples, a number of guidelines are distilled that can be used for splitting other stories.

The advice in this chapter can be used any time a story needs to be split. However, the guidelines are specifically targeted at the user stories or features that seem difficult to split.

When to Split a User Story

There are times when it may be necessary to split a user story into multiple, smaller parts. First, a user story should be split when it is too large to fit within a single iteration. Sometimes a user story won't fit in an iteration because it is bigger than a full iteration. Clearly, a story in this situation needs to be split.

Alternatively, a story may be small enough to fit within an iteration, but it won't fit within the iteration being planned because there isn't enough room left. The team may feel they will have time to develop a portion of a story in the iteration but not the entire story.

Second, it can be useful to split a large user story (an *epic*) if a more accurate estimate is necessary. For example, one of my clients was contemplating new features that would provide enhanced access into their system to customer service representatives (CSRs) who worked at other companies. The first question the product owner had to answer was whether these features were worth pursuing. Rather than writing a bunch of individual user stories, she wrote one large story and described the vision behind that story to the team. They estimated it as seventy story points. That was good enough for her to know she wanted to add these features. She knew there was a great deal of uncertainty in the estimate, but even if the estimate were off by 100% these features were still worth doing. If seventy story points had put her on the border of whether or not to include the CSR features in the release, she could have chosen to split the large story and have the team estimate the multiple smaller stories.

Splitting across Data Boundaries

One of the best ways to split a large user story is by the data that will be supported. For example, on a recent project the team was developing a product to collect financial information. They started with one epic user story: "As a user, I can enter my balance sheet information." A balance sheet in this case could include a great many fields. At the highest level, it includes assets and liabilities. Assets included such items as cash, securities, real estate, automobiles, loans, and so on. The system was such that the user could interact with this balance sheet at various levels of detail. A user could enter a single value representing all of his assets. Or he could enter slightly more detailed information (a total value of all loans, for example) or much more detailed information (an itemization of all loans). Considering the number of fields on the screen and the interactions among them, this was far more than the team felt they could complete in a single two-week iteration.

The team split this story by the type of data that the user could enter. Their first story was "As a user, I can enter summary balance sheet data." This story was very small (almost too small), as it covered only creating the basic form and two fields: one for assets and one for liabilities. Their next story was "As a user, I can enter categorized balance sheet data." This story covered the next level of detail (such as cash, securities, real estate, loans, and so on). When this story was implemented, there would be two dozen input fields on the screen. Their next story covered data validation, "As a user, I want the values I enter to be validated so that I don't make any mistakes." They discussed what this meant and agreed that positive and negative amounts would be allowed, that decimals could be entered but that amounts would be automatically rounded to the nearest dollar, and so on.

Their next user story was "As a user, I can enter detailed loan information." This story would allow a user to enter up to 100 loans (this number was discussed, agreed to, and noted as a condition of satisfaction on the story card). This story was larger than it sounds because it addressed a number of user interface issues, such as how new rows of loan data would be displayed on the screen. The story was much larger than the others that had been split out from the original story. However, even this story was much smaller than the original story because this one called for supporting detailed data only for loans. The loan story was used as a pattern for many other user stories that were split from the original, such as "As a user, I can enter detailed information about my real estate holdings" and "As a user, I can enter detailed information about my cash holdings, including checking and savings accounts."

By splitting the initial story in this way, the team created about a dozen user stories from the initial one. Each of the new stories was now well within the size they could complete in a two-week iteration. This leads to our first guideline:

> **Split large stories along the boundaries of the data supported by the story.**

Splitting a user story along data boundaries is a very useful approach and one you should definitely have in your bag of tricks. As another example, a few years ago I was working with a team developing an automated fax subsystem. The team was faced with some large user stories about how the system could be configured. The stories were made much smaller by splitting support for U.S. and international phone numbers.

In some cases a large story can be made much smaller by removing the handling of exceptional or error conditions from the main story. Suppose you are working on a system to process loan repayments and have this user story: "As a borrower, I want to pay off my loan." When the team discusses this story, the product owner points out that if the borrower inadvertently sends a check for more than the outstanding loan amount, a refund check has to be printed and mailed back to the borrower. She adds that this applies only for amounts over ¤2. This story could be split by writing the following stories:

- As a borrower, I want to pay off my loan. Note: Allow overpayments.
- As a borrower, if I accidentally repay too much, I get a refund if it's over ¤2.

Splitting on Operational Boundaries

I worked with a team recently that was tasked with developing a very complex search screen. There were dozens of fields on the top half of the screen, a middle-tier query builder that assembled formulated database queries based on what had been entered, and then a complex data display grid on the bottom of the screen. All of this work was initially described by a single user story. I had the team split the work into three pieces that were spread across three iterations.

In the first iteration they laid out the basic user interface, including about half of the search criteria fields that were on the top of the screen. They also wrote the portions of the query builder that worked with those fields. The bottom part of the screen was to hold the complex data display grid. This was too much to do in one two-week iteration. So at the end of the first iteration, that portion of the screen displayed a simple message such as "This search found 312 matches." This certainly wasn't very useful for a user who wanted to know what those 312 matches contained. However, it represented significant progress and made that progress visible to all project stakeholders.

The second iteration on this project added the data display grid, and the third iteration added the remaining search criteria fields to the top of the screen. These iterations were prioritized this way because there was a lot of uncertainty about how long it would take to develop the data display grid. Removing that uncertainty in the second iteration was deemed better than leaving it until the third. Because the team had already achieved a solid understanding of what was necessary to create the query builder, they considered that work to be low risk. This leads to our next guideline:

> **Split large stories based on the operations that are performed within the story.**

A common approach to doing this is to split a story along the boundaries of the common CRUD operations—Create, Read, Update, and Delete. To see how this works, suppose you are working on the SwimStats system, and the team is ready to develop this story: "As a coach, I can manage the swimmers on my team." The team talks to the coaches/users and finds out that this means the coach wants to add new swimmers, edit existing data for swimmers, and delete swimmers who have left the team. This initial story can easily be split into three stories:

- As a coach, I can add new swimmers to my team.
- As a coach, I can edit information about swimmers already on my team.
- As a coach, I can delete swimmers who are no longer on my team.

These stories very closely correspond to the Create, Update, and Delete portions of CRUD. Splitting a large story into these three stories is a very common pattern and leads to our next guideline:

> Split large stories into separate CRUD operations.

Removing Cross-Cutting Concerns

There are many orthogonal or cross-cutting features in a typical application. Security, error-handling, and logging, for example, each cut across all of the other features of an application. A story that is too big to fit in an iteration can often be reduced by isolating it from one or more of these cross-cutting concerns.

For example, many applications contain screens that behave differently depending on the privileges of the current user. If that is too much to develop in a single iteration, develop the screens in one iteration and add support for user-specific privileges in a later iteration.

On a recent project a client needed to split a story that involved searching for data and displaying the results. Each search would span the entire database, but only those results the user had privileges to see were to be displayed. The team's solution was to ignore this security restriction, and in the first iteration on this feature, users could see the entire result set.

As another example, suppose the team plans to work on a story that says "As a user, I am required to log in with a username and password before using the system." The team discusses the story and comes up with a list of constraints on the password: It must be at least eight characters, must include at least one digit, must not include any characters repeated three or more times, must be encrypted when transmitted and stored, and so on.

None of this may be particularly time-consuming, but in aggregate it may make the story a little too big to fit in an iteration. This can be resolved by removing the security precautions from the login story and creating nonsecure and secure versions of the story. The second story could list the planned security precautions, such as password length, character restrictions, and so on. You probably would not choose to release the product with only the first, nonsecure story developed, but there could be value in splitting the initial, large story in this way.

This leads to our next guideline:

> Consider removing cross-cutting concerns (such as security, logging, error handling, and so on) and creating two versions of the story: one with and one without support for the cross-cutting concern.

Don't Meet Performance Constraints

In software development we often forget (or ignore) Kernighan and Plauger's (1974) advice to "Make it work, then make it faster." A few years ago I was on a project to display charts of stock market prices. Web users would request a chart by the stock's ticker symbol. Our code would then retrieve the price history of that stock (over any of a variety of time periods from the current day to the last five years) and display a line chart of the stock. Among the conditions of satisfaction associated with that feature were ones covering the accuracy of the line, the handling of missing data, and the performance. To meet the performance target, we would need to cache the most frequently requested charts, regenerating each once per minute. Because caching would be a significant part of the effort to deliver this new feature, we separated it into a new user story and scheduled it into the next iteration. More generally, this same approach can be applied to any nonfunctional requirement, which leads to our next guideline:

> Consider splitting a large story by separating the functional and nonfunctional aspects into separate stories.

For example, this approach can be applied if a new feature must consume less than a defined amount of memory, be drawn with fewer than a number of shapes, or use a critical resource for less than a defined amount of time.

Split Stories of Mixed Priority

Occasionally, one story comprises multiple smaller substories that are of different priority. Suppose a project includes a typical login story: "As a user, I am required to log into the system." The product owner expresses her conditions of satisfaction for this story, and they include the following:

◆ If the user enters a valid username and password, she is granted access.

◆ If the user enters an invalid password three times in a row, she is denied access until she calls customer service.

◆ If the user is denied access, she is sent an email stating that an attempt was made to use her account.

This story is too big to fit in one iteration, so it must be split. The story can be split by looking for low-priority elements. In this case the product owner would not ship the product if it did not support the core login functionality. She might, however, be willing to release the product without a retry time-out mechanism or without sending an email about the access attempt. This leads to another guideline about splitting stories:

> Separate a large story into smaller stories if the smaller stories have different priorities.

Don't Split a Story into Tasks

Sometimes, we come across a feature that is difficult to split. In these cases, it is tempting to split the feature into its constituent tasks. For most software developers, considering a feature and decomposing it into its constituent tasks is such a habit that we often do it without even being aware of it. Do not, for example, split a story into the following:

◆ Code the user interface.

◆ Write the middle tier.

The best way to avoid this temptation is to follow Hunt and Thomas' advice (1999) to fire a tracer bullet through the system. A tracer bullet travels through all layers of a feature. That may mean delivering a partial user interface, a partial middle tier, and a partial database. Delivering a cohesive subset of all layers of a feature is almost always better than delivering all of one layer. This leads to another guideline:

> Don't split a large story into tasks. Instead, try to find a way to fire a tracer bullet through the story.

Avoid the Temptation of Related Changes

Once you've split a story and have it at an appropriate size, don't make things worse by adding work to the story. Often, this comes in the form of the temptation of related changes. We tell ourselves, "While I'm in that code, I might as well take care of these other lingering changes." It can very possibly be appropriate to fix a bug or address an old issue while working on a separate issue in the same part of the code. However, the priority of doing so needs to be considered in the same manner in which priorities were considered for other features. In other words, which is higher priority: spending half a day fixing a year-old bug or spending the same amount of time on something else? The answer is clearly entirely contextual and becomes this chapter's final guideline:

> Avoid making things worse by adding related changes to an appropriately sized feature unless the related changes are of equivalent priority.

Combining Stories

With all of this advice about splitting stories, it may be tempting to think that every user story about to be worked on should be made as small as possible. That's not the case. For teams working in two-week iterations, splitting features such that each can be done in two to five days or so is appropriate. (Stories may still be estimated in story points, but by the time a team needs to split stories they will know approximately how many story points or ideal days equate to around two to five days.) Stories will need to be a little smaller for one-week iterations and can, but don't need to, be a little larger for longer iterations. Stories of these approximate sizes flow best through the short iterations of an agile project.

Just as we may need to split large stories, we may need to combine multiple tiny stories. The combined stories are estimated as a whole rather than individually. When possible, try to combine related stories as that will make it easier to prioritize them. It is very common to combine multiple bug reports and treat them as one item.

Summary

It can be useful to split a story that does not fit in an iteration, either because it's too large for any iteration or it's too big to fit in the time remaining in an iteration being planned. It is also useful to split a large story if you need to provide a more accurate estimate than can be made of the one large story.

A story may be split by the type of data it will support. A story may also be split based on the operations inherent in the story. Splitting stories across the common CRUD operations (Create, Read, Update, Delete) is common. A story may be made smaller by segmenting out any cross-cutting concerns, such as security, logging, error handling, and so on. A story may also be made smaller by ignoring performance targets during the iteration in which the story is made functional. The performance target can be made its own story and satisfied in a later iteration. Many stories describe two or more needs. If these needs are of different priority, split the stories that way.

Avoid splitting a story into the development tasks that will be necessary to implement the feature. Splitting work into its necessary tasks is such a habit for us that it is easy for us to begin splitting user stories that way. Avoid the temptation of making a large story any larger by including related changes that are not necessary for the delivery of the user story.

Finally, remember that sometimes it is appropriate to combine user stories, especially in the case of bug fixes, which may be too small on their own.

Discussion Questions

1. What are some user stories on a current or recent project that you found difficult to split? How might you split them now?
2. What problems do you think are caused by splitting a story into tasks and then treating the tasks as user stories?

Part IV

Scheduling

The previous two parts covered estimating the size of each desired new piece of functionality, and then prioritizing so that the team is aimed at building the best possible product. In this part of the book, we focus on creating a schedule.

In the next two chapters, we begin by looking at the essential steps to planning a release and then to planning an iteration. The next chapter offers advice on selecting an appropriate iteration length. In addition to knowing the size of the work to be completed, if we want to estimate how long a project is likely to take, we must estimate the team's rate of progress through that work. Estimating velocity is, therefore, the topic of the next chapter.

The final two chapters in this part cover situations of greater complexity or uncertainty. First is how to plan a project when there are huge implications to being wrong about the schedule or when a preliminary schedule must be estimated far in advance and from very limited information. This part concludes with a chapter describing the additional things necessary in planning a project that involves multiple teams.

Chapter 13

Release Planning Essentials

> *"You improvise. You adapt. You overcome."*
> —Clint Eastwood in *Heartbreak Ridge*

Release planning is the process of creating a very high-level plan that covers a period longer than an iteration. A typical release will cover perhaps three to six months and maybe three to twelve or more iterations, depending on how long the iterations are. A release plan is important for a number of reasons.

First, it helps the product owner and the whole team decide how much must be developed and how long that will take before they have a releasable product. The sooner the product can be released (and the better it is when it's released), the sooner the organization will begin earning a return on its investment in the project.

Second, a release plan conveys expectations about what is likely to be developed and in what timeframe. Many organizations need this information because it feeds into other strategic planning activities.

Third, a release plan serves as a guidepost toward which the project team can progress. Without the concept of a release, teams move endlessly from one iteration to the next. A release plan provides context that allows iterations to combine into a satisfying whole. This is a fundamental concern with any iterative process, not just agile ones. A hiker who wishes to reach the summit of a mountain may head for the highest peak he sees. However, once he reaches that summit he learns that it was a false peak. A higher summit had been obscured by the one he has reached. The hiker sets off toward the higher summit, only to find that it, too, is a false peak, and an even higher summit is now visible. This rather circuitous way of hiking up a mountain can apply equally to iterative projects. Fortunately, the problems it creates are eliminated by having a release plan that shows a team's current expectation of where they ultimately wish to arrive.

The Release Plan

Part of planning a release is determining how much can be accomplished by what date. In some cases, we start with a date and see how much can be finished by then. In other cases, we start with a set of user stories and see how long it will take to develop them. In both cases, once a team has an initial answer, it is assessed against the organization's goals for the project: Will the product developed make the desired amount of money? Will it save enough money? Will the product capture the target market share? If not, perhaps a longer or shorter project may achieve an acceptable set of goals.

At a cursory level, determining how much work will fit into a release and what user stories that will be is a very straightforward process. Multiplying the planned number of iterations by either the expected or known velocity of the team gives us the total amount of work that can be performed. We then select the number of user stories that will fit and are done. Suppose that we wish to ship a new product in six months. We plan to work in two-week iterations, so there will be thirteen iterations during the project. We expect the team's velocity to be twenty story points or ideal days per iterations. The size of the total project is then $13 \times 20 = 260$ story points or ideal days. The product owner and team could then discuss all of the stories and prioritize them to deliver the most value possible while paying attention to not going above 260. The release plan itself is usually documented as simply a list of the user stories that will be developed during the project.

During release planning, we do not want to create a plan that indicates which developers will work on which user stories or tasks, or the sequence in which work will be performed within an iteration. Creating a plan with that level of detail during release planning is dangerous and misleading. Decisions about who works on what and the sequence of activities are best left to the individuals working on those tasks and are best deferred as long as possible. Additionally, remember that items in a release plan are user stories, which are descriptions of the functionality to be delivered, not individual engineering tasks to be performed. During release planning, it is too early, and some user stories may be insufficiently understood to be disaggregated into engineering tasks. As you'll see in Chapter 14, "Iteration Planning," the team will eventually disaggregate the user stories of the release plan into their constituent tasks. But they won't do this until the beginning of the iteration containing those stories.

Naturally, should your project, organization, and work environment warrant it, you can include additional information in a release plan. For example, you may wish to communicate some key assumptions underlying the plan. Most notably, you may want to state assumptions about who is on the team, how long the iterations will be, the date the first iteration will start, and the date the last iteration will finish. Chapter 21, "Communicating about Plans," will describe some additional useful information you may want to include when communicating about a release plan.

The general steps in planning a release are shown in Figure 13.1. Each of these steps will be described in the sections that follow.

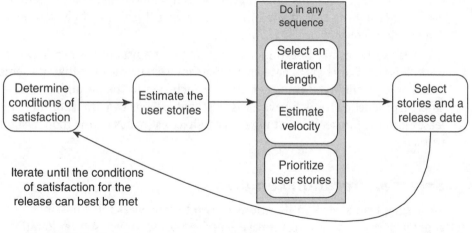

Figure 13.1   The steps in planning a release.

Determine the Conditions of Satisfaction

Before starting to plan a release, it is important to know the criteria by which the project will be evaluated as a success or a failure. For most projects, the ultimate scorecard is the amount of money saved or generated. As leading indicators of whether a project is likely to achieve these financial goals, most projects use the triumvirate of schedule, scope, and resources. For most projects, this means that the product owner's conditions of satisfaction are defined by a combination of schedule, scope, and resource goals.

The product owner will bring desired targets for each of these factors into almost every release planning meeting. A product owner may want four themes (worth 200 story points) developed in three months without adding personnel, for example. Although a target for each factor is often identified, one factor is usually preeminent. Projects are typically either date-driven or feature-driven. A *date-driven* project is one that must be released by a certain date but for which the feature set is negotiable. A *feature-driven* project is one that we would probably like to release as soon as possible but for which we consider the completion of a set of features to be more important.

Estimate the User Stories

Because an estimate represents the cost of developing a user story, it is important that each has been estimated. Imagine that you've decided to replace every item of clothing in your closet. You arrive at the mall and start shopping. However, you notice that all the price tags have been removed and that you have no way of knowing the cost of anything. This is what it feels like to be a product owner who is not provided any estimates.

It is not necessary to estimate everything that a product owner may ever want. It is necessary only to have an estimate for each new feature that has some reasonable possibility of being selected for inclusion in the upcoming release. Often, a product owner will have a wish list that extends two, three, or more releases into the future. It is not necessary to have estimates on the more distant work.

Select an Iteration Length

Most agile teams work in iterations of two to four weeks. It's possible to go slightly longer, and some teams have experimented with even shorter iterations. When planning a release, an appropriate iteration length will need to be chosen. Guidance on doing this is provided in Chapter 15, "Selecting an Iteration Length."

Estimate Velocity

If the team has experience working together, your best bet is often to use the velocity the team exhibited most recently. Naturally, if the technology or business domain has changed dramatically, it may not be appropriate to use a team's past velocity. Still, there are techniques you can apply that enable you to make an informed estimate of velocity based on past results. In Chapter 16, "Estimating Velocity," we will look at such techniques and will also explore options for estimating velocity.

Prioritize User Stories

Most projects have either too little time or too many features. It is often impossible to do everything that everyone wants in the time allowed. Because of this, the product owner must prioritize the features she wants developed. A good product owner will accept ultimate responsibility for prioritizing but will listen to advice from the development team, especially about sequencing. User stories are prioritized based on the guidelines given in the previous part of this book.

Select Stories and a Release Date

At this point, you have an estimate of the team's velocity per iteration and have an assumption about how many iterations there will be. It's time to see whether a release can be planned that meets the conditions of satisfaction for the project.

If the project is feature-driven, we can sum the estimates of all needed features and divide by the expected velocity. This will give us the number of iterations necessary to complete the desired functionality.

If the project is date-driven, we can determine the number of iterations by looking at a calendar. Multiplying the number of iterations by the expected velocity will tell us how many story points or ideal days will fit in the release. We can count off that many points or ideal days into the prioritized list of user stories and see how much functionality can be delivered in the desired time.

The next question to be addressed regards how detailed the release plan will be. Some teams in some environments prefer to create a release plan that shows what they expect to develop during each iteration. Other teams prefer simply to determine what they think will be developed during the overall release, leaving the specifics of each iteration for later. This is something for the team to discuss and decide during release planning.

There are advantages and disadvantages to each approach. Obviously, assigning specific features to specific iterations takes more time. However, the additional detail this provides can be useful when coordinating work among multiple teams. On the other hand, not allocating work to specific iterations provides less detail, but it takes much less time. Further, even if we do preliminarily assign work to specific iterations, we do so with less knowledge than we'll have at the start of each iteration. Undoubtedly, the plan will change as we learn more throughout the project. So the investment of time and effort to assign work to specific iterations should be weighed against this. Still, on some projects it may be worth doing. What I find to be a good compromise is to place specific work into the first one to three iterations, treating the rest of the release plan as one large bucket. It's almost always worth allocating specific work to the first iteration, especially if it is starting immediately.

Because there are a lot of give-and-take and what-if questions during a typical release planning session, we want an easy way to manipulate what's in and out of the release and its iterations. The best way of achieving this, assuming everyone is collocated, is to work with 3" x 5" note cards or sticky pads with user stories or features written on them. Unlike software, cards are tangible and easily shared.

To plan a release, the product owner selects her top priority items that will fit in the first iteration. Cards are stacked or arranged to indicate which stories comprise each iteration. Figure 13.2 shows one way of doing this. Cards can be arranged like this on a table or a wall. If you're using a wall, a corkboard is very effective, because cards can be pinned to the board rather than taped to the wall. Because each story card is annotated with an estimate, it is possible to look down each column of an arrangement like Figure 13.2 and verify that each iteration holds the right amount of work.

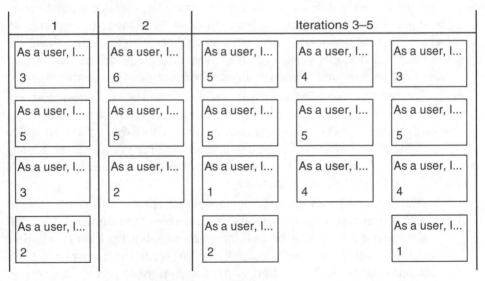

Figure 13.2   Arranging iterations in columns.

Updating the Release Plan

At this point, the release plan is done. However, it's important that the release plan isn't filed away somewhere or put up on a shelf, never to be touched again.

The release plan should be revisited and updated with some regular frequency. If the development team's velocity has remained fairly constant, and iteration planning hasn't introduced any big surprises, you may want to go as long as four to six weeks without formally updating the release plan. On the other hand, many projects benefit from establishing a rule that the release plan will be revisited after each iteration.

An Example

To tie all of the preceding together, let's consider a very brief example. We will again use the SwimStats website. Through market research we've discovered that coaches and swimmers in our target audience want the features described by the following user stories:

- As a coach, I can define practice sessions.
- As a coach, I can define custom fields I want to track for each swimmer.
- As a swimmer, I can run a report that shows my improvement in all events since a date in the past.
- As a swimmer, I can update my demographic information.
- As a coach, I can send an email to all swimmers on the team.
- As a system administrator, I can configure permissions and user groups.
- As a coach, I can purchase SwimStats and use it for my team.
- As a swimmer, I can compare my times with national records.
- As a coach, I can enter enter the names and demographic information of all swimmers on my team.
- As a swimmer, I can see my best times in each event.
- As a user, I am required to log in and can see only data for which I have permission.
- As a swimmer, I can see all of my times for a specific event.

Determining the Conditions of Satisfaction

The spring swim season starts in four months. The first release of the SwimStats website needs to be available a month before that. The product owner would like as many features as possible, but this is a date-driven project. Something must be releasable in three months, even if it is only the basics for small swim teams.

As a start-up, budget is also fixed. The project needs to be done with the one programmer, one database administrator, and one tester who are already on staff.

Estimating

The three developers who will work on the project meet with the product owner. They ask questions about the user stories, and the product owner clarifies the intent of each. The team elects to estimate in story points and assigns the estimates shown in Table 13.1.

Table 13.1 The Prioritized List of Stories

Story	Estimate
As a coach, I can purchase SwimStats and use it for my team.	5
As a user, I am required to log in and can see only data for which I have permission.	5
As a coach, I can enter enter the names and demographic information of all swimmers on my team.	8
As a swimmer, I can see all of my times for a specific event.	5
As a swimmer, I can update my demographic information.	5
As a swimmer, I can see my best times in each event.	5
As a swimmer, I can run a report that shows my improvement in all events since a date in the past.	5
As a swimmer, I can compare my times with national records.	8
As a coach, I can define practice sessions.	8
As a coach, I can send an email to all swimmers on the team.	3
As a coach, I can define custom fields I want to track for each swimmer.	8
As a system administrator, I can configure permissions and user groups.	3
Total	**68**

Selecting the Iteration Length

Because the entire project will only be three months, the developers and the product owner agree that four-week iterations are too long. Running four-week iterations just won't give them enough checkpoints on the team's progress or enough opportunities for the product owner to steer the project by adjusting priorities. Based on points that will be presented in Chapter 15, "Selecting an Iteration Length," everyone agrees to run two-week iterations.

Estimating Velocity

This project will be worked on by two programmers and a tester. Using the techniques you'll learn in Chapter 16, "Estimating Velocity," they forecast a velocity of eight story points per iteration.

Prioritizing the User Stories

The product owner, based on market research that has been done, prioritizes the stories. The prioritized story list, along with the estimate for each story is shown in Table 13.1.

Selecting the User Stories

Because this is a date-driven project, we know how many iterations there can be. The product owner wants a release out in three months so there is time for six two-week iterations followed by an extra week in case it's needed. With an estimated velocity of eight points per iteration, this means the release will be planned to include $6 \times 8 = 48$ story points. The product owner will be able to select up to forty-eight points from Table 13.1 to include in the release.

The user stories in Table 13.1 have been sorted by the product owner in descending order of how valuable she thinks each will be to the initial release of SwimStats. The product owner is allowed to select up to forty-eight points. She initially indicates that she'd like to select the first eight stories, through "As a swimmer, I can compare my times with national records." This is a total of forty-six points, which is close enough to forty-eight that the product owner agrees to stop there.

However, the developers point out that the story prioritized as the lowest by the product owner is necessary: "As a system administrator, I can configure permissions and user groups." This story is estimated at three points, which would put the release at forty-nine and over the planned forty-eight. The forty-eight points is a fairly rough guess, and an extra week is planned after the sixth iteration. Some teams may allow for forty-nine points under these circumstances.

The SwimStats team, however, decides not to allow forty-nine points. If a three-point story is being added, at least one point needs to be dropped from the release. The product owner decides to drop the eight-point "As a swimmer, I can compare my times with national records." This brings the release down to forty-one points. The product owner could add the three-point story, "As a coach, I can send an email to all swimmers on the team" to the release, but she decides to hold off on doing so. If the team gets even one point ahead of schedule, she'd prefer to add back the eight-point story she dropped. This makes the final release plan as shown in Table 13.2.

Table 13.2 The Final Release Plan for SwimStats

Story	Estimate
As a coach, I can purchase SwimStats and use it for my team.	5
As a system administrator, I can configure permissions and user groups.	3
As a user, I am required to log in and can see only data for which I have permission.	5
As a coach, I can enter enter the names and demographic information of all swimmers on my team.	8
As a swimmer, I can see all of my times for a specific event.	5
As a swimmer, I can update my demographic information.	5
As a swimmer, I can see my best times in each event.	5
As a swimmer, I can run a report that shows my improvement in all events since a date in the past.	5
Total	**41**

Summary

A release plan is a high-level plan that covers a period longer than an iteration. For most teams a release occurs every three to six months, but it is not unusual to have releases more or less frequently, depending on the type of software. At its simplest level, release planning is trivial: Multiply the expected velocity by the number of planned iterations and then select stories whose estimates sum to fill up the release.

A release plan does not have to describe exactly what will be worked on during each iteration. In fact, that level of detail is rarely needed. For most projects it is quite adequate to identify the stories that will be worked on in the first couple of iterations, leaving the remaining stories to be prioritized into specific iterations later.

Release planning is an iterative process that begins by identifying the product owner's conditions of satisfaction for the project. These usually include goals for the schedule, scope, and resources. If a project cannot be planned that meets the set of initial conditions of satisfaction, the planning process is repeated to see if a lessened set of conditions can be met; perhaps the desired functionality can be delivered a little later or with a larger team.

Once a release plan has been created, it is not left hanging on a wall to rot. It is usually updated at the start of each iteration.

Discussion Questions

1. Is your current project date-driven or feature-driven? What makes it so?
2. In your organization or on your current project, how often should a release plan be updated?

Chapter 14

Iteration Planning

> *"It is a capital mistake to theorize*
> *before one has data."*
> —Sherlock Holmes, *Scandal in Bohemia*

A release plan is an excellent high-level view of how a team intends to deliver the most valuable product they can. However, a release plan provides only the high-level view of the product being built. It does not provide the short-term, more detailed view that teams use to drive the work that occurs within an iteration. With an iteration plan, a team takes a more focused, detailed look at what will be necessary to implement completely only those user stories selected for the new iteration.

An iteration plan is created in an iteration planning meeting. This meeting should be attended by the product owner, analysts, programmers, testers, database engineers, user interaction designers, and so on. Anyone involved in taking a raw idea and turning it into a functioning product should be present.

Tangibly, an iteration plan can be as simple as a spreadsheet or a set of note cards with one task handwritten on each card. In either case, tasks and stories should be organized so that it's possible to tell which tasks go with which stories. For example, see Table 14.1, which shows an iteration plan in a spreadsheet. Tasks are shown one per row and are indented beneath the story to which they apply.

As an alternative to a spreadsheet, see Figure 14.1, which illustrates using note cards for iteration planning. The cards can be arranged as in that figure on a table or floor, or by taping or pinning them to a wall. For collocated teams, my preference is to do iteration planning with note cards. The team may walk out of an iteration planning meeting and immediately type the cards into a software system, if they desire, but there are very real benefits to using cards during the meeting.

Table 14.1 An Iteration Plan Shown as a Simple Spreadsheet

Row	User Story / Task	Hours
1	As a coach, I can assign swimmers to events for a meet.	
2	Determine rules about who can swim in which events.	6
3	Specify acceptance tests to show how this should work.	8
4	Design user interface.	16
5	Code user interface.	8
6	Add tables and stored procedures to database.	6
7	Automate tests.	6
8	As a swimmer, I can update my demographics.	
9	Specify acceptance tests.	5
10	Change view-only demographics page to allow edits.	6
11	...	

One of the most significant advantages to using note cards during iteration planning is that it allows everyone to participate in the process. If tasks are being typed into a system during the iteration planning meeting, someone has his or her fingers on a keyboard. There is tremendous power to having control over the keyboard. All conversations had better involve the typist, or nothing will get entered into the release plan. Worse, whoever has the keyboard can change what gets entered into the release plan.

Two examples attest to this power. In the first case, the team discussed a particular item and decided it should be estimated at twelve hours. The keyboard was in the control of a combination project manager/technical lead. He entered an estimate of eight into the system because "there's no way it will take that long," even though he was extremely unlikely to be the one who would do the task.

Story	Tasks	
As a coach, I can assign swimmers to events for a meet.	Determine rules about who can swim in which events. 6	Specify acceptance tests to show how this should work. 8
	Design user interface. 16	Code user interface. 8
As a swimmer, I can update my demographics.	Specify acceptance tests. 5	Change view-only demographics page to allow edits. 6

Figure 14.1 Iteration planning can be done with note cards on a table or wall.

In the second case, the team I was coaching discussed how a new feature would be implemented—would it be server-side Java code or a stored procedure in the database? Everyone but the team lead, who had the keyboard, agreed it would be implemented through stored procedures. He was asked to create a task of "add stored procedures" on their spreadsheet. Instead, he typed "Write data storage code." His message was clear: This issue has not been resolved.

Compare these two situations to an iteration planning meeting in which anyone can grab a card and write a task at any time. Using cards is a much more democratic and collaborative approach and is likely to lead to better results throughout the iteration and the project, not just during that meeting.

Tasks Are Not Allocated During Iteration Planning

Before looking at the things that are done during iteration planning, it's important to clarify one thing that is not done. While planning an iteration, tasks are not allocated to specific individuals. At the start of the iteration, it may appear obvious who will work on a specific task; however, based on the progress of the whole team against the entire set of tasks, what is obvious at the start may not be what happens during the iteration. For example, when planning an iteration we may assume that our database administrator will complete the "tune the advanced search query" task because she has the best SQL skills on the team. However, if she's unable to get to this task, someone else may step forward and do it.

Individuals do not sign up for tasks until the iteration begins and generally sign up for only one or two related tasks at a time. New tasks are not begun until previously selected ones are completed.

There's nothing to gain and quite a bit to lose by assigning individuals to specific tasks during iteration planning. Projects do best when they foster a "we're all in this together" attitude—when team members pick up slack for each other knowing that the favor will be returned. When individuals sign up for specific tasks at the beginning of the iteration, it works against fostering a unified commitment to achieving the goals of the iteration.

How Iteration and Release Planning Differ

The release plan looks forward through the release of the product, usually three to six months out at the start of a new project. In contrast, the iteration plan looks ahead only the length of one iteration, usually two to four weeks. The user stories of the release plan are decomposed into tasks on the iteration plan. Where the user stories of a release plan are estimated in story points or ideal days, the tasks on the iteration plan are estimated in ideal hours.

Why are the tasks of an iteration plan estimated in hours but the stories of a release plan are estimated in story points or ideal days? Primarily because it is possible to do so. The work of an iteration is no more than a few weeks off, and the team should have a reasonable level of insight into the work, especially after discussing during the iteration planning meeting. This allows them to credibly estimate the tasks of an iteration in hours. The user stories that comprise a release each represent multiple tasks, are more vague, and less understood so they must be estimated in more abstract units such as story points or ideal days.

These primary differences between a release plan and an iteration plan are summarized in Table 14.2.

The primary purpose of iteration planning is to refine suppositions made in the more coarse-grained release plan. The release plan is usually intentionally vague about the specific order in which user stories will be worked on. Additionally, at the time of iteration planning the team knows more than when the release plan was last updated. Planning the iteration as it begins allows the team to make use of their recently acquired knowledge. In this way, agile planning becomes a two-stage process. The first stage is the release plan, with its rough edges and general uncertainties. The second stage is the iteration plan. An iteration plan still has some rough edges and continues to be uncertain. However, because it is created concurrent with the start of a new iteration, an iteration plan is more detailed than a release plan.

Creating the iteration plan leads a team into discussions about both product design and software design. Product design discussions, for example, may be around topics such as the best combination of stories for optimizing value, interpretation of feedback from showing working software to customers, or the extent to which a desired feature should be implemented (that is, will 20% of the feature and effort deliver 80% of the value?). Software design discussions may, for example, involve the appropriate architectural tier in which to implement a new feature, which technologies should be used, whether existing code can be reused, and so on. As a result of these discussions the team comes to a better understanding of what should and will be built, and they also create a list of the tasks needed to achieve their goal for the iteration.

Table 14.2 The Primary Differences between a Release and an Iteration Plan

	Release Plan	**Iteration Plan**
Planning horizon	3–9 months	1–4 weeks
Items in plan	User stories	Tasks
Estimated in	Story points or ideal days	Ideal hours

Velocity-Driven Iteration Planning

At a broad level, there are two ways of planning an iteration, which I refer to as *velocity-driven* and *commitment-driven*. Different teams use different approaches, and each can be successful. Additionally, the two general approaches can be combined to varying degrees. In this section, we'll consider velocity-driven iteration planning; in the next, we'll focus on commitment-driven iteration planning.

The steps involved in velocity-driven iteration planning are shown in Figure 14.2. First, the team collaboratively adjusts priorities. They may have learned something in the preceding iteration that alters their priorities. Next, they identify the target velocity for the coming iteration. The team then selects an iteration goal, which is a general description of what they wish to accomplish during the coming iteration. After selecting an iteration goal, the team selects the top-priority user stories that support that goal. As many stories are selected as necessary for the sum of their ideal-day or story-point estimates to equal the target velocity. Finally, each selected story is split into tasks, and each task is estimated. These steps are described in more detail throughout the rest of this chapter.

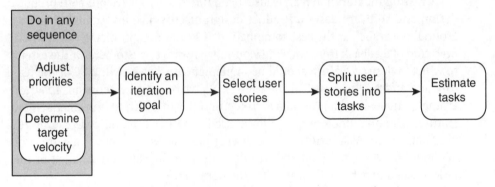

Figure 14.2 The sequence of steps in velocity-driven iteration planning.

Adjust Priorities

Imagine all of the user stories either physically stacked up or sorted within a spreadsheet such that the most valuable story is at the top and the least valuable is at the bottom. The project could progress by always taking stories from the top of this prioritized list to start each iteration. However, business and project conditions change quickly, so it is always worth a quick reconsideration of priorities.

One source of changes to priorities is the *iteration review meeting*, which is held after an iteration is finished. During the iteration review, the new functionality and capabilities that were added during the iteration are demonstrated to stakeholders, the extended project community, and anyone else who is interested. Valuable feedback is often received during these iteration reviews. The product owner herself should generally not come up with new ideas or changes during the iteration review, because she's been involved daily throughout the iteration. However, many others (including potential customers and users) may be seeing the results of the iteration for the first time. They will often have good new ideas that could preempt previously high-priority items.

As described in Chapter 9, "Prioritizing Themes," user stories and themes are prioritized based on their financial value to the product, their cost, the amount and significance of what the team will learn, and the amount of risk reduced. Ideally, a team should wait until after the iteration review meeting before discussing priorities for the coming iteration. After all, what they hear during the iteration review may influence them, and it's hard to prioritize next iteration's work if you are not entirely sure of what will be completed in this iteration. However, in many organizations I've found it useful to hold a prioritization meeting a few days before the start of a new iteration. I do this to fit the iteration review and the iteration planning meetings into the same day more easily.

An iteration review will typically take thirty to sixty minutes. For a large product with multiple teams, it's quite feasible that the product owner and other key stakeholders necessary for prioritization discussions could spend half a day in iteration reviews. Add another four hours to plan an iteration, and there may not be time to discuss priorities on the same day.

I usually schedule the prioritization meeting for two days before the end of the iteration. By that time, it's normally clear if there will be unfinished work from the current iteration. This allows the product owner to decide whether finishing that work will be a priority for the coming iteration. The product owner conducts the prioritization meeting and involves anyone she thinks can contribute to a discussion of the project's priorities. After having this meeting, the product owner can usually quickly and on the fly adjust priorities based on anything that happens during the iteration review.

Determine Target Velocity

The next step in velocity-driven iteration planning is to determine the team's target velocity. The default assumption by most teams is that their velocity in the next iteration will equal the velocity of the most recent iteration. Beck and Fowler (2000) call this *yesterday's weather*, because our best guess of today's weather is that it will be like yesterday's weather. Other teams prefer to use a moving average over perhaps the last three iterations.

If a team has not worked together before or is new to their agile process, they will have to forecast velocity. Techniques for doing so are described in Chapter 16, "Estimating Velocity."

Identify an Iteration Goal

With their priorities and target velocity in mind, the team identifies a goal they would like to achieve during the iteration. The goal succinctly describes what they would like to accomplish during that period. As an example, the SwimStats team may select "All demographics features are finished" as an iteration goal. Other example iteration goals for SwimStats could include the following:

- Make progress on reports.
- Finish all event time reports.
- Get security working.

The iteration goal is a unifying statement about what will be accomplished during the iteration. It does not have to be very specific. For example, "Make progress on reports" is a good iteration goal. It does not have to be made more specific, as in "Finish 15 reports" or "Do the meet results reports." If "Make progress on reports" is the best description of what will be worked on in the coming iteration, it is a good statement of that goal.

Select User Stories

Next, the product owner and team select stories that combine to meet the iteration goal. If the SwimStats team selected an iteration goal of "All demographics features are finished," they would work on any demographics-related stories that were not yet finished. This might include

- As a swimmer, I can update my demographics.
- As a coach, I can enter demographic data on each of my swimmers.
- As a coach, I can import a file of all demographic data.
- As a coach, I can export a file of all demographic data.

In selecting the stories to work on, the product owner and team consider the priority of each story. For example, if exporting a file of demographic data is near the bottom of the prioritized requirements list for the product, it may not be included in the iteration. In that case, the iteration goal could have been better stated as "The most important demographics features are finished."

Split User Stories into Tasks

Once the appropriate set of user stories has been selected, each is decomposed into the set of tasks necessary to deliver the new functionality. Suppose the highest-priority user story is "As a coach, I can assign swimmers to events for an upcoming meet." This user story will be turned into a list of tasks, such as:

- Determine rules that affect who can be assigned to which events.
- Write acceptance test cases that show how this should work.
- Design the user interface.

- Get user interface feedback from coaches.
- Code the user interface.
- Code the middle tier.
- Add new tables to database.
- Automate the acceptance tests.

A common question around iteration planning is what should be included. All tasks necessary to go from a user story to a functioning, finished product should be identified. If there are analysis, design, user interaction design, or other tasks necessary, they need to be identified and estimated. Because the goal of each iteration is to produce a potentially shippable product, take care to include tasks for testing and documenting the product. Including test tasks is important because the team needs to think right at the start of the iteration about how a user story will be tested. This helps engage testers right from the start of the iteration, which improves the cross-functional behavior of the team.

Include Only Work That Adds Value to This Project

The iteration plan should identify only those tasks that add immediate value to the current project. Obviously, that includes tasks that may be considered analysis, design, coding, testing, user interface design, and so on. Don't include the hour in the morning when you answer email. Yes, some of those email messages are project-related, but tasks like "answer email, 1 hour" should not be included in an iteration plan.

Similarly, suppose you need to meet with the company's director of personnel about a new annual review process. That should not be included in the iteration plan. Even though project team members will be reviewed using the new process, the meeting to discuss it (and any follow-on work you need to do) is not directly related to developing the product. So no tasks associated with it become part of the iteration plan.

Be Specific Until It's a Habit

New agile teams are often not familiar with or skilled at writing automated unit tests. However, this is a skill they work to cultivate during the first few iterations. During that period, I encourage programmers to identify and estimate unit testing tasks explicitly. A programmer may, for example, identify that coding a new feature will take eight hours and that writing its unit tests will take five hours. Later, once unit testing has become a habit for the programmers, the programmer would write only one card saying to code the new feature and would give it an estimate that included time to automate the unit tests. Once something like unit testing becomes a habit, it can be included within another task. Until then, however, making it explicit helps keep awareness of the task high.

Meetings Count (A Lot)

You should identify, estimate, and include tasks for meetings related to the project. When estimating the meeting, be sure to include the time for all participants, as well as any time spent preparing for the meeting. Suppose the team schedules a meeting to discuss feedback from users. All seven team members plan to attend the one-hour meeting, and the analyst plans to spend two hours preparing for the meeting. The estimate for this task is nine hours. I usually enter this into the iteration plan as a single nine-hour task, rather than as a separate task for each team member.

Bugs

An agile team has the goal of fixing all bugs in the iteration in which they are discovered. They become able to achieve this as they become more proficient in working in short iterations, especially through relying on automated testing. When a programmer gives an estimate for coding something, that estimate includes time for fixing any bugs found in the implementation, or a separate task ("Correct bugs") is identified and estimated. My preference is for identifying a single task but not considering it complete until all of its tests pass.

A defect found later (or not fixed during the iteration in which it was discovered) is treated the same way as a user story. Fixing the defect will need to be prioritized into a subsequent iteration in the same way that any other user story would be. Outside an iteration, the whole idea of a defect starts to go away. Fixing a bug and adding a feature become two ways of describing the same thing.

Handling Dependencies

Often, developing one user story will depend upon the previous implementation of another. In most cases, these dependencies are not a significant issue. There is usually what I consider a natural order to implementing user stories—that is, there is a sequence that makes sense to both developers and the product owner.

It is not a problem when there are dependencies among stories that lead to developing them in their natural order. The natural order is usually the order the team assumed when they estimated the stories. For example, the SwimStats team would probably assume that swimmers can be added to the system before they can be deleted. When stories are worked on in a sequence other than what was assumed when estimating, during iteration planning the team will often have to include additional tasks that make it possible to work on stories in the new order.

As an example, the natural order for the SwimStats website would be to complete the features that let a user add new swimmers to the system and then the features that let a user view an individual swimmer's fastest times in each event. It's a little unusual to think about seeing a swimmer's fastest times before having the screens through which swimmers are added to the system. However, it could be done if the product owner and team wanted to develop the features in that order. To do so, they would, of course, need to design enough of the database to hold swimmers and their times. They would also have to put at least one swimmer and her times into the database. Because this is part of the feature they don't want to do first, they would add the swimmer (and her times) to the database directly rather than through any user interface and software they developed.

For the SwimStats team to do this, during iteration planning they will need to identify a few tasks that would not have been identified if these two stories had been worked on in their natural order. For example, if the ability to add swimmers existed already, the team would not need to include a task of "Design database tables for information about individual swimmers." However, because the stories are being worked on out of their natural order, they will need to include this task.

Does that mean that working out of the natural order will cause the project to take longer? Two answers: Probably not, and it doesn't matter.

First, the project will probably not take longer; all we've done is shift some tasks from one user story to another. Designing the swimmer tables in this example would have happened sooner or later. When the time comes to work on the story about adding new swimmers to the system, that story will be done more quickly because part of its work is already complete.

You may be worried about the impact this task shifting has on the estimates given to the two stories. We may, for example, have shifted a point or an ideal day of work from one story to the other. In most cases, this isn't a big deal, and the differences will wash out over the course of the project. If anything, I've observed this to be a pessimistic shift, in that a five-point story becomes a six-point story. But because the team gives itself credit for only five points when they're finished, they slightly understate their velocity. Because the impact is small with a slightly pessimistic bias, I usually don't worry about it. However, if you're concerned about these impacts or if the task shifting is much more significant, re-estimate the stories involved as soon as you decide to work on them in other than the natural order.

Second, even if working on the stories in this order does cause the project to take longer, it doesn't matter, because there presumably was some good reason for working on them out of their natural order. The team may want to work on stories in a particular order so that they can address a technical risk earlier. Or a product owner may want earlier user feedback on a story that would more naturally have been developed later. By developing the stories out of their natural order, the team is able to get early feedback and potentially save a month or two of rework near the end of the project (when the schedule is least likely to be able to accommodate such a change).

Work That Is Difficult to Split

Some features are especially difficult to split into tasks. For example, I was recently in a planning meeting discussing a small change to a legacy feature. No one was comfortable in his or her ability to think through all of the possible impacts of the change. We were certain that some sections of the code would be affected but were not sure whether other sections would be. The changes were small in the sections we were sure about; we estimated them at a total of four hours. If the other sections were affected, we thought the estimate could go much higher, possibly as high as twenty hours. We couldn't be sure without looking at the code, and we didn't want to stop a planning meeting for that. Instead, we wrote these two tasks:

- Determine what's affected—two hours.
- Make the changes—ten hours.

This first task is called a spike. A *spike* is a task included in an iteration plan that is being undertaken specifically to gain knowledge or answer a question. In this case, the team did not have a good guess at something, so they created two tasks: one a spike and one a placeholder with a guess at the duration. The spike would help the team learn how they'd approach the other task, which would allow them to estimate it.

Estimate Tasks

The next step in velocity-driven iteration planning is to estimate each task. Some teams prefer to estimate tasks after all have been identified; other teams prefer to estimate tasks as each is identified. Task estimates are expressed in ideal time. So if I think that a task will take me six hours of working time, I give it an estimate of six hours. I do this even if six hours of time on the task will take me an entire eight-hour day.

Although I agree with accepted advice that the best estimates come from those who will do the work (Lederer and Prasad 1992), I believe that task estimating on an agile project should be a group endeavor. There are four reasons for this.

First, because tasks are not allocated to specific individuals during iteration planning, it is impossible to ask the specific person who will do the work.

Second, even though we expect a specific individual will be the one to do a task, and even though he may know the most about that task, it does not mean that others have nothing to contribute. Suppose during an iteration planning meeting, James says, "It will take me about two hours to program that—it's trivial!" However, you remember that just last month James worked on a similar task and made a similar comment, and that it took him closer to sixteen hours. This time, when James says that a similar task is going to take only two hours, you might add, "But James, the last time you worked on a similar task, you thought it would be two hours, and it took you sixteen." Most likely, James will respond with a legitimate reason why this case truly is different, or he'll agree that there is some difficulty or extra work in this type of task that he has been systematically forgetting.

Third, hearing how long something is expected to take often helps teams identify misunderstandings about a user story or task. Upon hearing an unexpectedly high estimate, a product owner or analyst may discover that the team is heading toward a more detailed solution than necessary. Because the estimate is discussed among the team, this can be corrected before any unneeded effort is expended.

Finally, when the person who will do the work provides the estimate, the person's pride and ego may make him reluctant to admit later that an estimate was incorrect. When an estimate is made collaboratively, this reluctance to admit an estimate is wrong goes away.

Some Design Is OK

Naturally, it's necessary for there to be some amount of design discussion while creating this list of tasks and estimates. We can't create a list of tasks if we don't have some idea of how we're going to do the work. Fortunately, though, when planning an iteration, it isn't necessary to go very far into the design of a feature.

The product owner, analysts, and user interface designers may discuss product design, how much of a feature should be implemented, and how it will appear to users. The developers may discuss options of how they will implement what is needed. Both types of design discussion are needed and appropriate. However, I've never been in an iteration planning meeting where it's become necessary to draw a class diagram or similar model. A desire to do so is probably the best warning sign of taking the design too far during iteration planning. Save those discussions for outside iteration planning

It's not necessary to go so far as drawing a design, because all that's necessary at this point are guesses about the work that will be needed to complete the features. If you get into the iteration and discover the tasks are wrong, get rid of the initial tasks and create new ones. If an estimate is wrong, cross it out and write a new value. Writing tasks and estimates on note cards is a great approach because each card carries with it a subtle reminder of impermanence.

The Right Size for a Task

The tasks you create should be of an approximate size so that each developer is able to finish an average of one per day. This size works well for allowing work to flow smoothly through your agile development process. Larger tasks tend to get bottled up with a developer or two, and the rest of the team can be left waiting for them to complete the task. Additionally, if the team is holding short daily meetings (Schwaber and Beedle 2002; Rising 2002), having tasks of this size allows each developer to report the completion of at least one task on most days.

Naturally, there will often be tasks that are larger than this. But larger tasks should be generally understood to be placeholders for one or more additional tasks that will be added as soon as they are understood. If you need to create a sixteen-hour task during iteration planning, do so. However, once the task is more adequately understood, augment or replace it. This may mean replacing the initial card with more or less than the initially estimated sixteen hours.

Commitment-Driven Iteration Planning

A commitment-driven approach is an alternative way to plan an iteration. Commitment-driven iteration planning involves many of the same steps as velocity-driven iteration planning. However, rather than creating an iteration plan that uses the yesterday's weather idea to determine how many story points or ideal days should be planned into the current iteration, the team is asked to add stories to the iteration one by one until they can commit to completing no more. The overall commitment-driven approach is shown in Figure 14.3.

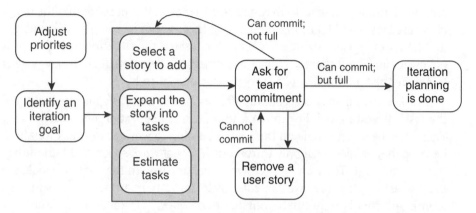

Figure 14.3 The activities of commitment-driven iteration planning.

The first steps—adjusting priorities and identifying an iteration goal—are the same as in the velocity-driven approach. The next step, selecting a story to add to the iteration, is different. The product owner and team still select the highest-priority story that supports the iteration goal. However, in commitment-driven iteration planning, stories are selected and decomposed into tasks, and the tasks estimated one story at a time. This is different from the velocity-driven approach, in which a set of stories whose estimates equaled the estimated velocity were selected.

Stories are selected one at a time because after each story is split into tasks and the tasks estimated, the team decides whether or not they can commit to delivering that story during the iteration.

Ask for a Team Commitment

In their study of what makes teams successful, Larson and LaFasto (1989) determined that a unified commitment made by all team members is one of the key factors contributing to team success. During an iteration planning meeting, I ask the team, "Can you commit to delivering the features we've discussed?" Notice that the question I ask is not "Can you commit to delivering the tasks we've identified?" That is a very different question and a far weaker commitment, because it is a commitment to complete a set of tasks rather than a commitment to deliver new functionality.

If new tasks are discovered during the iteration (and they almost certainly will be), a team that is committed to delivering the functionality described by a user story will try to complete the new tasks as well. A team that committed to only an identified list of tasks may not. In either case, it is possible that the newly discovered tasks will take long enough that they cannot be completed during the iteration. In that case, the team will need to discuss the situation with the product owner and see if there is still a way to meet the iteration goal; they may need to reduce the functionality of a story or drop one entirely.

I ask a team if they can commit after each user story is split into tasks and the tasks are estimated. For the first user story, the question often seems silly. There may be seven people on the team, planning to work a two-week iteration. Perhaps they've identified only thirty-four hours of work so far, and I ask if they can commit to it. Their answer (either verbal or through the confused looks on their faces) is "Of course we can commit to this. There are seven of us for two weeks, and this is only thirty-four hours of work." However, as the meeting progresses and as more user stories are brought into the iteration, the answer to my question, "Can you commit?" begins to require some thought. Eventually, we reach a point where the team cannot commit any further. If they cannot, they may choose to drop a story and replace it with a smaller one before finishing.

Summing the Estimates

The best way I've found for a team to determine whether they can commit to a set of user stories is to sum up the estimates given to the tasks and see if the sum represents a reasonable amount of work. There may very well be a large amount of uncertainty on some tasks, because the work hasn't been designed and requirements are vague. However, summing the estimates still gives some indication of the overall size of the work.

Suppose a team of seven is working in two-week iterations. They have 560 hours available each iteration (7 people × 10 days × 8 hours per day). We know that some amount of time will be spent on activities that are not shown on task cards—answering email, participating in meetings, and so on. Similarly, we know the estimates are wrong; they are, after all, *estimates*, not guarantees. For these reasons, we cannot expect this team to sign up for 560 hours of tasks. In fact, most teams are successful when their planned work (the sum of their task cards) represents between four and six hours per day. For our team of seven people, working two-week iterations means they can probably plan between 280 and 420 hours. Where a given team will end up within this range is influenced by how well they identify the tasks for a given user story, how accurately those tasks are estimated, the amount of outside commitments by team members, and the amount of general corporate overhead for the team. After as few as a couple of iterations, most teams begin to get a feel for approximately how many hours they should plan for an iteration.

Before committing to the work of an iteration, the team needs to look at the tasks and get a feel for whether they represent an appropriate distribution of work based on the various skills within the team. Is the Java programmer likely to be overloaded, while the HTML programmer has nothing to do this iteration? Are the selected user stories easy to program but time-consuming or difficult to test, thereby overloading the tester? Do the stories selected each need analysis and user interaction design before coding can begin?

A team in a situation like this should first try to find ways to better share work. Can the HTML programmer in this example help the tester? Can someone other than the user interaction designer do that work? If not, can we leave out of this iteration some stories that need user interaction design, and can we bring in some other stories that do not? The key is that everyone on the team is accountable for contributing whatever is within their capabilities, regardless of whether it is their specialty.

Individual Commitments

When assessing the ability to commit to completing a set of new functionality, some teams prefer to allocate each task to a specific person and then assess whether each individual is able to commit to that amount of work. This approach works well, and I've recommended it in the past (Cohn 2004). However, I've found that by not allocating tasks while planning the iteration and not doing the personal math needed to make individual commitments, the team benefits from the creation of a "we're all in this together" mindset.

If you do find a need to allocate tasks to individuals while planning an iteration, the allocations should be considered temporary and subject to change once the iteration is under way.

Maintenance and the Commitment

In addition to making progress on a project, many teams are responsible for support and maintenance of another system. It may be a prior version of the product they are working on, or it may be an unrelated system. When a team makes a commitment to complete a set of stories during an iteration, they need to do so with their maintenance and support load in mind. I am not referring to general bug fixes that can be prioritized in advance. Those should go through the regular iteration planning prioritization process. By maintenance and support activities, I mean those unpredictable but required parts of many teams' lives—supporting a production website or database, taking support calls from key customers or first-tier technical support, and so on.

I think of an iteration as an empty glass. The first things poured into the glass are the team's unchangeable commitments, such as support and maintenance of other products. Whatever room remains in the glass is available for the team when they commit to the work of an iteration. This is shown in Figure 14.4. Clearly, a team whose glass is 10% full with support work will have time to commit to more other work than will a team whose glass starts 90% full.

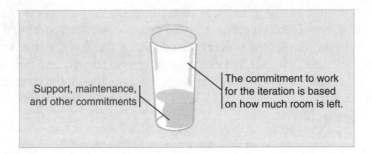

Figure 14.4   Other commitments determine how much a team can commit to during an iteration.

In most situations, the team will not be able to predict their upcoming support load very accurately. They should know a long-term average, but averaging twenty hours of support per week is not the same as having twenty hours every week. If the support and maintenance load exceeds expectations during an iteration, they may not be able to meet their commitment. They need to counter this by trying to exceed their commitment when the support and maintenance load is less than expected in some iterations. This variability is inescapable on teams with significant support and maintenance obligations.

My Recommendation

Both velocity-driven and commitment-driven iteration planning are viable approaches; however, my preference is for the commitment-driven approach. Although velocity plays a critical role in release planning, I do not think it should play an equivalent role in iteration planning. There are two reasons for this.

First, because velocity is a measure of coarse-grained estimates (story points or ideal days), it is not accurate enough for planning the work of short iterations. We can use these coarse-grained estimates for estimating the overall amount of work a team will complete during an iteration. We cannot, however, use them in the same way for planning the shorter-term work of a single iteration.

Second, a team would need to complete twenty to thirty user stories per iteration for errors in the story-point or ideal-day estimates to average out. Very few teams complete this many stories in an iteration.

To see the result of these problems, suppose a team has had a velocity of thirty in each of the past five iterations. That's about as consistent as it gets, and it's likely they'll complete thirty points again in the coming iteration. However, we know that not all five-point stories are the same. If we were to sort through a large collection of five-point stories, we know we could identify six five-point stories that all looked slightly easier than five points. We might be wrong on some, but if this was the first time we tried this, we'd probably succeed. We might increase our velocity from thirty to forty. On the other hand, we could instead select only the five-point stories that seem slightly harder. We still think they should be estimated at five points, but they are slightly harder than the other five-point stories.

On a project, we're not going to dig through our collection of user stories and try to find the "easy fives" or the "hard fives." However, most teams plan between three and a dozen stories into each iteration. When pulling that few stories into an iteration, a team will certainly get lucky and select all slightly easy ones or unlucky and select all slightly harder ones occasionally.

Because too few stories are completed in a single iteration for these to average out, I prefer not to use velocity when planning an iteration. However, because these differences do average out over the course of a release, velocity works extremely well for release planning.

Relating Task Estimates to Story Points

I'm often asked to explain the relationship between task estimates used during iteration planning and the story points or ideal days used for longer-range release planning. I see teams go astray when they start to believe there is a strong relationship between a story point and an exact number of hours. For example, I helped a team recently that had tracked their actual number of productive hours per iteration and their velocity per iteration. From this, they calculated that each story point took approximately twelve hours of work. Their view became the mistaken certainty that each story point always equaled twelve hours of work. However, the real case was something closer to that shown in Figure 14.5.

Figure 14.5 shows that on average, it will take twelve hours to complete a one-point user story. However, it also shows that some one-point stories will take less, and some will take more. Until the team estimates a story's underlying tasks, it is hard to know where a particular story lies on a curve such as this.

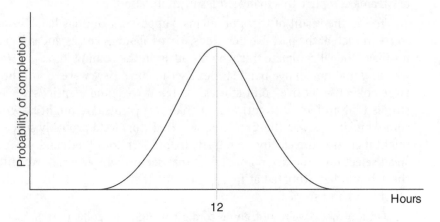

Figure 14.5   Distribution of the time needed to complete a one-point user story.

Although Figure 14.5 shows the distribution of hours for a one-point user story, Figure 14.6 shows the hypothetical distributions for one-, two-, and three-point stories. In this figure, each story point is still equivalent to twelve hours on average. However, it is possible that some one-point stories will take longer than some two-point stories.

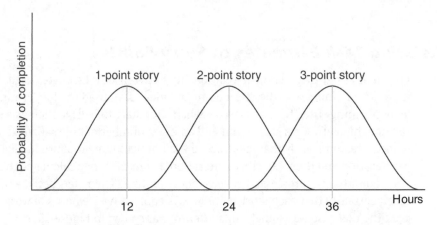

Figure 14.6   Distribution of times to complete one-, two-, and three-point stories.

That some two-point stories will take less time to develop than some one-point stories is entirely reasonable and to be expected. It is not a problem as long as there are sufficient stories in the release for these outliers to average out, and as long as everyone on the project remembers that some stories will take longer than others, even though their initial, high-level estimates were the same.

Days of the Week

When I started managing agile projects, my teams routinely started their iterations on a Monday and ended them on a Friday. We'd do this whether the specific team was using two-, three-, or four-week iterations. Mondays seemed like a natural day to begin an iteration, and Fridays were an obvious day to end on. I changed my mind about this after I began coaching a team that was developing a website that was busy during the week and barely used on the weekend.

The most logical night for this team to deploy new web updates was Friday evening. If something went wrong, they could fix it over the weekend, and the impact would be minimal because the site was very lightly used during that time. To accommodate this, this team decided to run two-week iterations that would start on a Friday and end on a Thursday. This worked wonderfully. Fridays were spent doing an iteration review and in planning the next iteration. This took until midafternoon most Fridays, after which the team would either get started on the work of the new iteration or occasionally head out for drinks or bowling. The iteration would start in earnest the following Monday. This was great because there was no dread of a Monday filled with meetings, as there was when Monday was review and planning day.

The team also benefited by occasionally using Friday morning to wrap up any last-minute work they'd been unable to finish on Thursday. They didn't make a habit of this, and it happened only a few times; however, spending a few hours on a Friday morning wrapping things up was preferable to coming in over the weekend (as they would have done with a Monday iteration start).

Summary

Unlike a release plan, an iteration plan looks in more detail at the specific work of a single iteration. Rather than the three-to-nine month horizon of a typical release plan, the iteration plan looks out no further than a single iteration. The fairly large user stories of a release plan are decomposed into tasks on the iteration plan. Each task is estimated in terms of the number of ideal hours the task will take to complete.

There are two general approaches to planning an iteration: velocity-driven and commitment-driven. The two approaches share many steps and often result in the creation of the same iteration plan.

Discussion Questions

1. Which approach to iteration planning do you prefer: velocity-driven or commitment-driven? Why?
2. What do you think of not having team members sign up for specific tasks during iteration planning?

Chapter 15

Selecting an Iteration Length

> *"Everything is vague to a degree you do not realize*
> *till you have tried to make it precise."*
> —Bertrand Russell

The majority of the agile processes, and teams using them, have settled on iteration lengths of two to four weeks. Some teams use longer iterations but two to four weeks is an accepted standard for most teams. There's no one magic iteration duration that is right for all teams under all circumstances. The right length for a team on one project may not be the right length for that same team on a different project.

Factors in Selecting an Iteration Length

Your selection of iteration length should be guided by the following factors:

- The length of the release being worked on
- The amount of uncertainty
- The ease of getting feedback
- How long priorities can remain unchanged
- Willingness to go without outside feedback
- The overhead of iterating
- How soon a feeling of urgency is established

There is no predetermined relative importance to these factors. The importance of each is entirely dependent upon the context of the project.

The Overall Length of the Release

Short projects benefit from short iterations. The length of a project's iterations determines

- How often the software can be shown (in potentially shippable form) to users and customers. Yes, of course, the software can be shown in miditeration form to these audiences, but the software usually is of potentially shippable quality only at the end of an iteration.
- How often progress can be measured. It's possible to get a sense of a team's rate of progress during an iteration, but only at the end of an iteration can we truly measure how much work has been truly completed.
- How often the product owner and team can refine their course, because priorities and plans are adjusted between iterations.

If a team is working toward a release that is perhaps only three months away, one-month iterations will give them only two opportunities to gather end-of-iteration feedback, measure progress, and adjust course. In most cases, this will be insufficient.

My general rule of thumb is that any project will benefit from having at least four or five such opportunities. This means that if the overall project duration will be four or more months, it might be worth considering monthly or four-week iterations. If the overall release will, however, be shorter, the project will benefit from proportionally shorter iterations.

The Amount of Uncertainty

Uncertainty comes in multiple forms. There is often uncertainty about exactly what the customer or users need, what the velocity of the team will be, and about technical aspects of the project. The more uncertainty of any type there is, the shorter the iterations should be. When there is a great deal of uncertainty about the work to be done or the product to be built, short iterations allow more frequent opportunities for the team to measure its progress through its velocity and more opportunities to gather feedback from stakeholders, customers, and users.

The Ease of Getting Feedback

Iteration length should be chosen to maximize the amount, frequency, and time-liness of feedback to the whole team. Depending on the environment, this may mean longer or shorter iterations. In some organizations, it is extremely easy to get informal feedback from internal stakeholders or users throughout an iteration but extremely difficult to get these same individuals to participate in a scheduled end-of-iteration review meeting. Other organizations have the opposite problem; it is difficult to get feedback on a day-to-day basis, but stakeholders, users, and others will attend a scheduled, formal review meeting (especially if food is provided).

Choose your iteration length to maximize the value of the feedback that can be received from those inside and outside the organization.

How Long Priorities Can Remain Unchanged

Once a development team commits to completing a specific set of features in an iteration, it is important that they not be redirected from that goal. It is, therefore, important that the product owner not change priorities during the iteration and that she help protect the team from others who may attempt to change priorities. Because of this, the length of time that priorities can go unchanged is a factor in selecting the iteration length.

A key consideration is how long it takes a good new idea to be turned into working software. Consider the case of a team using four-week iterations. If we assume that new ideas are equally likely to occur any time during an iteration, on average, a new idea can be said to occur in the middle of the iteration. That new idea will be prioritized into the next iteration, which starts in two weeks. It will take another four weeks (a full iteration) before the new idea shows up as potentially shippable, working software. This is shown in Figure 15.1. The key point to remember from this example is that the time from new idea to working software will be an average of 1½ times the length of the team's iterations.

As described in Chapter 14, "Iteration Planning," a team with maintenance or support duties concurrent with their new development work will hold some amount of time in reserve for those support and maintenance activities. Figure 15.1 is really illustrating the situation in which someone approaches the team with an idea that does not fit as part of their maintenance or support reserve.

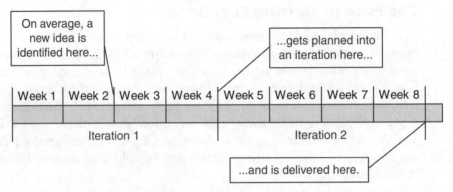

Figure 15.1   It takes an average of 1½ iterations to go from idea to software.

Willingness to Go without Outside Feedback

Even with a well-intentioned and highly communicative team, it is possible that the results of an iteration could be found worthless when shown to the broader organization or external users at the conclusion of the iteration. This may happen if the developers misunderstand the product owner (and don't communicate often enough during the iteration). It could also happen if the product owner misunderstands the needs of the market or users. The loss is almost never complete as long as we learn something from it. However, the less often a team receives outside feedback, the more likely we are to go astray and the greater the loss will be when that happens.

The Overhead of Iterating

There are costs associated with each iteration. For example, each iteration must be fully regression tested. If this is costly (usually in terms of time), the team may prefer longer, four-week iterations. Naturally, one of the goals of a successful agile team is to reduce (or nearly eliminate) the overhead associated with each iteration. But especially during a team's early iterations, this cost can be significant and will influence the decision about the best iteration length.

How Soon a Feeling of Urgency Is Established

Colleague Niels Malotaux (2004) points out that "As long as the end date of a project is far in the future, we don't feel any pressure and work leisurely. When the pressure of the finish date becomes tangible, we start working harder." Even with four-week iterations the end date is never very far in the future. But it is sufficiently far away that many teams will feel tangibly less stress during their first week than during the fourth and final week of an iteration.

The solution to this, of course, is to select an iteration length that evens out the pressure the team feels. The point is not to put the team under more pressure ("You *will* deliver today!"). Rather, it is to take the total amount of stress they'd normally feel and distribute it more evenly across a suitably long iteration.

Stick with It to Achieve a Steady Rhythm

Whatever duration you choose, you are better off choosing a duration and sticking with it rather than changing it frequently. Teams fall into a natural rhythm when using an unchanging iteration duration. When I started doing agile development using an early variation of Scrum (Takeuchi and Nonaka 1986; DeGrace and Stahl 1990), my teams used to select the duration of each iteration based on the amount of work we were bringing into that iteration. A two-week iteration could be followed by a six-week iteration, which could be followed by a four-week iteration, and so on. Through experimentation on many projects, I have since learned that teams are far better off sizing the work to the length of the iteration (rather than sizing the iteration to the work).

A regular iteration rhythm acts like a heartbeat for the project. Colleague Simon Baker, an agile coach with think-box ltd., describes it by saying that "Like a heart beats with a regularity that keeps the body going, a fixed iteration duration provides a constant which helps establish a development (and delivery) rhythm. Rhythm in my experience is a significant factor that helps achieve a sustained pace" (2004).

Making a Decision

One of the main goals in selecting an iteration length is finding one that encourages everyone to work at a consistent pace throughout the iteration. If the duration is too long, there is a natural tendency to relax a bit at the start of the iteration, which leads to panic and longer hours at the end of the iteration. Strive to find an iteration duration that smooths out these variations.

Having experimented with a variety of iteration lengths, my general preference is two weeks. One-week iterations (or anything shorter) can be very hectic and stressful. The next deadline is never more than four days away. Extremely short iterations leave no time for recovery if a team member is out sick or if anything goes wrong. Unless a project already has fully automated tests for all parts of the system, I do not often recommend starting with one-week iterations.

A four-week iteration, on the other hand, begins to feel like an eternity after having worked in one- and two-week iterations. With four-week iterations, I find that the team often has time to investigate and pursue more creative solutions than they may have time for with shorter iterations. An experienced agile team working on a highly exploratory phase of a project may benefit from a four-week iteration. However, four-week iterations have a feeling of very distinct beginnings, middles, and ends. I don't like how different the relaxed beginning feels from the more frantic end.

I find two-week iterations to be ideal. The overhead for planning and testing is much more manageable when amortized across two weeks. The first week of a two-week iteration may feel different from the second week, but the difference is not as dramatic as on a four-week iteration. Additionally, most organizations can (with sufficient training) learn not to adjust priorities for two weeks, whereas doing so for four weeks can be very difficult.

6 x 2 + 1

Working on endless two-week iterations can be a strain on a team because of the constant pressure to deliver and because a deadline is never further away than next week. My favorite technique to help reduce this strain is follow a macro-cycle of six two-week iterations followed by a one-week iteration. I refer to this cycle as "6 x 2 + 1." During the two-week iterations, the team works on items prioritized by the product owner. During the one-week iteration, however, the team chooses its own work. That doesn't mean it's play time or a week at the beach. Rather, the individuals on the team use this time to focus on what they view as priority work for the project. Programmers may perform refactorings they felt were too risky in the middle of other iterations or experiment with relevant new technologies. A tester may catch up on automating legacy manual tests. An analyst may work on an upcoming large feature that she feels hasn't received enough attention.

The chance to have one week of work they collectively prioritize themselves can be very reinvigorating for a team. It is important to stress that this one-week iteration is not a dumping ground for the sloppy work of previous iterations. Rather, it is a time when teams may work off some of the technical debt incurred either during early iterations while learning to be agile or from the project's pre-agile days.

Two Case Studies

To see how to apply these factors, let's consider two teams: the Napa team and the Goodman team. Each is a real team with only a few minor details changed.

The Napa Project

The seven-person Napa team was working on a client-server desktop application. The application would be used by 600 employees of the company. It would not be sold or used outside the company. Users were located in three cities, one of which was also home to the entire development team. The idea for the product began as a technology update of an existing system that had become expensive to maintain. However, due to changes in the company's core business, a great deal of new functionality was planned in the project as well. The project had been estimated to take thirteen months, but the company's rapid growth was creating pressure for an earlier release, even if it included only partial functionality.

For the Napa project, the team chose four-week iterations. We knew the project would be at least six months, so even four-week iterations gave us plenty of opportunities to bring the software to a potentially releasable state so that we could put it in the hands of real users. The project had a fair but not excessive amount of requirements and technology uncertainty. The developers were all experienced in the technologies being used (C++ and Oracle). And even though the new application would have features taking it well beyond what the current application did, we had the current application as a basic model of what was needed.

The project team was collocated with many of the intended users of the system. Most of the users were eager to participate in discussions about what would become their new system. However, the company was growing so quickly that access to these users was partially restricted. We had to be careful not to use too much of their time. Four-week iterations worked well in this situation. Showing them new versions every two weeks would have been too much in this environment. By making a new version available every four weeks, we were able to get more of the users to experiment with the software in a sandbox we had set up for that purpose.

As this was an entirely new application, there was very little overhead of iterating so this wasn't a factor in the decision. This project was critical to the continued success of the company and had extremely high visibility from the CEO down. For the most part, we were able to establish and maintain priorities for four weeks. Even with four weeks, a sense of urgency was maintained because the team remained aware of the need to get an initial release into users' hands as quickly as possible.

The Goodman Project

The Goodman team was working on the first version of an enterprise, commercial application. Over the course of the first three years, the company expected to sell no more than 5,000 licenses for the software. However, the product would be expensive, with an average price of $50,000 per user. Eighteen developers were split among two coordinated teams. The Goodman project was expected to take a year, but a preliminary release was planned to go to a handful of customers after six months.

For the Goodman project, the team chose two-week iterations. Because we were targeting an initial release six months out, the team could have used four-week iterations. However, there was a tremendous amount of uncertainty on this project. The company thought it knew who the product's users would be, but occasional debates about this raged within the company. It wasn't clear whether the product should be the high-end, high-price system that was initially conceived or whether we should aim for a larger audience at a lower price. This decision was made, remade, and then remade again, but never with sufficient force that the team could feel confident in the answer. There was also a large component of emergent requirements of the "I'll know it when I see it" variety.

Feedback was difficult to come by on this troubled project. Because it was a commercial product, we had no internal users. Many of the company's largest customers and prospects were overseas, which complicated matters. There were a number of people within the company who would have been likely users had they worked at our target customer companies, so we used them as proxies for our real users. Because of all the uncertainty and change on this project, we wanted to get feedback as often as possible, which pointed toward shorter iterations.

Priorities could not remain constant for more than a few days in this environment, which also pointed us toward the short, two-week iterations we chose. The test automation team on this project had been in place from the beginning of the project and did a very good job. This helped keep the overhead of iterating low and allowed us to be successful with short iterations. Finally, as the company was a recent start-up and newly public company, it was important that we maintain a sense of urgency. The company had gone public on the promise of some great software coming soon. Short, two-week iterations helped us keep a strong focus on getting that software developed as quickly as possible.

Avoid the End of the Quarter

Although it may be tempting to align iterations with the end of the month, I avoid doing so at all costs. If you tie iterations to the ends of months, one out of every three iterations will coincide with the end of a fiscal quarter. Although this is not quite as much of a problem with private companies, there is tremendous pressure in public companies to hit quarterly revenue goals.

I was on one project that had scheduled a significant new release for Friday, March 31, 2000. This release had been a key target for much of the company for nine months (which is the upper limit for how long a single release should be). With two weeks left before the release, our product owner left for a spring-break vacation with his school-age kids. While at Disney World, he valiantly tried to participate in some calls and answer some of our more important questions. Still, his absence came at a critical time, and some important work was not completed in what was to be the final iteration before the big release.

When the product owner returned, we were able to resolve all remaining open issues within a shorter-than-normal one-week iteration. This pushed our release date out from March 31 to April 7. Although a difference of one week may not seem highly critical to a nine-month project, the fact that the delay pushed delivery from one quarter to the next was hugely significant to this publicly traded company. When the planned initial shipment of hundreds of copies didn't happen on March 31, the revenue from those presales and upgrades could not be recognized until the second quarter. We might as well have delivered on June 30 as April 7.

I haven't planned a month-end release since then. There are too many unknowns, unknowables, and uncertainties in software development for me to want to risk recognizing revenue by targeting an end-of-the-quarter release.

Summary

Most agile teams work in iterations of two to four weeks. There is no universally correct iteration length that is right for all teams. Rather, each team should consider their unique situation and choose the right iteration length for them. Factors in this decision include

- The length of the release being worked on
- The amount of uncertainty

- The ease of getting feedback
- How long priorities can remain unchanged
- Willingness to go without feedback
- The overhead of iterating
- How soon a feeling of urgency is established

Discussion Questions

1. What is the appropriate iteration for your current project?
2. What differences would you expect on your project if you used one-week iterations? What differences would you expect if you used two-month iterations?

Chapter 16

Estimating Velocity

> *"It is better to be roughly right
> than precisely wrong."*
> —John Maynard Keynes

One of the challenges of planning a release is estimating the velocity of the team. You have the following three options:

- Use historical values.
- Run an iteration.
- Make a forecast.

There are occasions when each of these approaches is appropriate. However, regardless of which approach you are using, if you need to estimate velocity you should consider expressing the estimate as a range. Suppose you estimate that velocity for a given team on a given project will be 20 ideal days per iteration. You have a very limited chance of being correct. Velocity may be 21, or 19, or maybe even 20.0001. So instead of saying velocity will be 20, give your estimate as a range, saying perhaps instead that you estimate velocity will be between 15 and 24.

In the following sections, I'll describe each of the three general approaches—using historicals, running an iteration, and making a forecast—and for each, I'll also offer advice on selecting an appropriate range.

Use Historical Values

Historical values are great—if you have them. The problem with historical values is that they're of the greatest value when very little has changed between the old project and team and the new project and team. Any personnel or significant technology changes will reduce the usefulness of historical measures of velocity. Before using them, ask yourself questions like these:

+ Is the technology the same?
+ Is the domain the same?
+ Is the team the same?
+ Is the product owner the same?
+ Are the tools the same?
+ Is the working environment the same?
+ Were the estimates made by the same people?

The answer to each question is often yes when the team is moving onto a new release of a product they just worked on. In that case, using the team's historical values is entirely appropriate. Even though velocity in a situation like this is relatively stable, you should still consider expressing it as a range. You could create a range by simply adding and subtracting a few points to the average or by looking at the team's best and worst iterations over the past two or three months.

However, if the answer to any of the preceding questions is no, you may want to think twice about using historical velocities. Or you may want to use historical velocities but put a larger range around them to reflect the inherent uncertainty in the estimate. To do this, start by calculating the team's average velocity over the course of the preceding release. If they completed 150 story points of work during 10 iterations, their average (mean) velocity was 15 points.

Before showing how to convert this to a range, take a look at Figure 16.1. This figure shows the cone of uncertainty that was introduced back in Chapter 1, "The Purpose of Planning." The cone of uncertainty says that the actual duration of a project will be between 60% and 160% of what we think it is. So to turn our single-point, average velocity into a range, I multiply it by 60% and 160%.[1] So if

---

1. Technically, I should divide it by 0.60 and 1.6. However, because 0.60 and 1.60 are meant to be reciprocals ($0.6 \times 1.6 = 0.96 \cong 1$), you get approximately the same values by multiplying.

our average historical velocity is 15, I would estimate velocity to be in the range of 9 to 24.

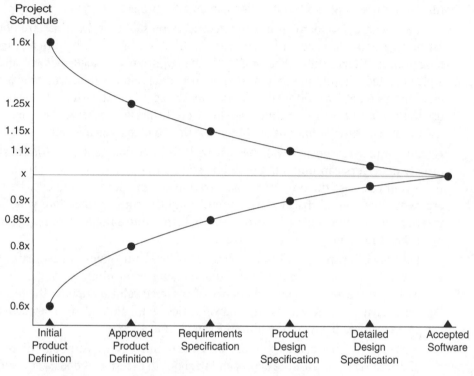

Figure 16.1   The cone of uncertainty around schedule estimates.

This range may feel large, but given the uncertainty at this point, it is probably appropriate. Constructing a range in this way helps the project team heed the advice offered in the quote at the start of this chapter that it is better to be roughly right than precisely wrong. A large range around the expected velocity will allow the team to be roughly right about it.

Run an Iteration

An ideal way to forecast velocity is to run an iteration (or two or three) and then estimate velocity from the *observed velocity* during the one to three iterations. Because the best way to predict velocity is to observe velocity, this should always be your default approach. Many traditional projects get under way with the

developers working on the "obvious" requirements or infrastructure, the analysts "finalizing" the requirements, and the project manager putting together a
comprehensive list of tasks that becomes the project plan. All of this takes
time—often, as long as a few iterations on an agile project.

I was with a development director recently who said that deadlines are not
set on traditional projects in his company until about two months into a year-
long project. It takes them that long to get the requirements "locked down" and
a plan created. He told me that even after that much effort, their project plans
were always off at least 50% and often more. We agreed that instead, he would
use this up-front time to turn the team loose on the project, observe their velocity over two or three iterations, and then use that to plan a release date.

For similar reasons, as was the case with this development director, most
project managers can hold off giving an estimate for at least one iteration. If
that's your case, use the time to run an iteration and measure the velocity. Then
create a range around that one data point, using the cone of uncertainty. So if
you ran one iteration and had a velocity of 15, turn it into a range by multiplying
by 0.60 and 1.6, giving a range of 9 to 24.

If a team can run three or more iterations before being giving an estimate of
velocity, they have a couple of additional options for determining a range. First
and easiest, they can simply use the range of observed values. Suppose the team
has completed three iterations and had velocities of 12, 15, and 16. They could
express velocity as likely to be within the range 12 to 16.

Alternatively, they could again use the cone of uncertainty. Although there's
no solid empirical basis for the approach I'm about to describe, it does work, and
it makes sense. Here's the approach: Calculate the average velocity for the iterations you've run. Then, for each iteration completed, move one step to the right
on the cone of uncertainty. So for a team that has run one iteration, use the
range for the "initial product definition" milestone. If the team has run two iterations, use the range for the "approved product definition" milestone (80% to
120%), and so on. For convenience, these numbers are shown in Table 16.1.

Table 16.1 Multipliers for Estimating Velocity Based on Number of Iterations Completed

Iterations Completed	Low Multiplier	High Multiplier
1	0.6	1.60
2	0.8	1.25
3	0.85	1.15
4 or more	0.90	1.10

Suppose that a team has run three iterations with an average velocity of twenty during that period. For three iterations the appropriate range is 85% to 115%. This means that if the team's average velocity is twenty after three iterations, their actual true velocity by the end of the project will probably be in the range seventeen to twenty-three.

I normally don't extend this analysis past three or four iterations. I don't use the cone of uncertainty, for example, to pretend that after six iterations, the team precisely knows their velocity, and it won't waver through the end of the project.

Some organizations will resist starting a project without having a more specific idea how long it will take. In such cases, stress that the need to run a few iterations first stems not from a desire to avoid making an estimate, but to avoid giving an estimate without adequate foundation. You'll want to stress that the purpose of these initial iterations is to assess the dark corners of the system, better understand the technologies involved, refine the understanding of the requirements, and measure how quickly the team can make progress.

Make a Forecast

There are times when we don't have historicals, and it is just not feasible to run a few iterations to observe velocity. Suppose the estimate is for a project that won't start for twelve months. Or suppose the project may start soon, but only once a client signs a contract for the work. There are two key differences in cases like this. First, you want to minimize the expenditure on the project so you won't actually start running iterations on a project that may not happen or that is too far in the future. Second, any estimate of velocity on these projects must reflect a high degree of uncertainty.

In cases like these, we need to forecast velocity. Forecasting velocity is rarely your first option, but it's an important option and one you should have in your bag of tricks. The best way to forecast velocity involves expanding user stories into their constituent tasks, estimating those tasks (as we do when planning an iteration), seeing how much work fits into an iteration, and then calculating the velocity that would be achieved if that work were finished in an iteration. This involves the following steps:

1. Estimate the number of hours that each person will be available to work on the project each day.
2. Determine the total number of hours that will be spent on the project during the iteration.

3. Arbitrarily and somewhat randomly select stories, and expand them into their constituent tasks. Repeat until you have identified enough tasks to fill the number of hours in the iteration.

4. Convert the velocity determined in the preceding step into a range.

Let's see how this works through an example.

Estimate the Hours Available

Almost everyone has some responsibilities outside of the specific project that is their primary responsibility. There are emails to be answered, phone calls to be returned, company meetings to attend, and so on. The amount of time this takes differs from person to person and organization to organization. What it amounts to, though, is that project participants generally do not spend 100% of their time working on the project.

From observation and discussion with colleagues, my opinion is that most individuals who are assigned full time to a project spend between four and six hours per day on that project. This fits with reports that individuals spend 55% (Ganssle 2004) to 70% (Boehm 1981) of their time on project activities. At the high end, Kennedy (2003) reports that engineers in Toyota—with its highly efficient, lean process—are able to spend 80% of their time on their designated projects.

Use these numbers as parameters in estimating the amount of time individuals on your project team will be able to dedicate each day to the project. If you are part of a large bureaucracy, you will most likely be at the low end of the scale. If you are part of a three-person start-up in a garage, you'll probably be at the high end. For the purposes of this example, let's assume that the SwimStats team estimates they will each be able to dedicate six hours per day to the project.

Estimate the Time Available in an Iteration

This step is simple: Multiply the number of hours available each day by the number of people on the team and the number of days in each iteration. Suppose the SwimStats team includes one analyst, one programmer, one database engineer, and one tester. Four people each working six hours per day is twenty-four hours each day. In a ten-day iteration they put about 240 hours toward the project.

When I introduce this approach to some teams, they want to factor in additional adjustments for vacations, sick time, and other such interruptions. Don't bother; it's not worth the extra effort, and it's unlikely to be more accurate anyway. These events are part of the reason why we don't plan on a team's being 100% available in the first place.

Getting More Time on Your Project

Regardless of how many hours team members are able to put toward a project each day, you'd probably like to increase that number. The best technique I've found for doing so was invented by Francesco Cirillo of XPLabs. Cirillo coaches teams to work in highly focused thirty-minute increments (Cirillo 2005). Each thirty-minute increment consists of two parts: twenty-five minutes of intense work followed by a five-minute break. These thirty-minute increments are called "pomodori," Italian for tomatoes and deriving from the use of tomato-shaped timers that ring when the twenty-five-minute period is complete.

Cirillo introduced this technique to Piergiuliano Bossi, who has documented its success with multiple teams (Bossi 2003; Bossi and Cirillo 2001). These teams would plan on completing ten pomodori (five hours) per day. If you find yourself with less productive time per day than you'd like, you may want to consider this approach.

Expand Stories and See What Fits

The next step is to expand stories into tasks, estimate the tasks, and keep going until we've filled the estimated number of available hours (240, in this case). It is not necessary that stories be expanded in priority order. What you really want is a fairly random assortment of stories. Do not, for example, expand all the one- and two-point stories and none of the three- and five-point stories. Similarly, do not expand only stories that involve mostly the user interface or the database. Try to find a representative set of stories.

Continue selecting stories and breaking them into tasks as long as the tasks selected do not exceed the capacity of the individuals on the team. For the SwimStats team, for example, we need to be careful that we don't assume the programmer and analyst are also fully proficient database engineers. Select stories until one skill set on the team can't handle any more work. Add up the story points or ideal days for the work selected, and that is the team's possible velocity.

Suppose we get the planned team together (or a proxy for them if the project will not start for a year), and we expand some stories as shown in Table 16.2. If we felt that the four-person SwimStats team could commit to this but probably no more, we'd stop here. This 221 hours of work seems like a reasonable fit within their 240 hours of available time. Our point estimate of velocity is then twenty-five.

Table 16.2 Hours and Points for Some SwimStats Stories

Story	Story Points	Hours for Tasks
As a coach, I can enter the names and demographic information of all swimmers on my team.	3	24
As a coach, I can define practice sessions.	5	45
As a swimmer, I can see all of my times for a specific event.	2	18
As a swimmer, I can update my demographics information.	1	14
As a swimmer, I can see a line chart of my times for a particular event.	2	14
As a coach, I can see a line chart showing the progress over the season of all of my swimmers in a particular event.	3	30
As a swimmer, I can see a pie chart showing how many first, second, third, and lower places I've finished in.	2	12
As a coach, I can see a text report showing each swimmer's best time in each event.	2	14
As a coach, I can upload meet results from a file exported from the timing system used at the meet.	5	50
Total	**25**	**221**

Put a Range Around It

Use whatever technique you'd like to turn the point estimate of velocity into a range. As before, I like to multiply by 60% and 160%. For the SwimStats team, this means our estimate of twenty-five story points per iteration becomes an estimate of fifteen to forty.

A Variation for Some Teams

Some teams—especially those with a significant number or part-time members—should not plan with a single number of hours that everyone is available. These teams may have members who are allocated for dramatically smaller portions of their time. In these cases, it can be useful to create a table like the one shown in Table 16.3.

For the SwimStats team, as shown in Table 16.3, Yury and Sasha are dedicated full time to the project. SwimStats is Sergey's only project, but he has some other managerial and corporate responsibilities that take up some of his time. Carina is split between SwimStats and another project. She has very few responsibilities beyond the two projects, and so she could put close to six hours per day on them. However, she needs to move back and forth between the two projects many times each day, and this multitasking affects her productivity, so she is shown as having only two productive hours on SwimStats per day.

Table 16.3 Calculating Availability on a Team with Part-Time Members

Person	Available Hours per Day	Available Hours per Iteration
Sergey	4	40
Yury	6	60
Carina	2	20
Sasha	6	60
Total		**180**

Remember Why We're Doing This

Keep in mind that the reason we're forecasting velocity in this way is that it is either impossible or impractical for the team to run an iteration, and they do not yet have any historical observations. This may be the case because the team doesn't yet exist, and you are tasked with planning a project that starts a few months from now.

If, for example, you are in an environment where you are doing strategic planning and budgeting well in advance of initiating a project, forecasting velocity in this way can be your best approach.

Which Approach Should I Use?

Determining which approach to use is often simpler than this variety of choices may make it appear. Circumstances often guide you and constrain your options. In descending order of desirability, follow these guidelines to estimate velocity:

- If you can run one or more iterations before giving an estimate of velocity, always do so. There's no estimate like an actual, and seeing the team's actual velocity is always your best choice.
- Use the actual velocity from a related project by this team.

◆ Estimate velocity by seeing what fits.

Regardless of which approach you use, switch to using actual, observed values for velocity as soon as possible. Suppose that you choose to estimate velocity by seeing what fits in an iteration because the project is not set to begin for six months and the organization needs only a rough guess of how long the project will take. Once the project begins and you are able to measure actual velocity, begin using those actuals when discussing the project and its likely range of completion dates.

Summary

There are three ways of estimating velocity. First, you can use historical averages if you have them. However, before using historical averages, you should consider whether there have been significant changes in the team, the nature of the project, the technology, and so on. Second, you can defer estimating velocity until you've run a few iterations. This is usually the best option. Third, you can forecast velocity by breaking a few stories into tasks and seeing how much will fit into an iteration. This process is very similar to iteration planning.

Regardless of which approach you use, estimates of velocity should be given in a range that reflects the uncertainty inherent in the estimate. The cone of uncertainty offers advice about the size of the range to use.

Discussion Questions

1. In Table 16.2, stories that were estimated to have the same number of story points did not have the same number of task hours. Why? (If you need a refresher, see the section "Relating Task Estimates to Story Points" in Chapter 14, "Iteration Planning."

2. Complete a table like Table 16.3 for your current project. What might you try to increase the amount of time each person is able to devote to the project?

Chapter 17

Buffering Plans for Uncertainty

> *"To be uncertain is to be uncomfortable,*
> *but to be certain is to be ridiculous."*
> —Chinese proverb

One of the complaints I often hear about agile planning is that it doesn't work well in some environments. Typically, the environments cited are ones in which:

- The project is planned far in advance.
- The project must meet a firm deadline and include a reasonably firm set of functionality.
- The project is contracted from one organization to another.
- Requirements are understood only at a very superficial level.
- The organization is uncomfortable allowing too much flexibility in schedules, even on projects that don't need firm deadlines and deliverables.

Being able to create reliable plans in these environments is extremely important. It is often not enough to use just the approach covered in the previous chapters. What projects in these environments have in common is that each comes with either an additional amount of uncertainty or with greater consequences to being wrong. For example, I was previously a vice president of software development at a Fortune 40 company, and our projects were typically scheduled onto the calendar twelve to eighteen months in advance, when we'd start setting the following year's budget. We certainly didn't lock down

187

requirements, but we would establish the nature of the products we would be building. Even though requirements were only vaguely understood, we had to make first-level commitments that would allow us to staff the organization appropriately. There was further uncertainty because I rarely knew who from my team would work on projects that far in advance. Often, they had not even been hired yet.

Compare this situation with a project on which you are required to state a firm deadline and commit to a core set of functionality. Missing the deadline, or delivering much less functionality, will damage your company's reputation in the industry and your reputation within the company. Even if you have a reasonable understanding of the requirements and know who will compose the team (unlike in my case above), the risk of being wrong is significant.

In these cases, there is either greater uncertainty or greater implication to being wrong about a release schedule. Because of this, it is useful to include a buffer in the determination of the schedule. A buffer is a margin for error around an estimate. In cases where there is significant uncertainty or the cost of being wrong is significant, including a buffer is wise. The buffer helps protect the project against the impact of the uncertainty. In this way, buffering a project schedule becomes an appropriate risk management strategy. In this chapter, we'll look at two types of buffers: feature buffers and schedule buffers.

Feature Buffers

I went to the grocery store last night with a list of thirty-seven items to get. I had only thirty minutes to shop and drive home because I wanted to watch a basketball game that was scheduled to start at that time. As always, I started at one end of the store and worked my way to the other. But as I went down each aisle, I was mostly focused on the twenty or so items that I knew we needed most. If I came home without milk, bread, or sliced turkey, I knew I'd be in trouble, and at halftime I'd be back at the store. But if I forgot items of lesser importance, my wife would be content, my daughters could eat, and I could watch the basketball game.

Buffering a project with features is exactly the same. We tell our customers, "We'll get you all of the functionality in this pile and ideally some of the functionality in that pile." Creating a feature buffer is simple to do on an agile project. First, the customer selects all of the absolutely mandatory work. The estimates for that work are summed. This represents the minimum that can be released. The customer then selects another 25% to 40% more work, selecting toward the higher end of the range for projects with more uncertainty or less tolerance for schedule risk. The estimates for this work are added to the original estimate, resulting in a total estimate for the project. The project is then planned as normal for delivery of the *entire* set of functionality; however, some amount of the work is optional and will be included only if time permits. The optional work is developed last, only after the mandatory work is complete.

To see how this works, assume that the product owner identifies 100 story points as mandatory. Each story selected is required to release a product that will be favorably accepted by the market. The product owner then selects an additional 30% more work, identifying user stories worth an additional 30 story points. These are added as optional work to the project. The total project is now expected to be 130 story points. Using the techniques described in Chapter 16, "Estimating Velocity," the team estimates velocity will be ten points per one-week iteration. The project is then planned to take thirteen iterations (130/10). If all goes well, the mandatory work will be done after the first ten iterations, and the remaining three will be spent on the optional features.

This feature buffering process is consistent with that used in the agile process, DSDM (Dynamic Systems Development Method). On DSDM projects, requirements are sorted into four categories: Must Have, Should Have, Could Have, and Won't Have. DSDM refers to this sorting as the MoSCoW rules. No more than 70% of the planned effort for a project can be targeted at Must Have requirements. In this way, DSDM projects create a feature buffer equivalent to 30% of the duration of the project.

Schedule Buffers

Suppose I need to go to the airport and catch a flight to Italy. (As long as I'm supposing, I might as well suppose I need to go somewhere nice.) An airplane flight has a very firm deadline. The flight will take off with or without me. In creating a plan for getting from my house to the proper gate at the airport, I need to leave early enough that I'm reasonably confident I'll make my flight, but not so early that I'm at the airport three days ahead.

I think about all of the steps involved: driving to the airport, parking my car, checking in and dropping off my luggage, and going through the security checkpoint. I think about how long that should take me if everything goes well and decide it should take seventy minutes. That's how long it *should take*. It may take even a few minutes less, but it could take a whole lot longer. If there's an accident on the highway, and if the parking lot is full, and if there's a long line to check in, and if there's a long line to go through security, it could take quite a while longer. I don't need to plan on all of these things going wrong on the same trip; but because this is an important trip, and I don't want to miss my flight, I should add some extra time to the seventy minutes it should take if everything goes well.

Let's say I decide to leave for the airport 100 minutes before my flight. If things go well, that will leave me thirty minutes to pass in the airport, which isn't bad. If things go really well (all the traffic lights are green, I park in the front row, no one is ahead of me to check in or at security) then maybe I have forty minutes in the airport. But if I get stuck in traffic or in a big line to check in, this extra time will most likely be enough to get me on the plane before it leaves. The extra thirty minutes are my schedule buffer; they protect the on-time completion of the overall project (getting to the airport).

For a trip to the airport, it is not appropriate to take a guess at my rate of progress (my velocity) and then provide the airline (the customer) with periodic updates about my expected arrival time. My expected arrival time and my rate of progress don't matter to the airline; the departure time is fixed, just like deadlines are on many software development projects. In this cases, a schedule buffer protects against uncertainty that can affect the on-time completion of the project.

Note that I am not concerned with whether any one activity (driving, parking, checking in, or going through security) takes too long. I am concerned only with whether the overall chain of activities takes too long. To make my flight, I add a thirty-minute buffer to my overall schedule for getting to the airport. What we'd like to do is add a similar schedule buffer to projects with greater uncertainty or with greater consequences for missing a deadline.

Reflecting Uncertainty in Estimates

To protect a project schedule against uncertainty, we need a way to quantify the uncertainty. When we estimate and assign a single value to a user story, we pretend that a single number reflects our expectations about the amount of time developing the feature will take. More realistically, though, we know the work may be completed within a range of durations. A team may estimate a particular user story as three ideal days, knowing that three ideal days typically represents four or five elapsed days of work. If the story takes six days to complete, however, no one will be shocked; things sometimes take longer than planned. If we graph the possible completion times for a task, it will look approximately like Figure 17.1.

The curve takes on this general shape because there normally is not much that can be done to accelerate the completion of a task, but there are an indefinite number of things that can go wrong and delay the completion of a task. For example, just as I'm about to finish coding a particular new feature, my computer crashes, and I lose unsaved changes. Then lightning hits the building and fries our source repository. We request a backup tape to be delivered tomorrow morning, but the delivery service loses the tape. But I don't care, as I'm run over by the proverbial bus on the way to work.

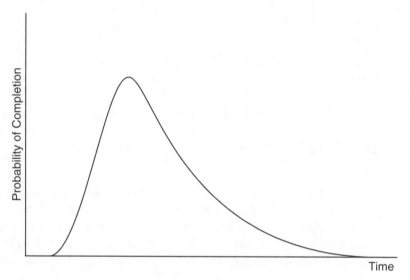

Figure 17.1   The distribution of completion times.

The single most likely completion time in Figure 17.1 is where the line peaks. Overall, however, finishing by that time is less than 50% likely. We know this because less than 50% of the area under the curve is to the left of the peak. If a developer were to provide an estimate corresponding to the peak of Figure 17.1, she would most likely take longer than that estimate to finish the work. A more useful way of visualizing this is in Figure 17.2, which shows the cumulative probability of finishing on or before the times on the horizontal axis.

Whereas Figure 17.1 shows the probability of finishing at a specific time, Figure 17.2 shows the probability of finishing at or before that time. When estimating and planning, this is more important to us than the probability of finishing on any one day (as shown in Figure 17.1).

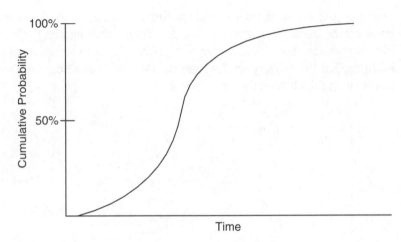

Figure 17.2 The cumulative distribution of completion times.

Another way to think about Figure 17.2 and cumulative probability of completion times is to assume that 100 different but equally skilled and experienced programmers independently develop a new feature. By what date would each finish? The results might be similar to those shown in Table 17.1. This table shows the number finishing on each day and, more important, the total number finished by a given date.

Table 17.1 Number of Developers Finishing a Feature on a Given Day

Day	Number Finishing That Day	Total Finished
Day 1	5	5
Day 2	40	45
Day 3	25	70
Day 4	15	85
Day 5	10	95
Day 6	5	100

Suppose we want to be 90% confident in the schedule we commit to. One initial approach to doing this might be to estimate the 90% likely duration for each user story in the project and then use those estimates. However, if we do this, the project schedule will almost certainly be too long. To see how a schedule buffer works, let's again consider my trip to the airport, a possible schedule for which is shown in Figure 17.3.

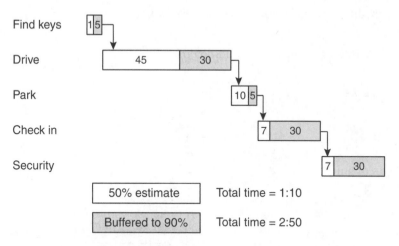

Figure 17.3   The 50% and 90% estimates for making a flight at the airport.

The first number for each task (in the clear box) is the 50% estimate of how long the task should take. I expect tasks to take longer half the time and shorter half the time. The second number (in the shaded box) is the additional amount of time to reach my 90% estimate. The additional time between the 50% and the 90% estimate is called *local safety*. We often add local safety to an estimate we want to be more confident of meeting. In this case, I think I can find my keys in one to six minutes. I can drive to the airport in forty-five to seventy-five minutes, and so on.

Adding up the 50% numbers gives me an expected duration of an hour and ten minutes. However, if I leave my house that close to departure time, the slightest delay will cause me to miss my flight. On the other end, adding up the 90% estimates gives a total of 2:50. I don't want to leave nearly three hours ahead of my flight, because there's very little chance that everything will go wrong. What I really want is a project plan that looks like Figure 17.4.

The plan in Figure 17.4 is built using the 50% estimates and then adding a project buffer. This type of plan makes much more sense than one built entirely from summing the 50% or the 90% estimates. The plan in Figure 17.4 protects the only deadline that matters: the overall project deadline. Because it isn't important if any one task on my way to the airport finishes late, I do not need to buffer the on-time completion of the tasks. This allows me to construct a schedule that removes local safety from the individual tasks and puts a fraction of that time into a buffer that protects the overall schedule. Notice that the buffered schedule of Figure 17.4 is only 1:58—nearly an hour shorter than the schedule created by summing the 90% estimates.

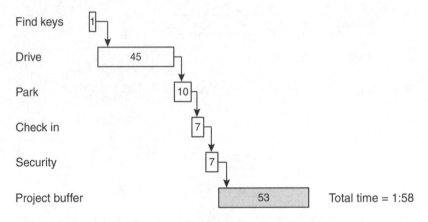

Find keys	1
Drive	45
Park	10
Check in	7
Security	7
Project buffer	53

Total time = 1:58

Figure 17.4   A buffered trip to the airport.

Even better, by moving local safety into an overall project buffer, we are able to avoid the impact of Parkinson's Law and student syndrome. As you'll recall from Chapter 2, "Why Planning Fails," Parkinson's Law says that work expands to fill the time available. Student syndrome (Goldratt 1997) refers to starting something at the last possible moment that doesn't preclude successful completion—for example, starting a college term paper three days before it's due. Because it averts the problems caused by Parkinson's Law and student syndrome, a shorter schedule that includes a schedule buffer is more likely to be met than is a longer schedule.

To create a schedule buffer for a software project, the first thing we need to do is revise our estimating process so that it generates two estimates for each user story or feature. Just like with the trip to the airport, we need to know the 50% and the 90% estimate for each. This is easy enough: When the team meets to estimate, start by estimating the 50% case for the first story. Then estimate the 90% case for that story before moving on to the next story or feature.

Sizing the Project Buffer

The project buffer in Figure 17.4 was sized to be fifty-three minutes. How did I come up with that duration? It was based on the 50% and 90% estimates for that project, as shown in Figure 17.4. The beauty of associating two estimates with each user story is that the numbers very clearly point out the degree of schedule risk associated with each item. For example, if one story is estimated as being three to five and another story is estimated as being three to ten, we know that the second story brings more schedule risk to the project. The project buffer will be sized to accommodate the amount of schedule risk brought by the work planned in the project. Think about an extreme example: If you are planning a project schedule, you will need a smaller project buffer for tasks estimated to be 3 to 7 than you will for tasks estimated to be 3 to 100. Clearly, if the project has some 3-point tasks that could turn into 100-point tasks, the project buffer needs to be larger than if the worst case for those tasks were 10 points. So the spread between the 50% and 90% estimates influences the size of the project buffer.[1]

Because our estimates are at the 50% and 90% points for each item, this means that the difference between these two estimates is about two standard deviations. The standard deviation for each item is then $(w_i - a_i)/2$, where w_i represents the worst case (90% estimate) for story i and a_i represents the average case (50% estimate) for the same story. We'd like the project buffer to protect the overall project to the same 90% level that each task was protected by its own 90% estimate. This means our project buffer should be two standard deviations and can be determined from this formula:

$$2\sigma = 2 \times \sqrt{((w_1 - a_1)/2)^2 + ((w_2 - a_2)/2)^2 + \ldots + ((w_n - a_n)/2)^2}$$

where σ is the standard deviation. This can be simplified to the following:

$$2\sigma = \sqrt{(w_1 - a_1)^2 + (w_2 - a_2)^2 + \ldots + (w_n - a_n)^2}$$

Let's see how we use this formula to determine the size of the schedule buffer. Suppose our project includes the six user stories shown in Table 17.2 and that each story has the 50% and 90% estimates shown. These estimates can be in story points or ideal days. The final column of Table 17.2 is calculated by taking the worst-case (90%) estimate of a story, subtracting the average case (50%) of that story, and squaring the result. The first story, for example, is $(13 - 5)^2 = 64$. The schedule buffer is the square root of the sum of these squares.[2] In this case, the schedule buffer equals the square root of 90, which is

---

1. Sizing a buffer in this way has been previously suggested by Reinertsen (1997), Newbold (1998), and Leach (2000).

9.4, so we'll round it to 9. The overall project duration is the sum of the 50% estimates plus the project buffer, or $17 + 9 = 26$ in this case.

Table 17.2 Calculating the Project Buffer for a Project with Six Stories

User Story	Average Case (50%)	Worst Case (90%)	(Worst–Average)^2
As any site visitor, I would like to see the personal records of any swimmer.	5	13	64
As any site visitor, I need to be authenticated before given access to sensitive parts of the site.	1	3	4
As a swimmer, I want to see when practices are scheduled.	3	5	4
As a swimmer or parent, I want to know where league pools are located.	5	8	9
As any site visitor, I want to see the national records by age group and event.	2	5	9
As any site visitor, I would like to see the results of any meet.	1	1	0
Total	**17**	**35**	**90**

Intuitively, the buffer calculated in Table 17.2 makes sense. The user story that contributes the most to the size of the schedule buffer (the first story) is the one with the most uncertainty (an eight-point difference between its 50% and 90% estimates). Similarly, a story with no uncertainty (the last story) doesn't contribute to the buffer at all.

Adding in a schedule buffer may or may not add one or more iterations to the length of a project. Most often it will. Suppose the team in this example had forecast their velocity to be nine points per iteration. If they had estimated the project to be seventeen points (the sum of the 50% estimates), they would have expected to finish in two iterations. However, with the project buffer included,

2. This is why this buffer-sizing technique is commonly called the "Square Root of the Sum of the Squares" approach.

the full project is twenty-six points and will take three iterations to complete if their velocity is nine.

A Simpler Buffer Calculation

The preceding approach to sizing the project buffer is the best way to size the project buffer. But if for some reason you cannot come up with both 50% and 90% estimates, there is a simpler way to size the project buffer. Estimate each story at the 50% level and then set the buffer at half the size of the sum of the 50% estimates. Be sure that the entire team is aware that their estimates are to be ones they are 50% confident in. We want estimates that are just as likely to be high as they are to be low.

Although this calculation is far simpler, it has the serious flaw of not being influenced by the actual uncertainty around the specific user stories in the project. Suppose there are two stories, each estimated at five story points. Each of these stories will contribute the same amount to the project buffer (half of their size, or 2.5 points each). This will be true even if one of the stories would have had a 90% estimate of 100 and the other a 90% estimate of 10.

For these reasons, and because it's extremely easy just to ask for two estimates at the time you're estimating, I prefer the approach based on the square root of the sum of the squares.

Buffer Guidelines

Regardless of whether you prefer to take the square root of the sum of the squares approach or the 50% approach, you should consider these additional guidelines based on advice from Leach (2000).

◆ The square root of the sum of the squares approach is most reliable if there are at least ten user stories or features being estimated. But if your project has fewer than ten items, you probably shouldn't be planning with a buffer anyway.

◆ The project buffer should represent at least 20% of the total project duration. A smaller buffer may not provide adequate protection for the overall project.

Combining Buffers

At first, it may seem like overkill to have multiple buffers. However, it is often appropriate to use multiple buffers, because we are protecting the project against multiple types of uncertainty. My car has shoulder belts and air bags because each buffers me against a different type of collision. We should always buffer a given type of project uncertainty with the right units, which means we buffer feature uncertainty with features and schedule uncertainty with time. Additionally, when multiple buffers are used, the size of each can be smaller.

It is when we combine feature and schedule buffers on a project that projects become truly protected against uncertainty. Consider the three projects shown in Figure 17.5. In this figure, (a) shows a project that must deliver a defined set of functionality but allows the schedule to vary. Figure 17.5(b) shows the opposite: a project whose date is fixed but has complete flexibility around the functionality to be built. Now look at Figure 17.5(c), and see that by including both a feature buffer and a schedule buffer the team is able to commit to both a delivery date and a minimum set of features. When creating a release plan, our goal is to use buffers so that the team can make these types of commitments.

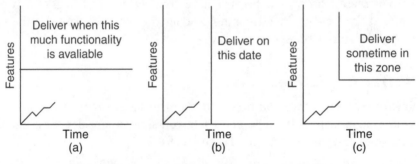

Figure 17.5 Three projects with different approaches to buffering.

Also, keep in mind that a project may use other buffers besides feature and schedule. A project may include a *budget buffer* where, for example, thirty developers are assigned to the project, whereas the budget allows up to thirty-three. This is a common practice on medium and large projects but is seen less frequently on small projects for two reasons.

1. The additional person or two who would make up the personnel buffer on a small project would almost certainly be able to make direct contributions to the project. There may be little or no productivity gains in fully staffing from

thirty to thirty-three developers. There will, however, almost certainly be productivity gains from fully staffing from four to five.

2. It is difficult to buffer anything in small numbers. When a thirty-person project has a three-person buffer to a full staff size of thirty-three, it has a 10% personnel buffer. A similar buffer on a three-person project implies a buffer of three-tenths of a developer. Clearly, it's easier to add whole rather than partial people to a project.

A Schedule Buffer Is Not Padding

The term *padding* has the pejorative meaning of excess time arbitrarily added to an estimate. I pad an estimate when I think it will take three days but decide to tell you five, just in case. Individuals add padding to an estimate if they expect to be beaten up if they are wrong. A schedule buffer is different: A schedule buffer is a necessary margin of safety added to the sum of estimates from which local safety has been removed.

When you put five car lengths between your car and the one ahead, you do that because you fully expect to use up most of that buffer if forced to brake suddenly. Yes, it's possible you could drive for hours with one car length separating you and the car ahead, but it's not likely. The buffer around your car is critical to your safety. Appropriate buffers around your project are critical to the safety of your project.

When we allow small amounts of flexibility in both delivery date and functionality, we can buffer two dimensions of the project. More important, we buffer each project constraint with the appropriate resource: We buffer the deadline with time; we buffer functionality with functionality. When we cannot buffer a constraint appropriately, we are forced to increase the size of other buffers. If I am forced to guarantee the functionality, I will support that guarantee with a larger schedule buffer.

Some Caveats

Although knowing how to add one or more buffers to a project is an important skill to have at your disposal, it is also good to be aware of some caveats on their use.

- When adding a schedule buffer, use the two-estimate approach described in this chapter or be sure that the single-value estimates represent estimates at the 50% point. Adding a schedule buffer on top of already pessimistic 90% estimates will result in an overly long schedule.

◆ On many projects, a precise deadline with a precise set of delivered functionality is not needed. Instead, the team simply needs to deliver high-quality software as fast as possible over a sustained period. If you're in this situation, don't take on the extra work of adding buffers to your project.

◆ Be careful with how you communicate buffers. You should not hide their existence or how they are used. However, a buffer (especially a schedule buffer) can appear to be padding. This means you'll need to communicate how you derived the estimates and the buffer, and how the buffer is intended to provide a schedule everyone can be highly confident of.

Summary

Most projects contain a tremendous amount of uncertainty. This uncertainty is often not fully reflected in the schedules and deadlines that project teams create. There are times when this uncertainty is so large or significant that extra steps should be taken when estimating the duration of the project. This may be the case when the project is planned far in advance, the project must absolutely meet a deadline with a reasonably firm set of functionality, the project is outsourced, requirements are still at a superficial level, or there is a significant impact (financial or otherwise) to being wrong about a date.

The two most common types of buffers are feature buffers and schedule buffers. A feature buffer is created when a product's requirements are prioritized and it is acknowledged that not every feature may be delivered. The agile process DSDM, for example, recommends that 30% of the effort of the project be considered optional, which creates a feature buffer for the project. If time runs short, the schedule can still be met by dropping items in the feature buffer.

A schedule buffer, on the other hand, is created by including in the schedule an amount of time that reflects the uncertainty inherent in a team's size. A feature buffer can be constructed by estimating both a 50% likely size and a 90% likely size for each user story. By applying the square root of the sum of the squares formula to each of the 50% and 90% estimates, an appropriately sized schedule buffer can be estimated.

A project should protect against feature uncertainty with a feature buffer and against schedule uncertainty with a schedule buffer. A feature buffer may be combined with a schedule buffer. In fact, this is usually a good idea, as it allows the size of each to be smaller.

Discussion Questions

1. Are there conditions in your organizations that could benefit from the extra effort of calculating a schedule buffer?

2. Is your current project buffered against any types of uncertainty? If so, how? If not, which types of buffer would be most beneficial?

3. Do you see evidence of Parkinson's Law or the student syndrome in your organization? Beyond the suggestions in this chapter, what might you be able to do to reduce the impact of these?

Chapter 18

Planning the Multiple-Team Project

> "Do the planning, but throw out the plans."
> —Mary Poppendieck

Agile teams are often described as having no more than seven to ten developers. Teams of this size can accomplish quite a bit, especially with an agile process that allows and encourages them to become more productive. However, there are some projects in which we'd like to bring a larger team to bear on the project. Rather than establishing a single 100-person team, the agile approach is to create multiple smaller teams. An agile project may have a dozen smaller teams instead of a single 100-person team.

In this chapter, we will take what we've learned in previous chapters and apply it to the challenge of planning a project comprising multiple teams. Planning a large, multiple team project may require

1. Establishing a common basis for estimates.
2. Adding detail to their user stories sooner.
3. Performing lookahead planning.
4. Incorporating feeding buffers into the plan.

A project may require some or all of these techniques, depending on how many subteams are involved, as well as how often and intensely they need to coordinate. In general, I advise teams to incorporate only as many of these additional techniques as necessary, starting with establishing a common basis and working in order toward introducing feeding buffers.

Establishing a Common Basis for Estimates

Although it would be nice to let each individual subteam choose whether to estimate in story points or ideal days, most projects with multiple teams will benefit from estimating in a common unit and establishing a baseline meaning for that unit. Imagine the difficulty of predicting how much longer is needed to complete a set of user stories if some of them are estimated in ideal days and some are estimated in story points. Worse, imagine how much harder it would be if one team estimated a set of stories as 20 points but another team estimated the same work as 100 story points.

At the start of a project, the teams should meet and choose between story points and ideal days. They should then establish a common baseline for their estimates so that an estimate by one team will be similar to that of another team if the other team had estimated the work instead. Each user story needs to be estimated by only one team, but the estimates should be equivalent regardless of which team estimated the work.

There are two good ways to establish a common baseline. The first approach works only if the teams have worked together on a past project. In that case, they can select some user stories from the past project and agree on the estimates for them. Suppose they are estimating in ideal days; they should find two or three stories they consider as one ideal-day each. Then they should find a few they consider to be two ideal-day stories, and so on. They may identify twenty or so old stories, agreeing upon a new estimate for each, knowing what they now know about the stories. Once these baseline stories are agreed upon, the teams may separately estimate stories by comparing them with the baseline stories (that is, estimating them by analogy).

The second approach is similar but involves collaboratively estimating an assortment of new user stories. A variety of stories planned for the new release are selected. The stories should span a variety of sizes and should be in areas of the system that most of the estimators can relate to. Either the entire large team—or representatives of each subteam, if the entire team is too big—meet and agree upon an estimate for these stories. As with the first approach, these estimates are then used as baselines against which future estimates are compared.

The only time separate teams should consider estimating in different units without a common baseline is when the products being built are truly separate and there is absolutely no opportunity for developers from one team to move onto another. Even then, my recommendation is to establish a common baseline, as it facilitates communicating about the project.

Adding Detail to User Stories Sooner

Ideally, an agile team begins an iteration with vaguely defined requirements and turns those vague requirements into functioning, tested software by the end of the iteration. Going from vague requirement to working software in one iteration is usually easier on a single-team project than it is when there are multiple teams. On a multiple-team project, it is often appropriate and necessary to put more thought into the user stories before the start of the iteration. The additional detail allows multiple teams to coordinate work.

To achieve this, larger teams often include dedicated analysts, user interaction designers, and others who spend a portion of their time during a given iteration preparing the work of the next iteration. In general, I do not advise having analysts, interaction designers, and others work a full iteration ahead. Rather, their primary responsibility should remain the work of the current iteration, but in planning the current iteration, they should include some tasks related to preparing for the next iteration.

What I've found to be the most useful outcome of work done in advance of the iteration is the identification of the product owner's conditions of satisfaction for the user stories that are likely to be developed during the iteration. A product owner's conditions of satisfaction for a user story are the high-level acceptance tests that she would like to see applied to the story before considering it finished. A user story is finished when it can be demonstrated to meet all of the conditions of satisfaction identified by the product owner.

Although it is extremely helpful to know the conditions of satisfaction for a user story before an iteration begins, it is unlikely (and unnecessary) that a team identify them for all user stories in advance of the iteration. Realistically, the exact set of stories that will be undertaken in the next iteration are not known until the end of the iteration planning meeting that kicks off the iteration. In most cases, however, the product owner and team can make a reasonable guess at the stories that will most likely be prioritized into the next iteration. Conditions of satisfaction can be identified for these stories in advance of the iteration.

Lookahead Planning

Most teams with either moderately complex or frequent interdependencies will benefit from maintaining a rolling lookahead window during release and iteration planning. Suppose two teams are working on the SwimStats application. Part of SwimStats involves displaying static information such as practice times, the addresses of and directions to pools, and so on. However, SwimStats must also provide database-driven dynamic information, including results from all meets over the past fifteen years and personal records for all swimmers in all events.

National and age-group records are stored in a database at the remote facility of the national swimming association. Accessing the database isn't as simple as the teams would like, and the national association is planning to change database vendors in the next year or two. For these reasons, the product owner and development teams agree that they want to develop an API (application programming interface) for accessing the database. This will make a later change to a different database vendor much simpler. The initial user stories and the estimates for each are shown in Table 18.1.

Table 18.1 The Initial User Stories and Estimates for SwimStats

User Story	Story Points
As SwimStats, we want to be able to change our database vendor easily.	30
As any site visitor, I need to be authenticated before being given access to sensitive parts of the site.	20
As a swimmer, I want to see when practices are scheduled.	10
As a swimmer or parent, I want to know where league pools are located.	10
As any site visitor, I want to see the national records by age group and event.	10
As any site visitor, I would like to see the results of any meet.	10
As any site visitor, I would like to see the personal records of any swimmer.	20

Velocity is estimated to be twenty points per iteration for each team. Because there are 110 points of work, this means the teams should be able to deliver all functionality in three iterations. However, thirty of the points are for developing the API, and another forty (the last three stories in Table 18.1) can be done only after the API. To finish these seventy points in three iterations, both teams will need to use the API. This leads them to an allocation of work as shown in Figure 18.1, which shows the team interdependency as an arrow between the API work of the first team and the personal records work done by the second.

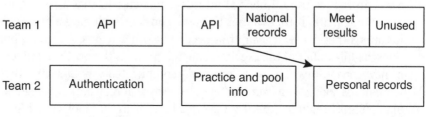

Figure 18.1 Coordinating the work of two teams.

You may recall that in Chapter 13, "Release Planning Essentials," I advised that the release plan show detail only for the next couple of iterations. This is because that is often enough to support the interdependencies encountered by many teams. When multiple teams need to coordinate work, the release plan should be updated to show and coordinate the work of the next two or three iterations. The exact number of iterations will, of course, depend on the frequency and significance of the dependencies among teams. As iterations are completed, details about them are dropped from the plan. The release plan then becomes a *rolling lookahead plan* that always outlines expectations about the new few iterations. Laufer (1996) refers to this as "peering forward."

Figure 18.1 shows the situation in which a handoff between teams occurs between iterations. This is safer than planning on a handoff occurring during an iteration. At the start of each iteration, each team identifies the work they can complete and commits to finishing it. In the case of Figure 18.1, at the start of the third iteration, Team 2 was able to make a meaningful commitment to completing the personal records user story because they knew that the API was finished. Suppose instead that when Team 2 planned its third iteration the API was not done but was expected to be finished in a few days. Even if Team 2 could finish the personal-records story without having the API on the first day, it is a much more tenuous commitment, and the overall schedule is at greater risk. Teams will often need to make commitments based on miditeration deliverables. However, to the extent possible, they should limit commitments to work completed before the start of the iteration.

Incorporating Feeding Buffers into the Plan

For most teams in most situations, a rolling lookahead plan is adequate. There are situations, however, in which the interdependencies between teams are so complex or frequent that the simple rolling lookahead planning of the preceding section is not enough. In these cases, your first recourse should be to try to find a way to reduce the number of interdependencies so that a rolling lookahead plan is adequate. If that cannot be done, consider including a *feeding buffer* in iterations that deliver capabilities needed by other teams. A feeding buffer, like the schedule buffer of the previous chapter, protects the on-time delivery of a set of new capabilities. This is a somewhat complicated way of saying that if your team needs something from my team tomorrow at 8:00 a.m., my team shouldn't plan on finishing it at 7:59. That is, we'd like a plan that looks like Figure 18.2.

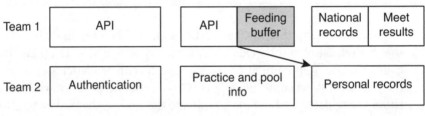

Figure 18.2   Adding a feeding buffer.

In Figure 18.2, a feeding buffer has been inserted between Team 1's completion of the API and the beginning of Team 2's work using the API on the personal records user story. The feeding buffer protects the start date on the personal-records story against delays in the completion of the API.

To include a feeding buffer in a release plan, all you need to do is plan temporarily for a lower velocity for the team that is delivering a capability to another team. In the case of Figure 18.2, Team 1's effort is evenly split between finishing the API and a feeding buffer so that we can be sure Team 2 is able to start on the personal records at the beginning of the third iteration. This does not mean that Team 1 gets to take it easy during the second iteration. In fact, the expectation is that they will complete ten points on the API, need only a portion of the buffer, and begin work on the national-records user story during the second iteration.

What Gets Buffered?

In the case shown in Figure 18.2, adding a feeding buffer did not extend the length of the overall project, because Team 1's third iteration was not already full. In many cases, however, adding feeding buffers will extend the expected duration of a project. But it usually does so in a way that represents a realistic expectation of the likely schedule, not in a "let's pad the schedule so we don't have to work hard" way. Because feeding buffers can prolong a schedule, you want to add them only when necessary.

To determine where feeding buffers are necessary, first allocate user stories among teams and iterations. Then look for critical dependencies between iterations and teams. Finally, add a feeding buffer only between these critical dependencies. That is, add a feeding buffer only if a team will be unable to do planned, high-priority work without the deliverables of another team. Even so, if the team can easily swap in other highly valuable work, a feeding buffer is unnecessary. Similarly, do not add a feeding buffer if the second team will be able to start making progress with a partial deliverable from the first team. If your team can start its work even if my team delivers only half of the planned functionality, a feeding buffer is not needed.

Sizing a Feeding Buffer

To size the feeding buffer, you can use the guidelines provided in Chapter 17, "Buffering Plans for Uncertainty." Fortunately, however, most interteam dependencies are based on no more than a handful of stories or features at a time. Because of this, you usually won't have enough stories to use the square root of the sum of the squares approach described in that chapter effectively. In these cases, set the size of the feeding buffer as a percentage of the stories creating the interdependency. You can use 50% as a default buffer size, but this should be adjusted based on team judgment.

It is possible to have a feeding buffer that is longer than a full iteration. However, it is rarely advisable to use a feeding buffer that long. A feeding buffer that is longer than an iteration is usually the result of planning to pass a large chunk of functionality on to another team. There are two reasons why a project probably doesn't need a large feeding buffer in these cases. First, the handoff from one team to another should almost certainly be divided so that the functionality is delivered incrementally. This will allow the second team to get started as soon as they receive the initial set of functionality from the first team. Second, rather than consume an extremely large feeding buffer, the teams would probably find ways of splitting the work or of making other adjustments between iterations as soon as they noticed one team slipping behind. Having the receiving team act as a product owner or customer of the delivering team will usually allow the two teams to work out an incremental delivery sequence that works for both teams.

I've never had to use a feeding buffer that was larger than a full iteration and have rarely used one longer than half an iteration. Whenever I encounter the possible need to do so, I question my assumptions and review the plan to see what I can do to shorten the chain of deliverables being passed from one team to another.

But This Is So Much Work

Well, yes, but so is a large, multiple-team project. Keep in mind that you don't need to do any of this if you've got a single team. You probably don't even need to do this if you have just three or four approximately seven-person teams as long as those teams communicate often.

However, many large projects need to announce and commit to deadlines many months in advance, and many large projects do have interteam dependencies like those shown in this chapter. When faced with a project like that, it is useful to spend a few more hours planning the project. Doing so will allow you to more confidently and accurately estimate a target completion date at the outset and will also provide some protection against easily avoided schedule delays.

Summary

Agile projects tend to avoid large teams instead using teams of teams to develop large projects. When multiple teams are working on one project, they need to coordinate their work. This chapter described four techniques that are useful in helping multiple teams work on the same project.

First, teams should establish a common basis for their estimates. All teams should agree to estimate in the same unit: story points or ideal days. They should further agree on the meaning of those units by agreeing upon the estimates for a small set of stories.

Second, when multiple teams need to work together, it is often useful to add detail to their user stories sooner. The best way to do this is to identify the product owner's conditions of satisfaction for a story. These are the things that can be demonstrated as true about a story once it is fully implemented.

Third, multiple teams benefit from incorporating a rolling lookahead plan into their release planning process. A rolling lookahead plan simply looks forward a small number of iterations (typically, only two or three) and allows teams to coordinate work by sharing information about what each will be working on in the near future.

Fourth, on highly complex projects with many interteam dependencies, it can be helpful to incorporate feeding buffers into the plan. A feeding buffer is an amount of time that prevents the late delivery by one team causing the late start of another.

These techniques are generally introduced to a project in the order described. They can, however, be introduced in any order desired.

Discussion Questions

1. How would you choose to establish a common baseline for your estimates on a project with multiple teams?

2. How significant are team interdependencies on your project? Which of the techniques introduced in this chapter would be most beneficial?

Part V

Tracking and Communicating

Part IV of this book described how to determine an appropriate schedule for a project. Once a plan and schedule have been created, the planning is not over. It is important to monitor progress against the plan, communicate about progress, and then refine the plan based on our observations.

In the first two chapters in this part, we look first at how to monitor a release plan and then at how to monitor an iteration plan. The part concludes by looking at various ways of communicating about estimates, plans, and progress. Also included is a sample end-of-iteration summary report.

Chapter 19

Monitoring the Release Plan

> *"The stars might lie, but the numbers never do."*
> —Mary Chapin Carpenter, "I Feel Lucky"

Ancient sailors had two problems. First, they had to know their latitude—that is, their north-south position on a map. Second, they had to know their longitude, or east-west position. Determining latitude by observing the North Star was relatively easy and had been done as early as 300 BC. Longitude presented a more difficult problem because it relied on the use of a relatively accurate clock, or chronometer. Unfortunately, there were no sufficiently accurate chronometers (especially that would fit and work aboard a ship) until the early eighteenth century.

Before the invention of the chronometer, a sailor could only guess at his longitude. To make these guesses, sailors applied a series of guesses and adjustments known as *dead reckoning,* which is generally considered to be short for *deduced reckoning*. Dead reckoning involved guessing how far east or west a ship had sailed and then adjusting that guess by guesses at the impact of the wind and the drift of the sea. Suppose that the speedometer on your yacht says you are traveling eight miles per hour. However, if you are heading into waves, wind, and current you may be making only five miles per hour of progress. Your dead reckoning guesses would need to reflect all of this, or you would incorrectly estimate your longitude.

Tracking the progress of a software team is very similar to charting a ship's position, especially by dead reckoning. We would like to sail our software

215

development project in a straight line from Point A to Point B. This rarely happens, though, because requirements change or are refined, our rate of progress isn't always what we expect, and we sometimes make mistakes in how we measure our position. The sections of this chapter describe techniques for tracking progress that are designed to minimize the effect of these and similar problems.

Tracking the Release

At the start of a release, we establish a plan that says something like "Over the next four months and eight two-week iterations we will complete approximately 240 story points [or ideal days] of work." As we learn more about our users' true needs and about the size of the project, this estimate may change. However, at any point we would like to be able to assess where we are relative to the goal of completing a certain amount of work in a given amount of time.

In doing so, there are many forces at work, and each needs to be considered. First, and ideally most significant, is the amount of progress made by the team. Second, however, is any change in the scope of the project. The product owner may have added or removed requirements. If the product owner adds forty story points and the team completes thirty, the team has more work to complete than when they started the prior iteration. The target has shifted, and it will be useful to know how far away the team is from the new target. Similarly, the developers may have learned things during the iteration that make them want to revise the story-point estimates assigned to some of the work coming later in the release plan.

These forces (completed work, changed requirements, and revised estimates) can be thought of as being similar to the forces of the wind (called *leeway*) and the forces of the sea (called *drift*) on a boat. Consider Figure 19.1, which shows the forces at work on a boat. The boat shown in this diagram will travel less distance than would be inferred from its speedometer. Similarly, even though the boat's compass pointed due east for its entire voyage, the wind will have caused it to make leeway to the south. Without course adjustments, this boat will take longer to get somewhere not quite its original destination. Mentally relabel the arrows of Figure 19.1 so that drift and leeway become requirements changes (adding or removing functionality) and changes to estimates. Figure 19.1 then reflects the challenges of tracking the progress of a software project against its schedule.

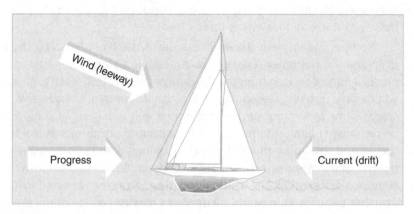

Figure 19.1   The forces at work on a boat.

Velocity

A boat measures its rate of progress in knots; an agile team measures its rate of progress with velocity. Velocity is expressed as the number of story points (or ideal days) completed per iteration. For a team that finished twelve stories worth a total of thirty story points in their last iteration, we say that their velocity is "thirty" or "thirty points per iteration." Assuming that the scope of the project hasn't changed, the team has that much less work to complete.

Because velocity is the primary measure of a team's progress, it is important to establish some ground rules for how it is calculated. The most important rule is that a team counts points toward velocity only for stories or features that are complete at the end of the iteration. Complete doesn't mean something like "The coding is done, but it hasn't been tested" or "It's coded but needs to be integrated." Complete means code that is well written, well factored, checked-in, and clean; complies with coding standards; and passes all tests. To know how much progress has been made, we count only the points for work that is complete. Opening the door to counting partially finished work, perhaps giving partial credit, makes it impossible to know exactly where we are.

There are three main problems with counting unfinished work. First, it is extremely hard to measure unfinished or incomplete work. Which is further along: A user story that has been programmed but has had no tests run against it or a story that has been partially programmed and partially tested? How far along is a programmer who has designed a solution for a story but hasn't started coding it? We're good at knowing when something hasn't been started, and we're fairly good at knowing when it's done. We should assess work to be in one of those two states and leave it at that.

Second, incomplete stories break down the trust between the developer team and the customer team on the project. If a story cannot be completed as planned during an iteration, the developers and the customer team need to collaboratively resolve the issue as soon as it's discovered. Usually, this means the story will be moved out of the iteration or split and parts of it moved out. The product owner and customer team can make these decisions in real time during the iteration and may choose to reprioritize based on the new knowledge about the cost of the story. Alternatively, the customer team may decide to alter the acceptance criteria for the story, accepting it under lessened criteria. They wouldn't go so far as to accept a buggy or untested version of the story, but they may reduce performance requirements, handling of special cases, and so on.

Third, and most important, unfinished work leads to a buildup of work in process in the development process. The more work in process a team allows to build up, the longer it will take new features to be transformed from raw ideas into functioning software. Over time, this will decrease the throughput of the whole team. Similarly, with large amounts of work in process, it takes longer for the team to get feedback on what they're developing. This means that learning is also delayed.

If a team has unfinished stories at the end of an iteration, they are working with features or stories that are too large. Small stories lead to a steady flow through the development process. If stories are left unfinished, they need to be split into smaller stories. Ideally, this should happen prior to the start of the iteration. However, if during an iteration a story is found to be larger than expected, it needs to be brought to the attention of the product owner. The product owner, in collaboration with the team, finds a way to split the story or reduce its scope such that a portion can ideally still be completed within the iteration, with the remainder moved to a future iteration.

So how should a team count a partially finished story when determining velocity? How they count such a story is less important than that they determine why it happened and how they can prevent it from happening again. It may have happened because it was underestimated. If so, the team should think about what type of work was underestimated or forgotten and try to remember to take care when estimating that type of work in the future. Or the story may have been unfinished because too many stories were pulled into the current iteration. If that was the cause, care should be taken to plan iterations more carefully.

Release Burndown Charts

Figure 19.2 shows a release *burndown chart* (Schwaber and Beedle 2002). The vertical axis shows the number of story points remaining in the project. (It could just as easily show the number of ideal days remaining.) Iterations are shown across the horizontal axis. A release burndown chart shows the amount of work remaining at the start of each iteration. This becomes a powerful visual indicator of how quickly a team is moving toward its goal. Figure 19.2 shows a hypothetical burndown for a project with 240 story points delivered in equal amounts over eight iterations.

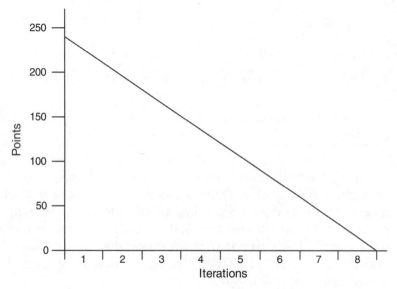

Figure 19.2   A 240-point project completed in eight iterations.

Of course, it's unlikely that a team that expects to have a velocity of thirty will have that exact velocity in each iteration. A more likely burndown chart of the 240-point release might appear as in Figure 19.3.

Figure 19.3 shows a team's progress after three iterations. Their progress has been inconsistent. During the first iteration they completed what appears to be about the planned thirty points of work. But at the end of the second iteration they actually had more work left to do than when they'd started that iteration. This could happen if, for example, the team realized that developing the user interface would be much more involved than they'd initially estimated and increased their estimates for all remaining user interface stories.

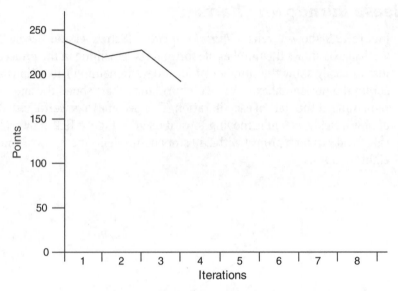

Figure 19.3   A more realistic burndown on a 240-point project after the third iteration.

Alternatively, the burndown chart may show a *burnup* because work has been added to the release. Think of this as equivalent to a sailboat making 8 miles per hour of progress but sailing directly into a current running 12 miles per hour in the opposite direction. In the sailboat's case, it ends up farther away from its initial target. However, in the case of the software project, the added work may be the result of the team's having learned something that directs them toward a more valuable release.

To see how this works, suppose that in the second iteration the team again completed the planned thirty points of work but that the product owner identified another forty points of work that is needed in the release. In this case, the net result is that there is more work to do at the end of the iteration than there was when it began. Because a burndown chart reflects the team's net progress, the chart is drawn to reflect this increase.

You may wonder why we'd draw the chart this way. We draw it this way because it allows a single burndown chart to show clearly and simply the two most important numbers we can use to see if a project is on track: how much work is remaining and the team's rate of progress net of all changes to the scope of the project. Imagine that you are on the team whose progress is shown in Figure 19.3. At the end of the third iteration, you are asked if the release will be finished within the planned eight iterations. And if it won't be, you are asked to provide a better estimate of when it will be finished. You can answer this question just by looking at the burndown chart in Figure 19.3. Simply line up a straight edge between the 240 points on the vertical axis and the number of points currently remaining in the project. Where the straight edge intersects the horizontal axis is when you can expect the project to finish. A casual look at Figure 19.3 tells you enough to know it won't finish in the planned eight iterations.

A Release Burndown Bar Chart

At one level, the release burndown chart of Figure 19.3 is great. It's easy to understand and can be explained quickly to anyone in the organization. A release burndown chart like this is very informative and tells us when the project is likely to finish if all factors affecting the project remain unchanged. However, sometimes it's useful to draw the release burndown chart so that you can easily see the team's velocity and the scope changes separately. To do this, draw a release burndown bar chart like the one shown in Figure 19.4.

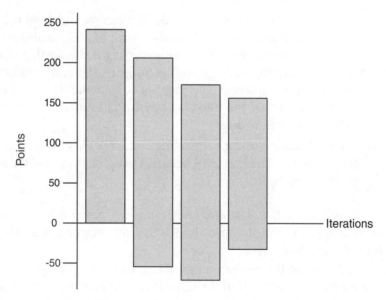

Figure 19.4   Separating the impact of velocity and scope changes.

Each bar in Figure 19.4 shows the amount of work in a release as of the start of an iteration. This type of burndown chart uses bars rather than lines to help distinguish the regions above and below the horizontal axis at 0. The bottom of the bar is lowered whenever work is added to the project. The bottom is moved up whenever work is removed from an iteration. If the bottom is below the horizontal axis at 0, it means that overall work has been added to the release.

An example is the best way to see how this works. In Figure 19.4, a release is planned to include 240 points of work. At the start of the first iteration the burndown chart is drawn with a single bar extending from 0 to 240. As before, the team expects an average velocity of thirty and expects to be done after eight iterations. During the first iteration, the team achieves the expected velocity, and the top of the second bar is drawn at 210. However, the product owner has realized that the release needs more features than originally thought. An additional fifty story points of work is identified that will be needed in this release. This causes the bar for the second iteration to extend below the 0 line. The second bar is drawn ranging from –50 to 210. In other words, the release now needs 260 points of work, which is more than when it was begun. By the end of the second iteration Figure 19.4 reveals three interesting facts.

1. The velocity of the team is as expected. This can be seen from the burndown across the top of the first two bars.

2. A great deal of work has been added. You can see this from the drop at the bottom of the second bar. Presumably, work has been added because it will lead to a more valuable release. However, it may be worth paying attention to the rate of scope change on this project—so far, more has been added than has been completed. This may not be something to worry about; it will depend on whether the trend is likely to continue and how important the initial target release date is.

3. The total amount of work remaining in the release is greater than when the project started. This is evident because the overall height of the second bar is greater than the first.

Clearly, there is a great deal more expressive power in drawing a burndown chart in this way. The drawback to it is that the meaning of the chart is not as immediately clear.

Let's look at the second and third iterations of the project in Figure 19.4. During the second iteration the team again achieves their target velocity. The product owner has again added work, but at least less was added than during the previous iteration.

But what happened during the third iteration? During this iteration, velocity has slowed to only twenty. This may be the result of underestimating some stories done in that iteration, a team member's being sick or on vacation, or the re-estimation of some of the remaining work. The team may have completed their planned thirty points of work but may have increased estimates on some remaining stories such that net progress is twenty rather than thirty.

What is most interesting, however, about the third iteration is shown at the bottom of the fourth bar. During this iteration, the product owner removed features from the release. When it's released, this project will still involve more story points than initially planned. We can tell this because the bar still extends below the x-axis at 0. However, at this point the project contains fewer planned points than it did at the start of the previous iteration. It's not important whether the features removed were ones in the original release plan or ones the product owner added in previous iterations. Prioritization of work is still up to the product owner, who can add or remove functionality as desired. The net effect is shown at the bottom of the burndown bar.

There are four simple rules to keep in mind when drawing this type of burndown chart.

- Any time work is completed, the top is lowered.
- When work is re-estimated, the top moves up or down.
- When new work is added, the bottom is lowered.
- When work is removed, the bottom is raised.

Let's take a look at a release burndown bar chart from a real project, as shown in Figure 19.5. What we see here is that the team made good progress during the first two iterations. The product owner added a small amount of work prior to the start of the second iteration, which is a fairly common occurrence on many teams. During the third iteration, the team discovered that some of their user stories were underestimated, and they re-estimated some of the remaining work. This led to the increase at the top of the fourth bar in Figure 19.5. Prior to the start of the fourth iteration, the product owner removed work from the release plan. This resulted in the bottom moving upward, even above the 0 line. During that iteration, the team made good progress. From that point on, the release plan stayed the same, and consistent progress was made until the end.

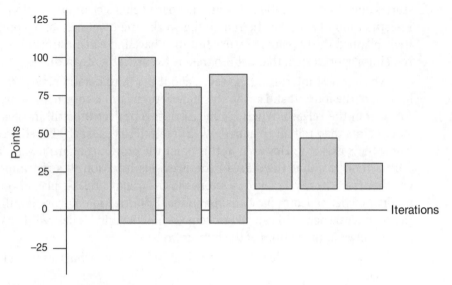

Figure 19.5   Removing work from a release.

A Caveat on Using the Release Burndown Bar Chart

Although I find the release burndown bar chart more expressive (and, therefore, often more useful) than the traditional burndown chart, I do have a couple of caveats on its use. First, the burndown bar chart is harder to understand, so I almost always start a new team with the simpler burndown line chart. Second, the burndown bar chart is for use only in organizations mature enough not to argue about whether something belongs above the line or below the line. At the first sign of an argument of this nature, I tell everyone involved that we can't use the burndown bar chart and we're reverting to the line chart.

A Parking-Lot Chart

Jeff DeLuca (2002) has suggested another useful way of visualizing how a team is doing at completing the planned functionality of a release. Figure 19.6 shows a variation of what DeLuca calls a parking-lot chart. A *parking-lot chart* contains a large rectangular box for each theme (or grouping of user stories) in a release. Each box is annotated with the name of the them, the number of stories in that theme, the number of story points or ideal days for those stories, and the percentage of the story points that are complete.

Figure 19.6   A parking-lot chart shows how much of each theme has been completed.

In the Swimmer Demographics box of Figure 19.6 you can see that this theme comprises eight stories, which are estimated at an aggregate of thirty-six story points. Eighteen of these story points are done, because we know that 50% of the feature is complete. We cannot tell how many of the specific user stories are done. The individual boxes on a parking lot chart may even be colored to indicate whether a theme is done or on schedule, needs attention or is significantly behind schedule.

A parking-lot chart is a powerful method for compressing a great deal of information into a small space. In many cases, all of a release's themes can be summarized on one page using a parking-lot diagram.

Summary

Velocity measures the amount of work completed by a team each iteration. Velocity should be calculated using an all-or-nothing rule. If a story is finished, the team counts its full estimate when counting velocity. If a story is partially completed during an iteration, it is not counted at all when determining velocity.

A release burndown chart shows the number of story points or ideal days remaining in the project as of the start of each iteration. A team's burndown is never perfectly smooth. It will vary because of inaccurate estimates, changed estimates, and changes in scope, for example. A burndown chart may even show a burnup during an iteration. This means that even though the team probably completed some work, they either realized that the remaining work was underestimated or increased the scope of the project. A key to interpreting a release burndown chart is understanding that it shows the team's net progress—that is, their progress minus any work added to the release.

A release burndown bar chart offers a sometimes-useful variation on the standard release burndown chart. It does so by separating a team's progress against planned work and changes to the scope of the release. Scope changes are shown by dropping the bar below the horizontal axis. This type of chart is more expressive than a standard burndown chart but must be used with care, as it may cause arguments in some organizations about whether a change affects the top or the bottom of a bar in the chart.

A parking-lot chart is useful for presenting a high-level view of a team's progress toward implementing the various themes planned in a project.

Discussion Questions

1. If you are not using a release burndown chart on your current project, what would be the result of producing one at the end of each iteration?

2. Which of the progress monitoring and reporting techniques described in this chapter would be most beneficial to your current project?

3. Which stakeholders on your project are not receiving information about the project that they would find useful?

Chapter 20

Monitoring the Iteration Plan

"Facts are better than dreams."
—Winston Churchill

In addition to tracking progress toward the high-level goal of a release, it is always helpful to track the development team's progress toward completing the work of a single iteration. In this chapter, we'll look at the two tools for iteration tracking: the task board and iteration burndown charts.

The Task Board

A task board serves the dual purpose of giving a team a convenient mechanism for organizing their work and a way of seeing at a glance how much work is left. It is important that the task board (or something equivalent to it) allow the team a great deal of flexibility in how they organize their work. Individuals on an agile team do not sign up for (or get assigned) work until they are ready to work on it. This means that except for the last day or two of an iteration, there typically are many tasks that no one has yet signed up for. A task board makes these tasks highly visible so that everyone can see which tasks are being worked on and which are available to sign up for. An example task board is shown in Figure 20.1.

The task board is often a large whiteboard or, even better, a corkboard. Taped or pinned to the task board are the story cards as well as the task cards that were written during iteration planning. The task board includes one row for each story or feature that will be worked on during the iteration. In Figure 20.1, the first row contains information about the five-point story. The first column of the task board holds the story card. Because the story card shows the point estimate assigned to the story, anyone looking at the task board can quickly determine the number of story points for each story included in the iteration.

Story	To Do	Tests Ready	In Process	To Verify	Hours
As a user, I can... 5	Code the... 8 Code the... 5 Test the... 6	√	Code the... SC 6 Code the... DC 4	Code the... LC 4	33
As a user, I can... 2	Code the... 8 Code the... 5				13
As a user, I can... 3	Code the... 3 Code the... 6	√	Code the... MC 4		13

Figure 20.1 A task board in use during an iteration.

The second column holds all of the task cards that the team identified as necessary to implement the story or feature. Each of these cards shows the estimate of the work remaining to complete the task.

The third column indicates whether the acceptance tests are ready for the story. I am a big fan of test-driven development (Beck 2002), both at the code level, where I encourage developers to write a failing unit test before writing code, and at the feature level, where I encourage teams to design high-level acceptance tests before they begin coding. If the conditions of satisfaction for each story were identified as part of iteration planning (as advised in Chapter 14, "Iteration Planning"), this is easy, as the conditions of satisfactions are essentially a user story's high-level acceptance tests. This type of specification by example is very beneficial for the programmers, as they can refer to specific examples of how each function and business rule is expected to work.

I have teams put a big checkmark in the Tests Ready column when they have specified the high-level tests for a story. Further, I encourage teams not to move many cards to the fourth column, In Process, unless the tests are specified. You may not need a Tests Specified column, but it's a useful, visible reminder to a team that is trying to become accustomed to specifying acceptance tests before coding a feature.

The In Process column holds cards that developers have signed up for. Typically, a developer takes a card from the To Do column, puts her initials on it, and moves it to the In Process column. This happens throughout the day as developers are finishing work and selecting what they'll work on next. No one should sign up for more than one or two cards at a time. This helps maintain a consistent flow of work through the process and reduces the cost of context switching among multiple tasks. As a constant reminder of this, when I have a team set up their task board I have them make the In Process column the width of one card. The To Do column is typically wider (and wider than shown in Figure 20.1) because cards are often taped four across there.

The To Verify column is another that you may or may not need but that I find useful, especially when working with a team that is learning how to become agile. Ideally, each test activity is thought of and a task card written during iteration planning. If so, when a programming task card ("Code the boojum user interface") is finished, it is removed from the task board (or moved to a final column called Done). At that time, someone can sign up for the associated test card ("Test the boojum user interface"). However, I find there are times when a developer considers a task card done but would like a fresh pair of eyes to take a quick, verifying look. In those cases, and when there is no associated test task, the task card is placed in the To Verify column.

The developers are encouraged to change the estimate on any task card on the board at any time. For example, if I start working on a card and realize that the estimate of two hours on it is wrong, I will go over to the task board, cross out the two, and replace it with perhaps a six. If I believe the estimate is even further off, I may rip up that task card and replace it with two or three task cards, each with its own estimate. The final column on the task board is simply a sum of the hours of work remaining on the feature or story. I usually sum the hours for each row every morning. I use these totals to draw an iteration burndown chart, which is the second tool for tracking the progress of an iteration.

Tracking Bugs on a Task Board

Many teams, when they begin the transition to an agile development process, are faced with a large number of legacy bugs. Not only is there usually a large backlog of bugs to be fixed "someday," but also bugs continue to come in at a rapid rate. A common challenge for teams moving to an agile process is how to deal with these bugs. The task board provides a convenient mechanism for starting to correct this problem.

As an example of how the task board can help, suppose the product owner includes "Fix ten 'high' bugs" in the new iteration. The product owner selects the ten bugs, and the developers write a task card (with an estimate) for each. The cards are taped in the To Do column of a row on the task board. As the iteration progresses, the developers work on the ten bugs in the same way they work on other task cards. Now suppose a user finds a new bug halfway through the iteration. If the new bug is considered a higher priority than one or more bug remaining in the To Do column, the product owner can swap out an equivalent amount of bug fixing work in favor of fixing the new bug.

This approach allows a team to correct legacy defects at whatever rate the product owner chooses. The team could allocate 40 hours to bug fixing, or they could allocate 100 hours. The product owner selects how much of an iteration should be directed toward bug fixing rather than new feature development. The product owner and team then collaboratively select which bugs fit within that amount of time.

Iteration Burndown Charts

Drawing a release burndown chart is a great way to see whether a project is going astray or not. Depending on the length of your iterations, it can be useful to create an iteration burndown chart. If you're using one-week iterations, it probably isn't necessary. By the time a trend is visible on an iteration burndown chart, a one-week iteration will be over. However, I've found iteration burndown charts to be extremely useful with iteration lengths of two weeks or longer. An iteration burndown chart plots hours remaining by day, as shown in Figure 20.2.

To create an iteration burndown chart, simply sum all of the hours on your task board once per day and plot that on the chart. If the team's task board is drawn on a whiteboard, I usually draw the iteration burndown by hand on one side of the task board. If the task board is on a corkboard, I tack a large piece of paper to the corkboard and draw the burndown chart on it.

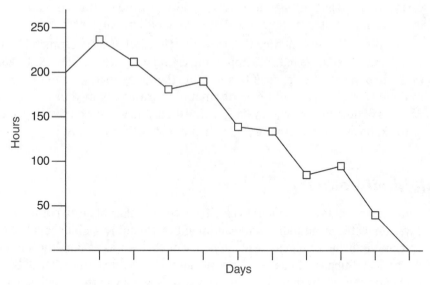

Figure 20.2   An iteration burndown chart.

Tracking Effort Expended

In the previous chapter, the analogy of a project as a sailboat was introduced to make the point that a sailboat's progress is not always easily measured. A sailboat that sailed for eight hours yesterday and then anchored may or may not be eight hours closer to its destination. Wind and current may have pushed the sailboat off what was believed to be its course. The boat may be closer to or farther from its destination. When this is the case, the most useful thing the crew can do is assess where they are relative to the destination. Measuring the distance traveled or time spent traveling are not helpful if we're not sure all progress was in the right direction.

On a project, it is far more useful to know how much remains to be done rather than how much has been done. Further, tracking effort expended and comparing it with estimated effort can lead to "evaluation apprehension" (Sanders 1984). When estimators are apprehensive about providing an estimate, the familiar "fight or flight" instinct kicks in, and estimators rely more on instinct than on analytical thought (Jørgensen 2004).

Tracking effort expended in an effort to improve estimate accuracy is a very fine line. It can work (Lederer and Prasad 1998; Weinberg and Schulman 1974). However, the project manager or whoever is doing the tracking must be very careful to avoid putting significant evaluation pressure on the estimators, as doing so could result in estimates that are worse rather than better.

Additionally, keep in mind that variability is a part of every estimate. No matter how much effort is put into improving estimates, a team will never be able to estimate perfectly. Evidence of this is no further away than your morning commute to work. There is an inherent amount of variability in your commute regardless of how you travel, how far you must go, and where you live. If you drive to work, no amount of driving skill will eliminate this variability.

Individual Velocity

Some teams refer to individual velocity as the number of story points or ideal days completed by an individual team member. Do not track individual velocity. Tracking individual velocity leads to behavior that works against the success of the project. Suppose it has been announced that individual velocity will be measured and tracked from iteration to iteration. How do you think individuals will respond? If I am forced to choose between finishing a story on my own and helping someone else, what incentive does measuring individual velocity give me?

Individuals should be given every incentive possible to work as a team. If the team's throughput is increased by my helping someone else, that's what I should do. Team velocity matters; individual velocity doesn't. It's not even a metric of passing interest.

As a further argument against measuring individual velocity, you shouldn't even be able to calculate it. Most user stories should be written such that they need to be worked on by more than one person, such as a user interface designer, programmer, database engineer, and a tester. If most of your stories can be completed by a single person, you should reconsider how your stories are written. Normally, this means they need to be written at a higher level so that work from multiple individuals is included with each.

Summary

A task board—which is often a whiteboard, corkboard, or just a designated space on a wall—helps a team organize and visualize their work. The columns of a task board are labeled, and team members move task cards through the columns as work progresses.

An iteration burndown chart is similar to a release burndown chart but is used to track only the work of the current iteration. It graphs the number of hours remaining on the vertical axis and the days of the iteration on the horizontal axis.

Teams should be reluctant to track the actual hours expended on tasks to get better at estimating. The risks and the effort to do so usually outweigh the benefits.

Teams should not calculate or track individual velocity.

Discussion Questions

1. In your organization, would the benefits of tracking the actual effort expended on tasks and comparing these with the estimates outweigh the risks and costs of doing so?

2. If your current project team is not collocated, what can you do to achieve some of the same benefits that collocated teams experience when using a task board?

Chapter 21

Communicating about Plans

> *"The more elaborate our means of communication,*
> *the less we communicate."*
> —Joseph Priestley

In this chapter, we will look at some specific ways to communicate about plans. However, more important than specifically what we communicate is how we approach the work of communicating about estimates and plans. We want all communication, but especially communication about estimates and plans, to be frequent, honest, and two-way.

Frequent communication about plans is important because of how often an agile plan is updated. For example, even if a team does rolling lookahead planning (as described in Chapter 18, "Planning the Multiple-Team Project"), their release plan may show only what will be developed in the next few iterations. The user stories that will be developed through the rest of the release may be included in the release plan, but they will not be sequenced beyond the horizon of the lookahead plan and may be listed only as broad themes.

We cannot (and do not want to) produce a plan on the first day and leave it alone for three to six months. Plans are updated throughout the project, and these updates need to be communicated. Failing to do so ignores the valuable feedback loops that can improve the desirability and success of the product and the usefulness of the plan. During the short timebox of an iteration, it is important for team members to see daily variations in the iteration burndown chart so that they can make adjustments to complete all the work of the iteration. Over the longer period of a release, project stakeholders and participants need insight into progress against and revisions to the release plan.

Honest communication is important if the development team and customer team are to trust each other. If the developers learn, for example, that the product owner has been telling them artificial dates, they will no longer trust her. Similarly, if developers give estimates that the product owner knows are unrealistic, trust will disappear here as well. I worked with a team recently that told me their executives ask for more work than can reasonably be expected because "That way, if they get 80%, they're happy." The theory was that the executives would get 80% of whatever they asked for, so they knew to ask for more than needed.

Without trust, it is hard to have honest communication, so the loss of trust must be taken very seriously. If a developer knows that a given task will take much longer than currently expected, she needs to feel safe sharing that knowledge with the rest of the team, including her manager. If this type of honest communication is discouraged, problems such as this will remain hidden longer.

It is important that communication about estimating and planning be two-way, because we want to encourage dialogue and discussion about the plan so that we make sure we always have the best possible plan (given current knowledge) for delivering value to the organization. We want to iterate and refine plans based on feedback and new knowledge. Because of this, we need dialogue about plans, not one-way presentations.

Finally, make it your responsibility to make sure that all recipients understand the message you are delivering. They need not only to hear the message, but also to understand it. If you are a project manager delivering the message that the project is behind schedule, do it in such a manner that no one can fail to understand. This is one of the reasons that agile teams favor big, visible charts as a way of communicating—with no more than a handful of big, visible charts hanging in the team's workspace, it is likely that everyone on the project team will understand the significance of each. To the contrary, if the news that a project is behind is "clearly" shown on page thirty-two of a forty-page weekly status report, it's quite likely that no one knows it.

With these goals in mind, the rest of this chapter provides some specific guidance and tips on how to communicate about estimates and plans.

Communicating the Plan

When asked about the schedule for a project, it is tempting to sum the number of story points to be delivered, divide by a guess of velocity, and say something like "We'll ship on June 14, which is 7.2 iterations from now." This is wrong because it gives the impression that the knowledge from which we construct the plan is sufficiently precise as to support this type of estimate. When possible, include with your communication of a target date either your degree of confidence in the estimate, a range of possible dates, or both. For example, you may say:

- I am 90% sure we'll complete the planned functionality by July 31.
- Based on our assumptions about the project size and team performance, the project will take three to four months.

As an example of this type of communication, Ron Jeffries (2004) of www.XProgramming.com has suggested saying something like this:

Right now, this appears to be a 200-point project. Based on our performance on other projects (or a random guess), with N programmers on it, and your intimate involvement in the project, a project of this size will take between four and six months. However, we will be shipping software to you every two weeks, and we'll be ticking off these feature stories to your satisfaction. The good news is that if you're not satisfied, you can stop. The better news is that if you become satisfied before all the features are done, you can stop. The bad news is that you need to work with us to make it clear just what your satisfaction means. The best news is that whenever there are enough features working to make the program useful, you can ask us to prepare it for deployment, and we'll do that. As we go forward, we'll all see how fast we're progressing, and our estimate of the time needed will improve. In every case, you'll see what is going on, you'll see concrete evidence of useful software running the tests that you specify, and you'll know everything as soon as I know it.

Some companies have become accustomed to communicating project schedules through the familiar Gantt chart, as shown in Figure 21.1. Gantt charts have earned a bad reputation, but this is because of how they are often used to predict, schedule, and coordinate tasks. Despite these challenges in their use, Gantt charts can be great tools for showing the allocation of features to iterations.

There are a couple of minor but key differences between what is shown in Figure 21.1 and a more traditional Gantt chart. First, Figure 21.1 stops at the feature level and does not decompose each user story into its constituent tasks. What is shown then is a *feature breakdown structure* rather than a work breakdown structure of the project. Because it is the completion of features, rather than the completion of the tasks that add up to a feature, that adds value to a product, the Gantt chart is drawn showing features.

Second, each feature is shown to take the full length of the iteration into which it is scheduled. A feature may be done midway through an iteration, but it is not made available to the organization until the end of the iteration, so that is what the Gantt chart reflects.

ID	Description	Start	End	Chart
1	Iteration 1	July 1	July 14	
2	As a user, I want ...	July 1	July 14	
3	As a user, I want ...	July 1	July 14	
4	As a user, I want ...	July 1	July 14	
5	Iteration 2	July 15	July 28	
6	As a user, I want ...	July 15	July 28	
7	As a user, I want ...	July 15	July 28	
8	As a user, I want ...	July 15	July 28	
9	As a user, I want ...	July 15	July 28	

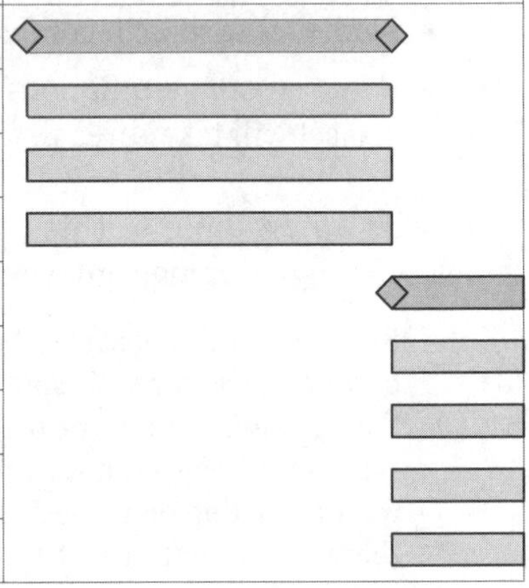

Figure 21.1 Showing iteration contents in a Gantt chart.

Third, no resource allocations are shown in Figure 21.1. Because the whole team is responsible for the delivery of all features, there is no benefit in putting Mary's name next to one feature and Vadim's next to another. Of course, if you're producing a Gantt chart showing the work of multiple teams, you may want to indicate whole-team responsibility by assigning features (or really entire iterations) to Team 1 or Team 2, and so on.

Communicating Progress

Naturally, the release burndown charts of Chapter 19, "Monitoring the Release Plan," are a primary way of communicating progress. Progress on a release burndown chart is a function of the amount of work remaining and the velocity of the team. The simple way to predict the number of iterations remaining is to take the number of points remaining to be developed, divide this by the team's velocity, and then round up to next whole number. So if there are 100 points remaining and the team's velocity is 10, we could say there are 10 iterations remaining.

However, measures of velocity are imprecise, and we expect velocity to fluctuate. If a team has determined their average velocity is ten, it is not inconceivable that it averages nine or eleven for the next few iterations. In fact, it's not inconceivable for velocity to be seven or thirteen over the next few iterations. In those cases, there could be as few as eight or as many as fifteen iterations left. When forecasting the number of iterations remaining, it generally is best to use a range of probable velocities.

To see one way of selecting the range of velocities, consider Figure 21.2, which shows a team's velocity over their preceding eight iterations. Velocity in the most recent iteration was nineteen. However, the average velocity over the past eight iterations is seventeen, and the average of this team's worst three iterations is fourteen. Each of these values will lead to a different expectation about when all of the currently planned work will be complete. This is why it is often best to use more than one velocity value and to present conclusions as a range of likely outcomes.

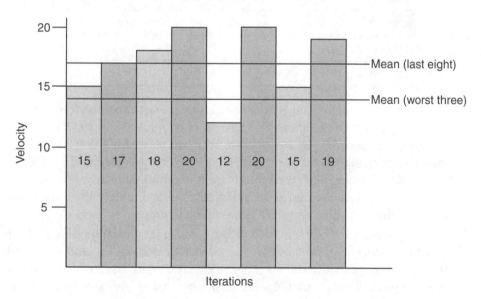

Figure 21.2   Velocity as measured for the last eight iterations.

In selecting a range of velocity values, I typically consider up to the last eight iterations. Many teams stay together that long, but going back beyond eight

iterations starts to feel like ancient history to me. If you don't have eight iterations, use what you have. From these previous iterations, I look at three values.

1. The velocity of the most recent iteration
2. The average (mean) velocity
3. The average (mean) velocity of the three slowest iterations

These three values present a good picture of what just happened, a "long
term" average, and a worst-case of what could happen. I use these three different
velocity values to forecast approximately how much more work may be completed by a given date. For example, if we would like to release the product after
five more iterations, and the team's most recent velocity was 19, we can predict
that the team might complete another 95 points. Similar math can be done with
the other measures of velocity. Doing so results in a range of the likely amount
of work the team will complete. I usually summarize this as shown in Table 21.1.

Table 21.1 The Expected Number of Points Based on Velocities in Figure 21.2

Description	Velocity	Iterations	Total Points
Worst three	14	5	70
Last eight	17	5	85
Most recent	19	5	95

Although I look for trends in velocity, many projects have too few iterations
for velocity trends to become either apparent or relevant. If I notice what appears
to be a trend toward an increasing velocity, I am pleased but don't act on it. I
would never draw a trend line through Figure 21.2, for example, and predict that
the team's velocity will be twenty in the next iteration. Similarly, if velocity ap-
peared to be headed downward, I would figure out and remove the cause of the
decline rather than plan on velocity continuing to drop.

Calculating the three expected velocity values (as shown in Table 21.1) allows the product owner and team to make predictions about the amount of work
that can be completed before a planned release date. Based on Table 21.1, for example, a product owner should feel comfortable that at least seventy additional
story points will be added during the next five iterations. However, the product
owner probably should not take out advertising space on a blimp about anything
beyond eighty-five more story points.

An End-of-Iteration Summary

Yes, it may not seem agile to suggest writing an end-of-iteration summary report. But almost every manager I talk to asks me if I do so. After I answer in the affirmative, I am almost always asked to share the template I use. You'll have to decide for yourself whether you want to take the time to do this. I find that I can complete this summary document in less than thirty minutes per iteration. I tend to favor two-week iterations on most projects, so this means I invest at most fifteen minutes per week in this.

The following sections present a sample iteration summary for the Swim-Stats project. I tend to include most of this information for most projects, but you may want to drop or add sections as appropriate.

Context

Dates

First Day of Iteration	September 1
Last Day of Iteration	September 14
Number of Working Days	9

Personnel

The following personnel were available during the iteration. Also listed are the days they were expected to work and the number of days they did work.

Name	Days Planned	Days Worked
Carina	9	9
Vadim	9	7
Sasha	8	9
Dmitri	9	9
Total	**35**	**35**

Working Days

Because holidays reduce the number of working days in an iteration, the number of planned working days may vary in some iterations. In this example, Vadim worked two days fewer than planned. He may have been sick. On the other hand, Sasha worked one day more than planned. Perhaps she'd tentatively planned a vacation day that she didn't take.

Metrics

Nightly Build Results

Date	Status
Monday, June 6	Build failed
Tuesday, June 7	812 unit tests passed; 1431 FitNesse tests passed; 104 user interface tests passed
Wednesday, June 8	826 unit tests passed; 1433 FitNesse tests passed; 104 user interface tests passed
Thursday, June 9	1 unit test failed
Friday, June 10	841 unit tests passed; 1442 FitNesse tests passed; 105 user interface tests passed
…	…

Color the Rows

The rows in this table are usually colored: green for a successful build and red for one that failed for any reason. Notice that the status column reports the number of successful tests only if all tests are successful. If any test fails, all that is shown is the number of failing tests. If one test fails, it doesn't matter how many tests pass. Reporting that 99 of 100 tests passed leads to the temptation to think that because 99% of the tests passed, we must be doing well. I want to avoid that temptation, so I report either the number of tests that passed (if they all did) or the number that failed otherwise.

Iteration Burndown

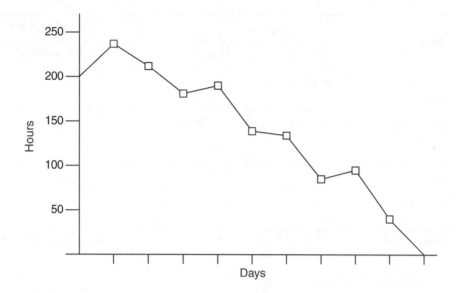

Velocity

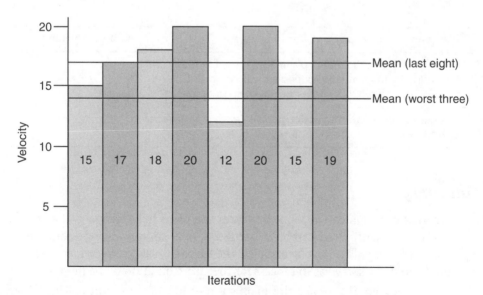

Contents and Assessment

Story	Result	Points Planned	Points Earned
As a coach, I can enter the names and demographic information of all swimmers on my team.	Finished	8	8
As a coach, I can define practice sessions.	Finished; bigger than planned	8	8
As a swimmer, I can see all of my times for a specific event.	Finished	3	3
As a swimmer, I can update my demographics information.	Started; not finished	1	0
Total		**20**	**19**

Iteration Review

The iteration review was held at 9:00 on September 15. The following items were identified:

Action Item	Responsible
Mark pointed out that the session planning logs used by most coaches he knows list information in the opposite order we show on the screen. We need to run those screens by some coaches.	Carina
Gary suggested we add a story about graphing a swimmer's results in an event.	Carina

Summary

We want communication about estimates and plans to be frequent, honest, and two-way. A Gantt chart can be a useful tool for communicating about a plan. However, it should not be taken below the feature breakdown level, and features on it should be shown as in process for the entire duration of the iteration.

Burndown charts are the primary method for communicating about progress, but they are often accompanied by a chart showing the development team's velocity per iteration. It is to useful to think of velocity as a range of values rather than one value. A good way to do this is to use the velocity of the most recent iteration, the average of the previous eight iterations, and the average of the lowest three of the previous eight iterations. These three values present a good picture of what just happened, a long-term average, and a worst case of what could happen.

On some projects an end-of-iteration summary can be useful, both in disseminating current information and as a historical document for use in the future.

Discussion Questions

1. Suppose a project has 150 points of work remaining to be done. Over the last 10 iterations the team have achieved a velocity of 10, 12, 13, 5, 14, 7, 6, 12, 16, and 14. You are asked when the project will be done. What do you say?

2. Is the deadline for your current project talked about as a specific date (September 18) or a range? Why?

3. Within what range of iterations or dates will your current project finish?

Part VI

Why Agile Planning Works

If it isn't clear by now why agile estimating and planning work, ideally it will be soon. Part VI, which comprises a single chapter, focuses solely on why agile estimating and planning work. In the following chapter, we'll quickly restate the purpose of planning and then consider some of the most important reasons why agile estimating and planning are successful in achieving that purpose.

The chapter concludes with a final set of a dozen guidelines for applying agile estimating and planning on your projects.

Chapter 22

Why Agile Planning Works

"If you want a guarantee,
buy a toaster."
—Clint Eastwood in *The Rookie*

Having arrived at this point, we are well equipped to look at why agile estimating and planning are successful. First, remember the purpose of estimating and planning. Planning is an attempt to find an optimal solution to the overall product development question: features, resources, and schedule. Changing any one of these causes changes in the others. While planning, we are exploring the entire spectrum of possible solutions of how to mix these three parameters such that we create the best product possible. The estimates and plans that we create must be sufficient for serving as the basis for decisions that will be made by the organization. In this chapter, we consider the agile estimating and planning process described so far by this book to see how it achieves these goals.

Replanning Occurs Frequently

One of the ways in which agile estimating and planning support the efficient exploration of the new product development solution space is through frequent replanning. At the start of each new iteration, a plan for that iteration is created. The release plan is updated either after each iteration or, at worst, after every few iterations. Acknowledging the impossibility of creating a perfect plan goes a long way toward reducing the anxiety that accompanies such a goal (Githens 1998).

Knowing that a plan can be revised at the start of the next iteration shifts a team's focus from creating a perfect plan (an impossible goal) to creating a plan that is useful right now.

For a plan to be useful, it must be accurate, but we accept that early plans will be imprecise. One of the reasons we replan is to remove that imprecision progressively. That is, an early plan may say that a project will deliver 300 to 400 story points in the third quarter. That plan may later turn out to be accurate (305 story points are delivered in August), but this plan is not particularly precise. During the early stages of a project, this plan may very likely be a sufficient basis for making decisions. Later, though, to remain useful, the plan will gain precision, and we may say that the project will deliver 380 to 400 story points in September.

An agile estimating and planning process recognizes that our knowledge is always incomplete and requires that plans be revised as we learn. As a team learns more about the product they are building, new features may be added to the release plan. As the team learns more about the technologies they are using or about how well they are working together, expectations about their rate of progress are adjusted. For a plan to remain useful, this new knowledge needs to be incorporated into the plan.

Estimates of Size and Duration Are Separated

A common planning flaw (on traditional as well as many agile teams) is confusing estimates of size and duration. Clearly, the size of an effort and the time needed to complete that effort are related, but many additional factors affect duration. A project of a given size will take programmers of different skill and experience levels different amounts of time. Similarly, duration is affected by the size of the team working on the project. A four-person team may take six months (twenty-four person-months). An eight-person team may reduce that to four calendar months but thirty-two person-months, even though the project is the same size in both cases.

To see the difference between estimates of size and duration, suppose I show you a book and ask you how long it will take you to read it. You can tell from its title that it's a novel, but I won't let you look inside the book to see how many pages are in it, how wide the margins are, or how small the type is. To answer my question about how long it will take you to read this book, you first estimate the number of pages. Let's assume you say 600. Then you estimate your rate of progress at one page per minute. You tell me it will take you 600 minutes, or 10 hours. In arriving at this estimate of duration (10 hours), you first estimated the size of the job (600 pages).

Agile estimating and planning succeed because estimates of size and duration are separated. We start by estimating the size of a project's user stories in story points. Because story points are abstract and notional, they are pure estimates of size. We then estimate a rate of progress, which we call velocity. Our estimates of size and velocity are then combined to arrive at an estimate of duration. Our estimating and planning process benefits from this clear and total separation of estimates of size and duration.

Plans Are Made at Different Levels

Because agile plans cover three different levels—the release, the iteration, and the current day—each plan can be made with a different level of precision. Having plans with different time horizons and different levels of precision has two main benefits. First, it conveys the reality that the different plans are created for different reasons. The daily plan, as committed to by each participant in a team's daily meeting, is fairly precise: Individuals express commitments to complete, or at least make progress on, specific tasks during the day. The iteration plan is less precise, listing the user stories that will be developed during an iteration and the tasks thought necessary to do so. Because each user story is imperfectly specified, there is also some vagueness around what it means to say that the story will be developed in the iteration. Finally, the release plan is the least precise of all, containing only a prioritized list of desired user stories and one or more estimates of how much of the desired functionality is likely to be delivered by the desired release date.

The second benefit of planning at different levels is that it helps the team view the project from different perspectives. An iteration plan is necessary for completing the highly coordinated work of a cross-functional team within a short iteration. A release plan provides a broader perspective on the project and ensures that the team does not lose the forest of the release for the trees of an iteration. A team that works iteration to iteration without awareness of a more distant goal runs the risk of continually pursuing short-term goals while missing out on targeting a truly lucrative longer-term goal. Short-term goals may be inconsistent with the desired long-term result.

Plans Are Based on Features, Not Tasks

A traditional plan in the form of a Gantt chart, PERT chart, or work breakdown structure focuses on the tasks needed to create a product. An agile plan focuses instead on the features that will be needed in the product. This is a key distinction, because it forces the team to think about the product at the right level—the features. When features are developed iteratively, there is less need for up-front thinking about the specific tasks necessary. The work of an iteration emerges, and the team will think of or discover all of the tasks as they are needed. What's more important is that the team think about the features that are being developed. Colleague Jim Highsmith (2004b) has stated that "agile planning is 'better' planning because it utilizes features (stories, etc.) rather than tasks. It is easy to plan an entire project using standard tasks without really understanding the product being built. When planning by feature, the team has a much better understanding of the product." At a task level, many project plans look the same; every agile plan is specific to the product being developed.

Small Stories Keep Work Flowing

From queuing theory (Poppendieck and Poppendieck 2003; Reinertsen 1997), we learn the importance of focusing on *cycle time*, the amount of time something takes to go from the start of a process to the end of that process. On a software project, cycle time is the time from when the team begins work on a feature until that feature delivers value to users. The shorter the cycle time, the better.

A key influence on cycle time is the variability in the time it takes to develop a new feature. One of the best ways to reduce variability is to work with reasonably small and similar size units of work. The estimating and planning process outlined in this book supports this by advising that teams estimate their short-term work within approximately one order of magnitude. Larger user stories can exist further down a project's prioritized requirements list. However, as those features near the top of the list (when they will be scheduled into an iteration that is beginning), they are disaggregated into smaller pieces.

Work in Process Is Eliminated Every Iteration

High amounts of work in process slow a team. On a software project, work in process exists on any feature that the team has started developing but has not yet finished. The more work in process there is, the longer any new feature will take to develop, as the new feature must follow the already-started work. (Or the new feature needs to be expedited, jumping ahead of the work in process, but that just compounds the problem for the next feature that cannot be expedited.) So work in process leads to increased cycle times. And in the previous section, we learned the importance of maintaining a short cycle time.

One of the reasons why agile planning succeeds is that all work in process is eliminated at the end of each iteration. Because work is not automatically rolled forward from one iteration to the next, each iteration is planned afresh. This means that work on a feature not fully implemented in one iteration will not necessarily be continued in the next. It often will be, but there's no guarantee. This has the effect of eliminating all work in process at the start of each iteration.

Because work in process is eliminated at the start of each iteration, teams are more easily able to work efficiently in short iterations. This means a shorter feedback loop from users to the project team, which leads to faster learning as well as more timely risk mitigation and control.

Tracking Is at the Team Level

Traditional approaches to estimating and planning measure and reward progress at the individual team member level. This leads to a variety of problems. For example, if finishing a task early results in a programmer's being accused of giving a padded estimate for the task, the programmer will learn not to finish early. Rather than finish early, she won't report a task as complete until its deadline.

Agile estimating and planning successfully avert this type of problem by tracking progress only at the team level. This is one of the reasons that Chapter 14, "Iteration Planning," included the advice that individuals should refrain from signing up for specific tasks during iteration planning. Similarly, there are no individual burndown charts prepared—only a teamwide burndown chart.

Uncertainty Is Acknowledged and Planned For

Many traditional, prescriptive plans make the mistake of believing that features can be locked down at the beginning of a project. Plans are then made that do not allow changes or force changes through an onerous change control process. This leads us to delivering projects with features that users don't want. When we create a plan early in a project and do not update the plan as we acquire new knowledge, we lose the opportunity to synchronize the plan with reality.

With an agile approach to estimating and planning, teams acknowledge both end and means uncertainty. End uncertainty (about the product ultimately being built) is reduced as product increments are shown to potential users and other stakeholders at the end of each iteration. Their feedback and responses are used to fine-tune future plans. Means uncertainty (about how the product will be built) is reduced as the team learns more about the technologies in use and themselves. Early discovery that a particular third-party component cannot meet performance requirements, for example, may lead the team to find an alternative. The time to find and switch to the new component will need to be factored into new plans once the need is identified.

A Dozen Guidelines for Agile Estimating and Planning

With all of these reasons in mind, the following is a list of a dozen guidelines for successful agile estimating and planning.

1. **Involve the whole team.** Primary responsibility for certain activities may fall to one person or group, as prioritizing requirements is primarily the responsibility of the product owner. However, the whole team needs to be involved and committed to the pursuit of the highest-value project possible. We see this, for example, in the advice that estimating is best done by the whole team, even though it may be apparent that only one or two specific team members will work on the story or task being estimated. The more responsibilities are shared by the team, the more success the team will have to share.

2. **Plan at different levels.** Do not make the mistake of thinking that a release plan makes an iteration plan unnecessary, or the other way around. The release, iteration, and daily plans each cover a different time horizon with a different level of precision, and each serves a unique purpose.

3. **Keep estimates of size and duration separate by using different units.** The best way to maintain a clear distinction between an estimate of size and one of duration is to use separate units that cannot be confused. Estimating size in story points and translating size into duration using velocity is an excellent way of doing this.

4. **Express uncertainty in either the functionality or the date.** No plan is certain. Be sure to include an expression of uncertainty in any release plan you produce. If the amount of new functionality is fixed, state your uncertainty as a date range ("We'll finish in the third quarter" or "We'll finish in between seven and ten iterations"). If the date is fixed instead, express uncertainty

about the exact functionality to be delivered ("We'll be done on December 31, and the product will include at least these new features, but probably no more than those other new features"). Use bigger units (iterations, months, and then quarters, for example) when the amount of uncertainty is greater.

5. **Replan often.** Take advantage of the start of each new iteration to assess the relevancy of the current release plan. If the release plan is based on outdated information or on assumptions that are now false, update it. Use replanning opportunities to ensure that the project is always targeted at delivering the greatest value to the organization.

6. **Track and communicate progress.** Many of a project's stakeholders will have a very strong interest in the progress of the project. Keep them informed by regularly publishing simple, very understandable indicators of the team's progress. Burndown charts and other at-a-glance indicators of project progress are best.

7. **Acknowledge the importance of learning.** Because a project is as much about generating new knowledge as it is about adding new capabilities to a product, plans must be updated to include this new knowledge. As we learn more about our customers' needs, new features are added to the project. As we learn more about the technologies we are using or about how well we are working as a team, we adjust expectations about our rate of progress and our desired approach.

8. **Plan features of the right size.** Functionality that will be added in the near future (within the next few iterations) should be decomposed into relatively small user stories—typically, items that will take one or two days up to no more than ten days. We are best at estimating work that is all within one order of magnitude in size. Working with user stories that fall within these ranges will provide the best combination of effort and accuracy. It will also provide stories that are small enough to be completed during one iteration for most teams. Of course, working with small user stories can become quite an effort on longer projects. To balance this, if you are creating a release plan that will look more than two or three months into the future, either write some larger stories (called *epics*) or estimate the more distant work at the theme level to avoid decomposing large stories into small ones too far in advance.

9. **Prioritize features.** Work on features in the order that optimizes the total value of the project. In addition to the value and cost of features when prioritizing, consider the learning that will occur and the risk that will be reduced by developing a feature. Early elimination of a significant risk can often justify developing a feature early. Similarly, if developing a particular

feature early will allow the team to gain significant knowledge about the product or their effort to develop it, they should consider developing that feature early.

10. **Base estimates and plans on facts.** Whenever possible, ground your estimates and plans in reality. Yes, there may be times in some organizations when it will be necessary to estimate things like velocity with very little basis in fact, and Chapter 16, "Estimating Velocity," presented some valid techniques for doing so. However, whenever possible, estimates and plans should be based on real, observed values. This goes, too, for an estimate of how much of a feature is complete. It's easy to tell when a feature is 0% done (we haven't started it), and it's relatively easy to tell when we're 100% done (all tests pass for all of the product owner's conditions of satisfaction). It's hard to measure anywhere in between—is this task 50% done or 60% done? Because that question is so hard, stick with what you can know: 0% and 100%.

11. **Leave some slack.** Especially when planning an iteration, do not plan on using 100% of every team member's time. Just as a highway experiences gridlock when filled to 100% capacity, so will a development team slow down when every person's time is planned to full capacity.

12. **Coordinate teams through lookahead planning.** On a project involving multiple teams, coordinate their work through rolling lookahead planning. By looking ahead and allocating specific features to specific upcoming iterations, interteam dependencies can be planned and accommodated.

Summary

The purpose of agile planning is to discover iteratively an optimal solution to the overall product development questions of which features with which resources in what timeline. An agile approach to estimating and planning succeeds in finding such a solution because plans are made at different levels and replanning occurs frequently; because plans are based on features rather than tasks; because size is estimated first and then duration is derived from the size estimate; because small stories keep work flowing, and work in process is eliminated at the end of every iteration; because progress is measured at the team, rather than the individual, level; and because uncertainty is acknowledged and planned for.

Discussion Questions

1. Are there other reasons you can think of why agile estimating and planning succeed?

2. Which of the dozen guidelines apply to your current estimation and planning process? Would that process benefit by following the others?

Part VII

A Case Study

Everything has already been said. But in the one chapter of Part VII, I'll say it all again in an entirely different way.

The following chapter is written as fiction but summarizes many of the key points of this book. In it, you will be introduced to a mythical company, Bomb Shelter Studios, as it undertakes its first agile project. Along the way, you will meet

- Allan, a programmer
- Carlos, an agile coach
- Delaney, an analyst
- Frank, a product manager
- Laura, the chief financial officer
- Phil, the chief executive officer
- Prasad, a tester
- Rose, an artist
- Sasha, a programmer

Chapter 23

A Case Study: Bomb Shelter Studios

The flight was a long one, but the conference had been a success. Flights back from the East Coast were always the hardest, but on this flight Frank had upgraded to first class, exchanging some of his frequent-flyer miles for a bit more room and comfort. Reflecting on the week's events, Frank settled into his seat.

As a product manager for Bomb Shelter Studios, Frank knew that the company's latest game, *Deep Black & White*, would do well. It played a game called Go that was extremely popular in Japan, China, and Korea but had only a moderate following in Europe, North America, and the rest of the world. The programmers on his team had come up with artificial intelligence breakthroughs that allowed *Deep Black & White* to play at a level known as 5-dan. This was still far from the 9-dan level of the best professional players, but it was far ahead of where any of Bomb Shelter's competitors were.

Frank was ecstatic that *Deep Black & White* would be released and marketed in Asia through the distribution deal he'd negotiated with a publisher at the conference. The revenue from sales in those markets would really help Bomb Shelter. Frank knew that the additional six months it took to complete *Deep Black & White* had almost been the end of the small, privately held game development company he had co-founded.

From its inauspicious beginnings three years ago, Bomb Shelter Studios had become recognized as a high-end developer of thinking and strategy games. In addition to the newly finished *Deep Black & White*, Bomb Shelter had developed games that played chess, backgammon, reversi, bridge, checkers, mancala, and similar games. Once a game was developed, distribution rights were sold to a publisher that would take care of all production and distribution, allowing Bomb Shelter to focus entirely on developing new games.

While Frank had been at the conference, his analyst and small team back in Santa Barbara had been thinking about the new game, Havannah, that they were nearly ready to start. Because of the problems with *Deep Black & White*—not just the six-month delay, but also finding too many bugs and uncovering some usability issues late—Frank knew that they had to find a different way of planning and developing projects. Sasha, the company's lead architect, researched some ideas the team had. She suggested using what they were calling an "agile process" for the next project. Frank wasn't exactly sure what that meant, but he was sure they needed to do something different. Being six months late on the next game wasn't going to work. Everyone on the team was excited to give an agile process a try, and they all knew what was at stake.

Day 1—Monday Morning

"Good morning, everyone," Frank said as he entered the conference room. It was still a minute before nine, and almost the entire team was already waiting for him. That was a good sign. Even though the team was tired from the final push on *Deep Black & White*, it looked like they were ready to get right back in it for Havannah.

"Good morning, Frank. I saw your email about *Deep Black & White*. That's great news on the distribution deal," said Allan, the C++ programmer who had coded the artificial intelligence engine that let *Deep Black & White* play such a strong game.

"Have a donut, Frank," Sasha said as she pushed the nearly empty box across the table."

"Thanks," Frank said, taking a maple bar from the box.

"Frank, this is Carlos," Sasha said. "Carlos is an experienced agile coach. We've brought him in to help us as we learn to work in this new, agile way."

Frank and Carlos shook hands and exchanged greetings.

"It looks like everyone is here except Rose," Frank said. "Let's go ahead and get started. We can fill her in later. We probably won't talk about the artwork much in this meeting anyway."

"We can't start, Frank," Carlos said. "This is important. We need the *whole team* here. A big part of the benefit we're after from trying an agile process requires everyone to participate. Rose may not have much to say about the artificial intelligence in the move engine. But even so, we need her perspective if we want to plan the best possible game we can."

"She always gets here about five minutes after nine on Monday. She drops Brooke at school on Monday, Wednesday, and Friday. She'll be here," Prasad said, finishing almost exactly as Rose opened the door to the conference room.

"Sorry. Traffic," Rose said, quickly sliding into a chair.

"So, Delaney, you've been doing the product research on Havannah," Frank said to the analyst. "It's been a while since I've thought about that game. I'm sorry to ask, but can you tell me how to play it again?"

"Sure, Frank. First, the board looks like this," Delaney said as she pulled a wooden board from her bag and placed it on the table. The board looked like Figure 23.1. "There are two players who take turns placing a piece on the board. Each player has different colored pieces. Once a piece is played on the board, it can't move."

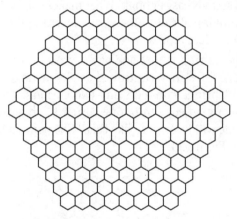

Figure 23.1   An empty Havannah board.

"Just like in *Deep Black & White*," Frank said.

"Right, but unlike in Go, pieces cannot be captured. The goal in Havannah is to be the first player to make a ring, a bridge, or a fork. Whoever does that wins the game."

"And what are rings, bridges, and forks?" Frank asked as Delaney grabbed a handful of pieces and began to arrange them on the board.

"A ring is the simplest. It looks like this," Delaney said as she drew Figure 23.2. "A ring is a set of connecting pieces that encloses one or more points."

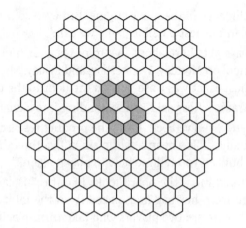

Figure 23.2   A ring.

"OK, that sounds easy enough. What makes this game hard?" said Allan, who was already thinking ahead to the work of writing the artificial intelligence engine that would select moves.

"Remember, a ring is just one of the ways to win. You can also win with a fork or a bridge," Delaney continued as she arranged the pieces as shown in Figure 23.3. "A bridge connects any two corners. The bridge could run in a straight line along an edge from one corner to an adjacent corner. More likely, though, a bridge will look more like this." She pointed to the bridge on the right of the board in Figure 23.3.

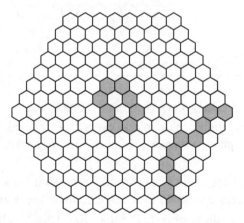

Figure 23.3   A ring and a bridge.

"Does a player have to say which shape he'll be trying to make before the game starts?" Allan asked.

"No, that's part of the fun and part of the challenge. You can start out trying to make a bridge, realize that's not going to work, and maybe try a fork."

"So what's a fork?"

"It's like this, Frank," Delaney said as she added some more pieces to the board, as shown in Figure 23.4. "A fork connects three edges, not corners. Corners aren't edges, so they can't be used in a fork—just in a bridge."

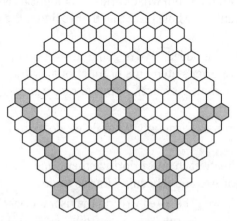

Figure 23.4   The winning shapes in a game of Havannah: a fork, a ring, and a bridge.

"Programming the move engine is going to be a challenge. With so many possible ways to win and so many spaces on the board, the options are tremendous."

"You're right, Allan," Delaney said. "Many people think this game is harder than chess because there are more options and because we can't use a huge end-game book, like we can in chess. In chess, once we get down to a few pieces left, it's possible to use a book of the best moves to play. At that point we don't need to rely on just the move engine to select a move. With Havannah, there are too many pieces and too many positions."

"You didn't want an easy game to program, did you, Allan?" Sasha teased the other programmer.

Allan looked like maybe he did want an easy game to program this time.

"Don't worry. The good news is that because so few people play Havannah right now, we don't need as strong an engine as we did with *Deep Black & White,*" Delaney said, noting the slight look of relief on Allan's face. "We'll want to get there eventually, but we won't need it in version 1.0. A decent engine that beats most humans most of the time will be fine."

"OK, Delaney. Are there any other rules we need to be aware of?" Frank asked.

"No, that's it. The rules are simple, but this game really makes you think. That's why we think it will do well with customers who've bought our other games."

"So, do you have a requirements document written?"

"Not yet, Frank. From what Carlos has taught us about agile software development, we want the whole team together to figure the requirements out collaboratively."

"Right," Carlos added. "We're going to start today's meeting by writing *user stories*. They're brief statements of functionality but told from the user's perspective. For example, *As a user, I want to save a game I'm in the middle of.* Stuff like that."

"That sounds easy enough. What do we do with those once we're done with them?"

"We'll estimate each one, prioritize them, and then figure out the best trade-off between features and schedule," Carlos said.

"So how do we get started writing the user stories?" Frank asked.

"We're going to use these note cards," Carlos said as he tossed a package of cards to each person in the room. "I like to write user stories in this template." Carlos picked up a marker and wrote "As a <user type>, I want to <goal> so that <reason>" on the whiteboard. "Delaney, you've done the most thinking about Havannah; can you get us started?"

"Sure," the analyst said. "Let's start with, *As a player, I can undo a move so that I can take back a big mistake.*"

"Is that our first story?" asked Prasad, the tester.

"Yes, so I'll write it on a note card so we don't forget it," Delaney said as she wrote Story Card 23.1.

As a player, I can undo a move so that I can take back a big mistake.

Story Card 23.1

"Do we estimate that story now?" Allan asked.

"Not yet, Allan. It will be easier if we write a bunch of stories first and then estimate them at the same time," Carlos said.

"My turn. If we've got an undo story, we need a redo story. *As a player, I want to redo a move that I've undone so that I can replay a sequence,*" Frank said.

"Good story, Frank. Write it on a card," Carlos told the product manager.

"Wouldn't it be better if we typed these into a spreadsheet?" Frank asked.

"Perhaps later. But in a meeting like this, it helps to have the physical cards. You'll see," Carlos said. "We can each write any story whenever we think of it. We don't need to wait for whoever is typing."

"And when we get to planning, the cards are even more useful," Sasha added. "We can stack the cards by priority or into what we'll do in each iteration."

Frank began to see some other advantages to using the note cards. He could write additional notes or draw on the cards. He couldn't do that in a spreadsheet. He still hadn't learned much about the team's new "agile process," but he liked what he'd seen so far. With growing enthusiasm, he wrote Story Card 23.2.

As a player, I want to redo a move that I've undone so that I can replay a sequence.

Story Card 23.2

"A good way to get all the stories is to…" Carlos began.

"Do you really mean *all*, Carlos?" Sasha asked the team's new coach.

"Yes. Kind of. I'd like to use this meeting to write as many story cards as we can. Undo and redo are pretty small. We don't need our stories to be that small. In fact, we should probably combine undo and redo."

"OK. I'll do that," Frank said as he wrote Story Card 23.3. "How do we indicate that this card is related to the other two cards? Do we number them?"

"No, just rip up the first two," Carlos said. "We won't need them."

Frank ripped the first two cards in half.

As a player, I'd like to undo and redo moves.

Story Card 23.3

"Carlos, Frank didn't include a reason on the reason card. There's no 'so that.' Is that a problem?" Allan asked.

"Hey, it's only my second story!" Frank mockingly defended himself.

"Actually," Carlos clarified, "we don't always need a 'so that' clause. If it helps make the story more clear, use one. But it's not worth worrying about, especially on a story like this one, where it's obvious why a user would want to do that."

"Carlos, you said we want to write all the stories today, even if some are written at a high level. I assume we can add more later. Right?" asked Rose.

"Absolutely. Ideally we do think of some additional stories later. Otherwise, it means we're not thinking creatively enough about the game. I'd hate to think that we don't come up with some ideas later that are better than the ones we start with today. The purpose of writing 'all' the stories today is so that we're all aware—again, just at a high level—of what features are likely. This especially helps Sasha and Allan as they think about the architecture of the game and even how they'll design the move engine."

"OK. That sounds great, Carlos. Let's keep going. Do we all just start writing cards?"

"We could," Carlos said. "But it works best if we apply some structure to it. Let's talk through what a user may want to do at various times in the game—before a game starts, during the game, and even after the game."

Various nods and comments of agreement came from the rest of the team as Carlos continued: "Right when Havannah loads, what might someone want to do?"

"Start a game."

"Restore a saved game."

"Select the computer's playing strength."

"OK, let's get those written," Carlos said. A few minutes later, the team had produced the stories shown in Table 23.1.

"Carlos," Frank asked, "if these stories are things a player may want to do before the game starts, why do we include *As a player, I want the system to play background music*? Isn't that something the player wants while playing the game, rather than before?"

"We're just brainstorming the user stories," Carlos answered. "We won't keep track of which stories happen before the game starts and which happen during it. I'm just using that approach to help us think through what we need in the game."

"OK. What do we do next?"

"Now we think about what a user might want to do during a game."

The team answered Carlos' question by writing the stories shown in Table 23.2.

Table 23.1 Stories Thought of While Thinking about What Users Want
before a Game Begins

Story Text
As a player, I can start a new game.
As a player, I can restore a saved game.
As a player, I can select the computer's playing strength.
As a player, I'd like to be able to use the system to play against another human on my computer.
As a player, I'd like the appearance of the game to be aesthetically pleasing.
As a player, I'd like to be able to choose between a wooden board and pieces and a metal board and pieces.
As a new player, I want to be able to view an interactive tutorial for the game.
As a player, I want the system to play background music.
As a player, I can select the background music played by the system.

"OK, I suppose we should move on to things that a user may want to do after a game is finished," Frank said.

"There isn't much a player would want to do after a game is over. We didn't think of saving a game earlier, so we can add that," Prasad said.

"A player may also want to go back and annotate moves. *Deep Black & White* supports that," Rose said. "I can put a note on a move like 'I also thought of playing on hexagon A3.'"

"OK, let's get these written as stories," Carlos said, which resulted in Table 23.3.

"What next, Carlos?" Allan asked.

"While you put the finishing touches on *Deep Black & White* over the next two weeks, Delaney is going to do some more product research."

"Yes," Delaney added. "I want to validate with prospective users the features they think are the most important."

"But before we finish today, we should create a high-level estimate for each story," Carlos said.

"OK, let's estimate. But let's take a ten-minute break first, though," Allan said.

Table 23.2 Stories from Thinking about What Users Want to Do during the Game

Story Text
As a player, I want to place a piece on the board using either my keyboard or my mouse.
As a player, I want to see a visual indicator of whose turn it is.
As a player, I'd like a visual indicator of the last piece played (make it blink, perhaps).
As a player, I'd like to undo and redo moves.
As a player, I'd like to ask for a hint sometimes.
As a player, I'd like to be able to save games.
As a player, I want to be able to quit the game.
As a player, I want to restart the game so that I can give up and start over.
As a new player, I want access to an online help system.
As a player, I want all pieces of the winning shape to blink or glow so that I can see the winning shape.
As a new player, I'd like to be warned after making a horrible move and be given the chance to take it back.
As a new player, when it's my turn to play I'd like to be shown any hex I should play in, because if I don't, the computer will play there next and win.
As a player, I'd like the computer to play a move in no more than two seconds on a 2.0GHz PC.

Estimating the User Stories

"What we're going to do," Carlos resumed the meeting, "is estimate each story as a number of story points."

"What's a *story point*?" asked Frank.

"A story point is a unitless estimate of the size and complexity of a story," answered Carlos. "Suppose we decide that saving a game is three points. If we think that restoring a saved game will be the same effort, we'll call it three points. If we think restoring a game will be a little less, we'll call it a two."

"So the numbers don't mean anything?" Frank asked.

Table 23.3 Stories Thought of While Thinking about What Users Want after a Game

Story Text
As a player, I want the system to keep track of how many games I win and lose. (By the playing strength of the computer?)
As a player, I'd like to add annotations to saved games.
As a player, I'd like to step forward through moves so that I can review a game I've already played.
As a player, I can save a game.

"Only relatively. A two is twice a one. An eight is four times a two. Like that. That's all that matters," Carlos clarified. "We're going to estimate by playing planning poker." Carlos handed each person a set of cards with the values 1, 2, 3, 5, and 8 written on them. "The way this works is Delaney will read us one of the story cards. We can talk about it and ask questions. Then we'll each pick one of the cards I just passed out. Those numbers are our estimates. When we've each picked a card, we'll turn them over at the same time. If we all agree, that's the estimate. If not, we'll discuss our estimates and the story for a couple of minutes, and then we'll do it again. We'll keep doing it until we agree on an estimate for the story."

Carlos answered a few questions about the technique and then asked Delaney to read the first story: "*As a player, I can start a new game.*"

"The first story or two are always hard to estimate," Sasha added. "Because we're estimating stories relative to each other, it's hard when there's nothing to compare with. We mostly just need to decide whether this initial story is one of the smaller ones or one of the larger ones we've got. If, after we've estimated four or five stories, we decide we need to change the estimate on this first one, we can."

"What do we mean by this story?" Allan asked. "It's not clear what starting a new game means."

"We wrote this story when we were thinking about what a user might want to do after first starting our software," said Delaney. "We said she'll probably want to start a new game or restore an old game. That's all we meant."

"Does this story include drawing a blank game board and setting things up so that the computer is ready to play a game?" Allan asked.

"I think it does. I don't think the board needs to be pretty for this story. We've got another story about making the screen aesthetically pleasing. But this story does require that we draw the Havannah board on the screen."

Carlos waited a few more seconds to see if there were any more questions. "OK, everyone pick a card with your estimate on it."

"It's a one," said Allan, showing everyone his card.

"Not yet, Allan," Carlos said. "Everyone needs a chance to think about it without seeing anyone else's estimate. Doing it that way prevents any bias." He paused. "It looks like everyone has picked a card. Turn them over."

Cards ranged from Allan's and Rose's ones to a five from Prasad.

"Why a five, Prasad?" Carlos asked.

"I think this story will be one of the larger ones we've got to do," he replied.

"Not even close," argued Allan. "All this story needs is a user interface where a player can choose a Start New Game button and then have it draw a blank Havannah board. The board doesn't have to be pretty, and it doesn't need to let the user place any pieces. We have separate stories for those. This story is easy."

"OK, I hadn't thought of it that way," said Prasad.

After allowing the discussion to continue a little longer, Carlos again asked everyone to select a card representing his or her estimate. Most estimates were now ones, with a two shown by Prasad. Carlos encouraged another short conversation and then asked Prasad if he could support an estimate of one. He said he could, and the first story was estimated at one story point.

"On to our next story," said Delaney, who read, "*As a player, I can restore a saved game.*" After two minutes of discussion about how this story would work, Carlos asked each team member to select a card. There was no consensus on the first round of cards. Sasha argued that this story was twice as big as the first story because it involved setting up a blank Havannah board, reading the saved game from a file, and placing the pieces that had already been played on the board. Convinced by Sasha's arguments, the team agreed on an estimate of two for the story.

"OK, next is *As a player, I can select the computer's playing strength.* Let's estimate that," said Sasha.

"That's the whole move-selection engine," said Allan. "That's going to be hard. Can we skip this one for now and come back to it after we've estimated some of the other big stories?"

"That's OK with me," Sasha said.

"Wait, though," Rose said. "I thought this story was about letting the user pick a playing strength, not about the computer playing at that strength. This is easy; it's just a field or two on the screen."

"That's how I meant the story when I wrote it," Frank said.

"That's fine but then we need a story like, *As a player, I can play against the computer at different playing strengths,*" Rose said.

"Can we split that up, though?" Allan asked. "I think that's going to be hard. How about *As a player, I can play against a weak computer opponent*? And then *As a player, I can play against a strong computer opponent* and a medium computer opponent?"

"Sure. Let's do that," Sasha said. "Let's start with the player selecting the computer's playing strength. Everyone pick one of your planning poker cards. OK? Ready; turn them over." Everyone turned over a one. "That seems reasonable to me. We're saying this is about the same size as *As a player, I can start a new game.*"

There were nods of agreement that the two stories were indeed about the same size.

"Let's move on to the *As a player, I can play against a weak computer opponent* story," Allan suggested, eager to talk about the move-engine stories that he'd probably be the one to program. "How strong does our weak engine need to be?"

"It can't play randomly," Delaney said. "But it doesn't have to be very strong. This game is deceptively hard, and it takes most people a while to figure out what's a good move. But even our weak level needs to know whether it's best to try to make a ring, a bridge, or a fork, based on what the human player is doing."

"OK, let's estimate it," Allan said.

"Wait," Prasad said. "How are we going to test this? It seems like it's going to be really hard to test."

"Good question," Carlos said. "Any ideas?" He looked around the room.

"One way would be to identify a bunch of positions, see what the engine suggests, and ask a good human player if those are decent moves," Rose said.

"That's good. Can we automate that, though?" Delaney asked. "We need to automate the tests so that if the engine starts making weird moves, like *Deep Black & White* did in April, we know about it immediately."

"Absolutely," Prasad answered. "We can have a file that describes a board position and then says how the computer should respond."

"There may not be just one acceptable move," Allan said. "That file should allow us to specify multiple good responses."

"Great answers. We don't need to design that file now, though, as long as we know there are some options. Let's estimate the story," Carlos said.

The room grew quiet as each person thought about all that would be involved in this story. When each had selected a card, they all held them up at the same time.

"Allan, I think you're supposed to hold up only one card, not all of them. Did you have a hard time making up your mind?"

"No, I don't have a card big enough. So I'm holding them all up. All these cards"—the programmer indicated the 1, 2, 3, 5, and 8 cards—"add up to 19. That seems about right."

"I've got some bigger cards—13, 20, 40, and 100," Carlos said. He passed a set of the additional cards to each person. "I was hoping we wouldn't need them, but we might."

"Why were you hoping we wouldn't need these?"

"Considering the stories that we've estimated so far, any story we estimate at 100 story points is not going to fit into a single iteration. It's going to be too big. The same is probably true of the rest of the numbers I just passed out. It's OK for us to have some big stories, and it's perfectly fine for us to estimate them with big values. But we need to remember that we'll have to split them up before working on them so that each fits into an iteration. And we need to remember that estimates of very large features are likely to be less accurate. That's why the ranges get bigger."

"So, Allan, you think this is a nineteen. Really?" Sasha asked while double-checking the eight in her hand.

"Absolutely. First, I need to learn more about this game. The engine is going to need to recognize whether the player is trying to make a ring, bridge, or fork. It's going to have to decide which shape it should try to make. It needs to decide whether a move should be offensive or defensive. Even a first, weak engine is going to take a while."

"Well, you'd know. But nineteen is huge," Sasha said.

"Prasad, why do you think this is a three?" Carlos asked, focusing the discussion on the estimators with the outlying values.

"The testing just doesn't sound hard. I don't think I'll have that much to do. I'll create those text files for the tests, and that's it."

"Sure but we're estimating the full story, not just our own parts of it. Testing may be a three, but Allan's time needs to be in there, too," Carlos explained.

"Oops. Yeah, then, Allan's right," Prasad said. "This one is going to be big."

"Let's see if he's right. Pick up your cards, and re-estimate based on what you just heard," Carlos instructed. He paused a few seconds to make sure everyone had time to think. "Turn them over."

All cards showed twenty this time.

"It looks like you convinced everyone, Allan," Carlos said. "A twenty is probably too big for one story, though. Allan, is there a way to split this story up? Maybe have an even weaker engine the first time? Then improve it before you ship."

"I don't see any good ways," Allan said. He thought for a moment and then continued, "We could have the engine play an offensive move every turn, always trying to make its own pattern, ignoring the human's moves. I don't think that's a good idea, though."

"What if a first engine recognized only rings?" Rose asked. "We could take away bridges and forks—just for now. Allan, couldn't you write an engine that played offensively and defensively but that tried to make—and block—only rings?"

"Absolutely. That could work. So let's split this into three stories—one for each shape."

Everyone agreed, and they estimated the three stories as shown in Table 23.4.

Table 23.4 Three Smaller Stories Split from the Weak-Engine Epic

Story Text	Estimate
As a player, I can play against a weak engine that recognizes rings.	8
As a player, I can play against a weak engine that recognizes bridges.	5
As a player, I can play against a weak engine that recognizes forks.	8

"When those were one story, the estimate was twenty. Now it's twenty-one. Should we take a point off of one story so it's still twenty?" Frank asked.

"No. The estimates are what they are, and they're not meant to be that precise," Carlos answered. "Breaking stories up helps us see more of what's involved. The sum of the estimates doesn't need to equal the estimate of the larger story."

"Allan, what should we do about the medium-strength and strong engines? Do you want one story for each, or do you want to split those up by rings, bridges, and forks as well?"

"One story each. I think that we should define our medium-strength engine as one that never makes an outright blunder," Allan said. "It may not always play the absolute best move, but it never makes an outright mistake. We can test that the way we described, and we can have some good human players test it. As long as it makes moves that they would consider reasonable, it's OK. For the strong engine, we can strengthen that condition and have it play the best move it can find. Based on performance, we can set how far ahead the move engine looks."

"So how do you want to write those as stories?" Frank asked.

"I think *As a player, I can play against a medium-strength engine* is fine," Delaney answered.

"Yes," agreed Carlos. "You can note on the story card that 'Always plays moves a good human player thinks are reasonable' is one of the conditions of satisfaction for that story. That will help you remember what a 'medium-strength engine' is without having to make another story about reasonable moves."

The team discussed this story a bit more, played planning poker, and then agreed to estimate it as eight story points.

"And then we'll have *As a player, I can play against a strong engine* as well, I suppose," Frank said.

"This is at least twice as big as the medium engine," Allan said. "We called that an eight. I don't have a sixteen, though. Do we use thirteen? That's the closest. Or do we make up a sixteen?"

"What you want to do," Carlos said, "is think of the cards as buckets. If this story is a sixteen, it won't fit in a bucket that holds thirteen. We don't want to make up new values because it starts to look too precise. We don't know if this is a thirteen or a sixteen or a nineteen. It's important to remember that these are estimates, not guarantees."

"OK, I think this is two to three times as big as the medium engine," Allan said. "That means it's sixteen to twenty-four. Because twenty-four won't fit in a twenty bucket, should I estimate it as forty? That seems high. It's not five times as big as the medium engine."

"No, I wouldn't," Carlos answered. "They're buckets, but think of the contents as sand, not water. You can overfill it a tiny bit at the top."

"Let's estimate, then," Allan said.

Based on the discussion they'd just heard, no one disagreed with Allan, and everyone held up a twenty.

"So we'll call this story a twenty," Carlos said. "That's OK for now. We'll probably need to find a way to split it into at least two discrete pieces of work later."

"We don't need to break it up into smaller stories, like we did for the weak engine?" Allan asked.

"No, we can do that later, when we're closer to working on that story," Carlos said. "We'll know more then, and there's nothing to gain by splitting it today."

"Good. Let's move on," Delaney suggested. "The next story is *As a player, I'd like to be able to use the system to play against another human on my computer*. This referred to two of us sitting at one computer passing the keyboard or mouse back and forth and making moves. All we want is for the computer to tell us when someone wins."

"The other features we identified still work, though, right?" Prasad asked. "Two human players may want to use undo and redo, or they may want to ask for a hint."

"Sure," Delaney answered.

"I think we should add a story: *As a player, I want the computer to recognize a winning shape*," Allan said.

"Isn't that part of the move-engine stories?"

"Yes, but if we pull it out we could do it separately and that would let us write a human-versus-human version of the game really quickly while we get the move engine working."

There were no objections, and the new story was estimated as two story points.

"Allan, does that lower any of the estimates for the weak move-engine stories?" Frank asked.

"Not really. I would still estimate each the way we have. We could lower the eight-point stories to seven, if you want."

"No, we don't want to do that," Carlos said. "That makes the numbers look too precise. If we want to lower it to a five, we can. Otherwise, let's leave it as an eight."

"No, five is too low," Allan said.

"OK. So we're back to estimating *As a player, I'd like to be able to use the system to play against another human on my computer*."

After two rounds of planning poker they reached agreement to call that story a three.

"Next is *As a player, I'd like the appearance of the game to be aesthetically pleasing*," Delaney read.

"Finally. One of my stories," Rose, the artist, said.

"Yeah, except I don't like the way this story is written," Sasha said. "It's kind of vague, and it's big. I like the next story: *As a player, I'd like to be able to choose between a wooden board and pieces and a metal board and pieces.* What else did we mean by 'aesthetically pleasing'?"

"It had to do with the overall look and feel of the game," Frank answered. "We probably won't have many menus, but we want them to look good. We want the menu items to be in logical places. We want an attractive splash screen when the game loads. The board and pieces are the entire user interface. There will probably be some background art behind the game board. Rose needs time to do that."

"Those are good. Can we split some of those out as separate stories?" Sasha asked.

"We could," Delaney said, "but it might be hard. I think the menu items need to be developed in the context of whatever features introduce the need for a new menu or menu item. Rose, what do you think of having one story for a splash screen and another for background art?"

"Fine with me. Obviously, I'd do them separately anyway."

The team made quick progress through the next set of stories.

"What do we do about this story?" Prasad asked, pointing to a card that read *As a player, I'd like to ask for a hint sometimes.*

"What do you mean?"

"If we've done the move engine, this story is really simple. All you do is ask the move engine to suggest a new move, but for the player instead of the computer. That would be trivial. But if we don't have the move engine written, this story has to be at least as big as writing the whole move engine."

"So we have a dependency that we can do hints only after we've done the move engine," Allan said.

"Yes, but I don't think that's a problem in this case," Sasha said. "Developing the move engine before the hint feature seems like the natural way to program those stories. The dependency won't be in our way. We can ignore it. Or if we're worried about forgetting this dependency, we can note it on the card. Either way, the story can be estimated with the assumption that the move engine exists."

Everyone agreed, and the story was estimated at one story point.

"What would we have done if we really wanted to have hints before the move engine?"

"Sometimes you can't get rid of a dependency and you have to live with it, just like before you started using an agile process," Carlos explained. "Most of the time, however, you can get rid of it. If we wanted to get rid of this dependency, you could write the code that lets a user ask for a hint, displays that hint, and makes the move for the user if she likes it. To get the hint, you would have an object in the system called HintGenerator. Eventually, HintGenerator would call the move engine to get a good hint. But for now, you could have it return either the first open space or a random open space. That way, you'd be done with the hint story before even starting the move engine."

"We'd have to remember to come back later and make HintGenerator actually call the move engine," Allan said.

"Yes," Carlos said. "We could make another story that was something like *As a player, I want to get good hints*, rather than just hints."

"That's probably a one-line change," Allan said. "We'd delete whatever Hint-Generator does to find an empty space and call the move engine instead. We'd have to estimate that as a one, the same as the original story. It doesn't seem like we'd gain anything."

"Ah," Carlos said, "this is where it's sometimes useful for us to have cards that say zero instead of just the numbers we have now. Because we have to come back and hook HintGenerator up to the right code, we want a story card so that we don't forget. On the other hand, it really is so simple that we want to call it a zero."

Carlos gave each person another planning poker card, this time with a zero on it. "I've been holding on to these because I didn't want you to use them before we talked about what a zero-point story would be." Each person now held a deck of cards containing 0, 1, 2, 3, 5, 8, 13, 20, 40, and 100.

"In this case, though, we're going to add support for hints after the move engine is finished, though. Right?" asked Frank.

"Yes, we'll just keep that as a one-point story," Sasha answered.

Estimating continued in this fashion until the team had estimated each of the stories they had written. The stories and their estimates are shown in Table 23.5.

"So where do we go from here? We need one more two-week iteration on *Deep Black & White* before we send it to the publisher," Frank said.

"While everyone else is working on that, I'm going to interview some likely buyers of this game," Delaney said. "I want to see what features are the most important."

"Will that take long?"

"No, I'll be done before the end of the iteration," Delaney said. "Let's meet again in two weeks, right after we ship *Deep Black & White* and after Frank takes us all out to celebrate finishing it."

"Sounds great. I'll get right on that celebration. Are hamburgers OK, Delaney? Or should we splurge for pizza?"

Table 23.5 Estimates for All Stories Written So Far

Story Text	Estimate
As a player, I can start a new game.	1
As a player, I can restore a saved game.	2
As a player, I can select the computer's playing strength.	1
As a player, I can play against a weak engine that recognizes rings.	8
As a player, I can play against a weak engine that recognizes bridges.	5
As a player, I can play against a weak engine that recognizes forks.	8
As a player, I can play against a medium-strength engine.	8
As a player, I can play against a strong engine.	20
As a player, I'd like to be able to use the system to play against another human on my computer.	3
As a player, I want the computer to recognize a winning shape.	2
As a player, I want a nice-looking splash screen when the program starts.	5
As a player, I want nice-looking background art that integrates with the game boards.	5
As a player, I'd like to be able to choose between a wooden board and pieces and a metal board and pieces.	8
As a player, I'd like to ask for a hint sometimes.	1
As a new player, I want to be able to view an interactive tutorial for the game.	8
As a player, I want the system to play background music.	5
As a player, I can select the background music played by the system.	1
As a player, I want to place a piece on the board using either my keyboard or my mouse.	3
As a player, I want to see a visual indicator of whose turn it is.	2
As a player, I'd like a visual indicator of the last piece played (make it blink, perhaps).	2
As a player, I'd like to undo and redo moves.	2
As a player, I'd like to be able to save games.	3

Table 23.5 *Estimates for All Stories Written So Far (Continued)*

Story Text	Estimate
As a player, I want to be able to quit the game.	1
As a player, I want to restart the game so that I can give up and start over.	1
As a new player, I want access to an online help system.	8
As a player, I want all pieces of the winning shape to blink or glow so that I can see the winning shape.	3
As a new player, I'd like to be warned after making a horrible move and be given the chance to take it back.	8
As a new player, when it's my turn to play I'd like to be shown any hex I should play in, because if I don't, the computer will play there next and win.	3
As a player, I'd like the computer to play a move in no more than two seconds on a 2.0GHz PC.	8
As a player, I want the system to keep track of how many games I win and lose. (By the playing strength of the computer?)	3
As a player, I'd like to add annotations to saved games.	3
As a player, I'd like to step forward through moves so that I can review a game I've already played.	5

Preparing for Product Research

In the quiet of the early morning of the next day, Delaney sat at her desk in the team's new open space, preparing the questionnaire she would use to interview prospective game buyers. Frank had asked to meet with her sometime during the day so she could explain to him how she was going to prioritize features. As the product manager, Frank would make the final decisions about what would be in the product, but Delaney knew that he would rely heavily on her research. She wanted to be prepared for meeting with him. By the time Frank arrived, Delaney had nearly finished the questionnaire.

"Good morning, Delaney," Frank greeted the analyst. "Do you still have time to get together this morning?"

"Absolutely. I came in early to finish the questionnaire I want to send. I'd like to show it to you."

"Let's do it," Frank said as he pulled up a chair. "Show me what you've got."

"I printed this about a half-hour ago," Delaney said as she handed Frank the page shown in Table 23.6. "I've added more questions since I printed that. But it's enough to give you an idea of what I'll send."

Table 23.6 The Beginnings of Delaney's Questionnaire

How do you feel if...	I like it that way	I expect it to be that way	I am neutral	I can live with it that way	I dislike it that way
...you can select to play against a fairly weak computer opponent?					
...you can NOT select to play against a fairly weak computer opponent?					
...you can select to play against a medium-strength computer opponent?					
...you can NOT select to play against a medium-strength computer opponent?					
...there is an interactive tutorial that helps you learn how to play?					
...there is NOT an interactive tutorial that helps you learn how to play?					

Frank reviewed the page Delaney had given him and then asked, "You seem to be asking each question twice. Why is that?"

"The first form of the question is called the functional form; the second is the dysfunctional form to indicate it means a feature is not present. Asking these two questions gives us a better understanding than just asking 'How much do you want this feature?' It tells us how the user will feel if the feature is there and how he'll feel if it isn't."

"Can you give me an example of how that might be important?"

"Sure. Suppose we ask, 'How do you feel if you can undo and redo moves?' and a user says that she expects to be able to do that. We then ask her, 'How do you feel if you cannot undo and redo moves?' and she says she would dislike that. That tells us that feature is mandatory for this user. She expects to be able to undo and redo; she dislikes it if she cannot."

"OK, I'm with you so far."

"Now suppose we ask the same user, 'How do you feel if there is an interactive tutorial to help you learn the game?' She likes that idea. We also ask the dysfunctional form of that question, 'How do you feel if there is not an interactive tutorial?' and she says neutral on that. This is what we call an attractive feature, or an *exciter*. We've found a feature that the user didn't expect to get or could live without. But she's told us she'd like the feature. So we've learned this feature isn't mandatory, but because it's one she'd like, she may be willing to pay extra for it."

"But couldn't we get that by asking users to rate the importance of features from one to five, like we did on *Deep Black & White*?" Frank asked.

"Not really," Delaney said. "A single scale like that just tells us how strongly a user values a feature. It doesn't tell us how strongly the user would react to the absence of the feature. I wouldn't prioritize wheels very highly if you asked me about features on a car, but I'd be mad if you took them away."

"Who are you going to give the questionnaire to?"

"I'm going to email about 500 members of some game clubs I know where they play Havannah. Many are in Europe or in the larger U.S. cities. We're offering a coupon for $10 off one of our existing games to anyone who responds. I expect to get fifty or so responses. I'm going to do some phone interviews as well."

"Isn't this going to be a lot of questions for people to answer if you have two questions for each user story?" Frank asked.

"Not really. I can group some of the user stories we identified into *themes*. For example, we've got two user stories about background music. They can be combined into a background music theme. I'll combine the background-art and splash-screen stories into one theme about the game being aesthetically pleasing. Similarly, I'm not going to waste time asking about saving games and restoring games. We know those are mandatory features."

"That's great. I want to make sure this stays lightweight and easy. How will we use the answers you get?"

"I want to separate our features into three categories. First are features we must have. These are cost-of-entry features like saving and restoring games. The second category is features that the more we have of them, the better. I suspect things like playing levels will be in this category. The more playing levels—like strong, medium, and weak—the better. The third category is the exciters. These are features that most users don't expect, but once they see them, they want them. The right mix of features from the latter two categories plus all the necessary must-have features can add up to a compelling product."

Before Frank could respond, Allan rolled his chair next to Frank and Delaney. "Good morning," he said. "I couldn't help but overhear part of that. It sounds really interesting. Will the rest of the team have access to the results of your interviews?"

"Absolutely, Allan."

"Good. You know, I might even want to listen in on one or two of your phone interviews to hear what users have to say. Would that be OK?" Allan asked.

"Absolutely," said Delaney. "Understanding our audience is something the whole team really benefits from. The more that you or the other techies want to be involved in this, the better from my perspective. I'll benefit from your insights, and you'll benefit from hearing what the customers say."

"I agree," Allan said. "I can't do any calls with you today. I need to fix a bug in the scoring engine of *Deep Black & White*. But any other day this week when you're making calls, let me know."

"I'll do that," Delaney said.

"It sounds like you've got a solid plan worked out," Frank said. "This is exciting. Will you still have some results next week?"

"Definitely. The IT group is going to put the questionnaire on our website tomorrow. We could start getting preliminary results any time after that."

"Great. Thanks for showing this to me," Frank said as he got up and excused himself.

Iteration and Release Planning, Round 1

Two weeks after the meeting in which they wrote and estimated user stories, the team again assembled in a conference room adjoining their open workspace. By nine, the whole team was present, even Rose who had begun dropping Brooke at preschool five minutes earlier so that she would be in the office by the time the team started their daily standup meetings.

"We have three goals for today," Carlos began. "First, we're going to plan your initial two-week iteration. After that, Delaney is going to tell us what she found during her product research about what prospective buyers want. Finally, we're going to take an initial very rough guess at what your release plan and schedule may look like. Any questions?"

Sasha waited a few seconds to see whether there were any questions. There weren't.

Planning the First Iteration

"So what should we develop first?" Rose asked.

"I want to get started on the move engine," Allan said. "That's our biggest risk."

"No argument from me," Sasha, the other programmer on the team, said. "Are there things I can do to help, Allan? Normally, all of the artificial intelligence work is yours."

"Yeah, there are things you can do. Thanks," Allan said. "That would help me a lot, because I'm worried about how hard it might be to do the strong engine."

"So let's start with the story *As a player, I can play against a weak engine that recognizes rings*. Isn't that the one you want to do first, Allan?" Delaney asked.

"Yes, it is. The first thing we need to do is code the classes that will keep track of the state of the board, keep track of whose turn it is, and stuff like that. Sasha, you can definitely help there."

"OK. How long do you think it will take? A couple of days?"

"A couple of solid days. Let's say sixteen hours," Allan answered.

"Allan, we want to capture each task on a note card. Write that on a card, and put sixteen in the corner of the card so we don't forget the estimate," Carlos said.

Allan wrote Task Card 23.1.

Code state management classes.

16 hours

Task Card 23.1

"Should I put my initials on it so we remember this is my card?"

"No. It sounds like you'll probably be the one to do it. But it works better if we don't assign work to specific individuals right now."

"I'm going to need to test this," Prasad said. "It shouldn't take long, but this is the first code on this project, and I want to make sure I set it up right. I'm going to say testing will take ten hours."

He wrote Task Card 23.2.

> Write automated tests for state management classes.
>
> 10 hours

Task Card 23.2

"Carlos, you told me earlier I need to break my work up into small pieces," Allan said. "I can't just say that writing the move engine for rings will take two weeks, can I?"

"No, you can't. When we're identifying tasks, we want them to be around one to sixteen hours. Ideally, you should be able to finish one each day, which means the average should be like five or six hours, because we always have a few other things to do each day."

"In that case," Allan said, "the way I plan to write this is to first have a move engine that will be smart enough to play six hexagons in a row to make a ring. There won't be an opponent trying to stop the engine. I'll have the engine start in a random place on the board and figure out how to make a ring in six moves. Next, I'll write it so that it tries to make a ring even if an opponent tries to block the ring. Then I'll switch to the defensive side of rings. I'll have the engine try to block another player that is trying to make a ring. That'll be it for this story for me."

"OK, I wrote a task card that says *Have move engine pursue an unblocked ring*. That's what you said you wanted to do first," Sasha said.

"That'll probably take me most of a day. Put six hours on that card, please," Allan said.

"Allan, no offense, but you are always optimistic at the start of a new engine," Rose, the artist, said.

"Yeah, you're right. You'd better double that," Allan agreed.

Sasha crossed out the six and wrote twelve hours on the card.

Carlos then led the discussion through estimates of the other tasks Allan had identified. "Are there other tasks we haven't identified for this story?" he asked.

"We might want to include some time for testing!" Prasad said. "If Allan can give me code after each of the tasks he identified, I can define and automate tests right along with him. Any bugs I find, he'll hear about while the code is fresh in his mind. I wrote the tasks on cards while Allan was describing how he'll code this, but I haven't estimated them yet. Can we do that together now?"

When they finished discussing the *As a player, I can play against a weak engine that recognizes rings* story, they had written the task cards summarized in Table 23.7.

Table 23.7 Tasks and Estimates for "As a player, I can play against a weak engine that recognizes rings"

Task	Hours
Code state management classes	16
Write automated tests for state management classes	10
Have move engine pursue an unblocked ring	12
Write automated tests for unblocked rings	12
Have move engine pursue a ring even if the human player tries to block it	8
Identify test cases for trying to make a blocked ring	4
Automate test cases for making a blocked ring	4
Have the move engine try to block a human player who is trying to make a ring	12
Identify test cases for blocking a human player making a ring	4
Automate test cases for blocking a human player making a ring	2

"That's about eighty-four hours in this iteration. The work is split across Allan, Sasha, and Prasad," Carlos said. "Based on what I've seen after being here a couple of days, I think you should plan on six hours per day per person of productive work. The rest of each day goes to answering emails, talking to other project teams, your own daily meetings, the half day every other week we'll spend doing this planning, and so on."

"Six seems reasonable to me."

"Me, too. It might be closer to five, but I can try to get six a day on this project and figure out how to make that happen by not doing some of the other little things that chew up my time every day," Sasha said.

"Now that you've split that first story into tasks," Carlos said, "the question you need to ask yourselves is whether you can commit to finishing the story."

"The story or the tasks?" Frank asked. "Which are we committing to?"

"Good question, Frank," Carlos said. "You commit to the story. We identify the tasks as a way of seeing how much work is involved and of helping us make the commitment. Because you're committing to the story, not just the tasks, it's important that you think about this as a whole-team commitment. At the end of the iteration, I don't want Sasha to say she's done with the state management classes but that Allan isn't done. That wouldn't do you any good. You can think about tasks, but you commit to stories."

"Interesting," Frank said. "I like the distinction."

"I can commit to this story," Prasad said. "I've got thirty-six hours of testing tasks. With six hours a day for ten days, I've got sixty hours available."

"And between Allan and me, we have forty-eight hours of tasks. That won't be a problem," Sasha said.

"Great. We've got our first story planned, and we've committed to it," Frank said. "Let's move on to the next most important story."

"Frank, before we do that, let's list everyone's availability for the next two weeks," Carlos said. "We've said we'll assume six hours per day, but is anyone planning any vacation or any time out of the office?"

"I'm taking two days off. I've got a couple of paintings in a show up in San Francisco, so I want to head up there for that," Rose said.

"I'll probably take one day off. Either a Friday or a Monday," said Allan.

"My mom and dad are going to be in town next week. Too much time with them drives me nuts, so I'll be working extra!" Delaney joked.

During this, Carlos had taken the notes shown in Table 23.8 on the whiteboard in the front of the room. "This will help us know how much we can commit to as we identify the next few stories we'll work on," Carlos explained.

Table 23.8 Carlos' Notes on Who Is Planning to Be Gone during the Iteration

Who	Gone
Frank	
Allan	1 day?
Rose	2 days
Sasha	
Prasad	
Delaney	

"Thanks, Carlos," Frank said. "What's the next most important thing to do?"

"I'd really like to have the game play human versus human," Delaney said.

"That's a good step," Allan agreed. "It would make us program the logic that recognizes when the game has been won. We could easily add the undo and redo features while I get a suitable first move engine programmed."

"Let's break *As a player, I'd like to be able to use the system to play against another human on my computer* into tasks," Frank said.

Everyone agreed. When they were done, they had identified the tasks listed in Table 23.9.

Table 23.9 Tasks and Estimates for "As a player, I'd like to be able to use the system to play against another human on my computer"

Task	Hours
Very simple board and graphics	4
Draw empty board	2
Clicking a hexagon adds a new piece of the right color	4
Computer knows when a piece completes a winning pattern	6
Design tests	6
Automate tests	8

"So as a team, can you commit to completing this story in addition to the first one?" Carlos asked.

"Wait—doesn't this story encompass another story we wrote? We have one that says *As a player, I want the computer to recognize a winning shape*. We've included that as part of playing against a human," Prasad said. "Should we remove it?"

"I don't know yet. We included it by accident. Let's see if we can commit to the work we just identified. If we can't, we can remove having the computer recognize winning shapes and let the players decide when a game is over," Delaney said. "What do you think? Can we commit to this story, too?"

"Yes," Allan and Sasha said nearly in unison.

"Seems fine to me," Rose said.

"Barely," Prasad said.

"What are you thinking, Prasad?" Carlos asked the tester.

"Between the two stories, I'm at fifty hours. I know we're saying I've got sixty but that seems high to me. We'll have to see how it goes."

"Keep in mind, testing tasks are not assigned specifically to you, Prasad," Carlos said. "Anyone can do them. If you fall a little behind, others will be expected to pick up testing tasks."

"Absolutely. I usually do some testing," said Rose. "I want to start on some board designs this iteration, but that can wait if I'm needed to test instead."

"Thanks, Rose," Prasad said. "Even without help, I think can commit to this story. But I'm starting to get close to full."

The discussion then turned to the next story, *As a player, I can play against a weak engine that recognizes bridges*. By the time they finished discussing what would be involved in this story and the amount of work involved, the team had identified the tasks and estimates shown in Table 23.10.

Table 23.10   Tasks and Estimates for "As a player, I can play against a weak engine that recognizes bridges"

Task	Hours
Engine can find path from one corner to another (that is, form a bridge)	4
Identify and automate tests for simple bridge design	6
Engine can form a bridge around obstacles	12
Identify tests for forming a bridge around obstacles	6
Automate tests for forming a bridge around obstacles	4
Engine knows when to give up on a particular bridge	8
Identify tests for giving up on a bridge	4
Automate tests for giving up on a bridge	2
Engine tries to prevent a another player from forming a bridge	4
Identify tests for blocking another player from making a bridge	4
Automate tests for blocking another player from making a bridge	4
Engine can choose appropriately between placing a piece that leads to making a bridge and one that leads to making a ring	16
Identify tests for choosing between making a bridge or a ring	6
Automate tests for choosing between making a bridge or a ring	2

"Can we commit to this story, too?" Rose asked.

Frank noticed and appreciated that this was one of the team members asking her peers if they could commit. He liked that so much better than asking them himself, as the product manager, "Can *you* commit?"

"I've been adding these up as we go," Sasha said, rising from her chair. "Here's how I've added them up." She drew Table 23.11.

Table 23.11 Sasha's Summary of Hours for the Three Stories

Story	Programming Hours	Testing Hours	Artwork Hours
As a player, I can play against a weak engine that recognizes rings.	48	36	0
As a player, I'd like to be able to use the system to play against another human on my computer.	12	14	4
As a player, I can play against a weak engine that recognizes bridges.	44	38	0
Total	**104**	**88**	**4**

"I don't know about the rest of you, but I can commit to four hours over the next two weeks," Rose joked.

"With two programmers each getting thirty hours a week and doing a two-week iteration, I think we're OK on the programming side," Sasha said.

"I agree," Allan said.

"I don't feel comfortable taking on any more, though," Sasha said. "And besides, that's too much testing for just Prasad."

"I plan to help with some testing," Rose said.

"Me, too," Delaney said. "I probably can't do any of the automation, but I can help specify good test cases."

"With some help, I'm OK on the testing hours," Prasad said. "I think we can commit to this."

"Everyone OK with it, then?" Frank asked.

Everyone was.

"I'd like to add a few more tasks to the iteration, just to make sure we account for them," Delaney said. "I really need to do a few more player interviews. We haven't talked about my product research yet, but a few things came up that I want to follow up on. Adding twelve hours or so for me of additional product research would be great. I can still spend most of my time on testing, though."

"And I'd like to do some preliminary board and piece drawings so we can get those circulating. It always takes a while to get enough feedback on those. I'd like to draw four board and piece sets at four hours each."

"Those seem reasonable to me," Frank said. "Let's add those."

"So with everything we've listed, are we all comfortable committing to this?" Sasha asked. "It's 224 hours in total now. With five of us on the project—Allan, Prasad, Rose, Delaney, and me—this works out closer to five hours a day. But that's if all the work and each of us is interchangeable. We're not."

"And besides," Carlos said, "you're better off adding something midway through the iteration than dropping something."

Everyone agreed that the level of effort was just right—not too hard, not too soft, just right. Everyone committed that as a team, they would deliver those three stories in two weeks.

"Fantastic," Frank said. "It is great to think that we'll make so much visible progress so quickly. Normally, it takes much longer before we have anything to show."

"Let's take a fifteen-minute break," Carlos said. "When we come back, I want to move on to the second goal for this meeting: release planning. I want to have some initial guess as to how long we think this project will take."

Release Planning

When everyone returned and was seated around the table, Frank began the meeting. "Delaney, tell us about the product research and what you found."

"What I did," Delaney said, "was send out just over 500 email invitations to complete a web-based questionnaire. I also spoke on the phone with thirty-five likely buyers of a game such as this. In total, we got answers from seventy-eight prospective buyers. The purpose of the survey was to find out which features we've identified are mandatory; they just need to be in the game. We also want to learn which features are exciting. They may not need to be in the game, but including a few exciters really makes a game more appealing and may let us charge a higher price for it. Finally, there are some features we call linear. The more of a linear feature present in a product, the more people will pay for it. Examples of linear features are horsepower in a car, the number of channels on satellite TV, and the number of playing levels in a game. I won't explain here exactly how I did the research. But if you're interested, I can point you to a chapter in a book [see Chapter 11, "Prioritizing Desirability"]. I've summarized the results, though, on this page," Delaney concluded as she distributed pages showing Table 23.12.

Table 23.12 Distribution of Results from Surveying Users

Story or Theme	Exciter	Linear	Mandatory	Indifferent	Reverse	Questionable	Category
Weak opponent	8	34	50	4	4	0	Mandatory
Medium opponent	12	34	51	1	1	1	Mandatory
Strong opponent	10	16	39	32	2	1	Indifferent Mandatory
Play another human	5	23	14	58	1	0	Indifferent
Aesthetically pleasing	20	63	24	2	0	1	Linear
Hints, bad-move warnings	47	21	21	0	0	1	Exciter
Interactive tutorial	35	24	21	18	2	0	Exciter
Background music	15	48	21	12	2	2	Linear
Online help	10	42	36	5	3	4	Linear
Winning shape blinks	18	12	55	9	3	3	Mandatory
Statistics	12	28	26	34	0	0	Indifferent
Annotate saved games	14	15	32	36	1	2	Mandatory Indifferent

"Delaney, there are a lot fewer items here than we have stories," Prasad said. "How come?"

"The longer the questionnaire, the lower the response rate," Delaney said. "So I merged stories based on my judgment. For example, 'aesthetically pleasing' in that table covers the three stories we had about nice graphics, a splash screen, and the ability to change the board and pieces between a metal look and a wood look. On the other hand, if I combine too many stories into one question, the answers we get back may not be very useful."

"I can relate the first three columns to your descriptions of the three types of features, Delaney. But what do 'indifferent,' 'reverse,' and 'questionable' mean?" Rose asked.

"Good question. Indifferent is easy; it just means that the person didn't have a strong preference either way," Delaney answered. "Because of how the questions are presented, it's possible for us to not be able to interpret an occasional opinion. For example, this could happen if someone said they dislike background music but that they also dislike it when there's no background music. That happens; people get confused or misinterpret questions when rushing. You'll notice the percentages for reverse and questionable are pretty low."

"Delaney, am I reading this right?" Rose asked. "It says that weak and medium-strength opponents are mandatory. But you've said that a strong opponent is both indifferent and mandatory. How can that be? Why not pick the answer with the highest percentage?"

"Yes, weak and medium opponents are mandatory. The reason we see two spikes in the values for a strong opponent is that we are probably selling into two audiences—those who already play Havannah and are good at it and those who aren't. Those who are good at it consider a strong opponent as mandatory if they're going to buy. Newer players are telling us they'll be happy with a medium-strength player."

"What strikes me, Delaney, is that there aren't many features on this list that your audience considered exciting," Frank said as more question than statement.

"True. But just because there aren't many exciters doesn't mean the product itself won't be exciting," the analyst answered. "Remember that exciters are unexpected features. If I got into a new Porsche, there's probably very little in there that would truly be unexpected. But the car itself would still be very exciting. But I agree with the point I think you were making. We haven't identified all the features this product needs. Every product should have at least one or two exciters—stuff that really makes the user say, 'Wow!' The survey seems to be saying we haven't found that yet. This is why I asked for time in the coming iteration to follow up on this research. I want to have a few open-ended discussions with some of the survey participants. I'm hopeful that will help us find an exciter or two."

"This is great, Delaney. Very helpful," Frank said. "Does anyone have any more questions for her?" Frank paused before continuing. "If not, let's talk about what we need in a release of Havannah."

No one had any additional questions. They immediately plunged into planning the release by prioritizing features.

"Here are the stories I considered mandatory and didn't even bother asking about in the questionnaire," Delaney said as she arranged some story cards on the conference room table. The story cards and estimates she included are shown in Table 23.13.

Table 23.13 Stories Delaney Considered so Obviously Mandatory She Didn't Include Them in the Questionnaire

Story Text	Estimate
As a player, I can start a new game.	1
As a player, I can restore a saved game.	2
As a player, I want the computer to recognize a winning shape.	2
As a player, I want to place a piece on the board using either my keyboard or my mouse.	3
As a player, I want to see a visual indicator of whose turn it is.	2
As a player, I'd like a visual indicator of the last piece played (make it blink, perhaps).	2
As a player, I'd like to undo and redo moves.	2
As a player, I'd like to be able to save games.	3
As a player, I want to be able to quit the game.	1
As a player, I want to restart the game so that I can give up and start over.	1
As a player, I'd like the computer to play a move in no more than two seconds on a 2.0GHz PC.	8
As a player, I'd like to step forward through moves so that I can review a game I've already played.	5
Total	**32**

"None of these stories should be surprising," Delaney continued. "We see these features in every game we make. Supporting them is really the cost of entry."

Delaney grabbed another set of cards. "On this part of the table, I'm going to arrange the stories that our customers told us are mandatory." In that group, she arranged the cards shown in Table 23.14.

Table 23.14 Mandatory Stories Based on Delaney's Initial Research

Story Text	Estimate
As a player, I can select the computer's playing strength.	1
As a player, I can play against a weak engine that recognizes rings.	8
As a player, I can play against a weak engine that recognizes bridges.	5
As a player, I can play against a weak engine that recognizes forks.	8
As a player, I can play against a medium-strength engine.	8
As a player, I can play against a strong engine.	20
As a player, I'd like to be able to use the system to play against another human on my computer.	3
As a player, I want all pieces of the winning shape to blink or glow so that I can see the winning shape.	3
Total	**56**

"Delaney, why do you include the strong engine in there?" Allan asked. "I like that. But according to what you showed us a few minutes ago, it was considered both a mandatory feature and one users were indifferent to."

"Good observation, Allan," Delaney said. "I'm making the recommendation that we consider that feature mandatory because I think many users will outgrow what you're defining as the medium-strength engine. Those users will get bored with the game if we don't include the strong engine."

"OK."

Frank was enjoying this. In his role as product manager and Delaney's as the analyst, the team had often left all the product definition up to them. He liked that they were engaged in these discussions and were attentive to what was being discussed. That could only help the new product.

"The other story I've included as mandatory that is worth discussing is *As a player, I'd like to be able to use the system to play against another human on my computer*. I've included that as mandatory because we've already said it's a good milestone. This next stack," Delaney said as she grabbed another handful of cards, "have linear value. That is, the more of them, the better, but none is mandatory."

Delaney arranged the stories of Table 23.15 on the table.

Table 23.15 Stories That Delaney's Research Indicates Add Value Linearly (the More of Them, the Better)

Story Text	Estimate
As a player, I want a nice-looking splash screen when the program starts.	5
As a player, I want nice-looking background art that integrates with the game boards.	5
As a player, I'd like to be able to choose between a wooden board and pieces and a metal board and pieces.	8
As a player, I want the system to play background music.	5
As a player, I can select the background music played by the system.	1
As a new player, I want access to an online help system.	8
Total	**32**

"Art isn't optional," said Rose. "We need a nice splash screen and attractive boards and backgrounds."

"I didn't say these are optional, Rose," Delaney said. "You're right—we do need these. There is a certain baseline we can't fall below, and the game does need to be aesthetically pleasing, which is how I asked the question on the survey. These are linear, because the more of them, the better. Two board choices are better than one, but three would be even better."

"OK. That makes sense," Frank said. "You've still got some story cards in front of you. What type of stories are those?"

"These next cards are exciters. Likely buyers don't expect any one of these, but we should include a couple because they really boost enjoyment of the game. And like I said earlier, a few exciters means we can charge more for it, too."

Delaney arranged the cards shown in Table 23.16 on the conference room table.

"After the exciters," Delaney went on, "the remaining two stories were ones that prospective players said they are indifferent about. I don't think we want to add these." She placed on the table the cards summarized in Table 23.17. "We're unlikely to sell more games or games at a higher price by adding features that players are indifferent about."

Table 23.16 Exciters According to Delaney's Research

Story Text	Estimate
As a player, I'd like to ask for a hint sometimes.	1
As a new player, I want to be able to view an interactive tutorial for the game.	8
As a new player, I'd like to be warned after making a horrible move and be given the chance to take it back.	8
As a new player, when it's my turn to play I'd like to be shown any hex I should play in, because if I don't, the computer will play there next and win.	3
Total	**20**

"Wow," Frank said. "This is more information than we normally have at this point. Great job, Delaney. You got all this from your surveys?"

"Yes. The questionnaire is intentionally lightweight and just asks users how they'd feel if a feature was present and how they'd feel if it was not present. Because I combined some of our individual user stories into themes, the questionnaire had only twenty-four questions on it. Including some chitchat, it took only about fifteen minutes over the phone. Our website tracked the time it took each respondent to fill out the form. The average time was seven minutes. One person took forty, but I suspect they walked away from it or took a phone call."

"So, Frank, what are our priorities?" Sasha asked.

"Well, we need to do all of the features that Delaney identified as mandatory or that her survey found to be mandatory."

"That's eighty-eight story points, according to our estimates," Sasha said.

"Of the features Delaney said are linear, I agree with Rose: We need nice artwork," Frank said. "All of those stories should be in. And I can't see going without background music. Maybe the user can't change songs, but that's only one point, so for now, I'm going to say we want it. And we need online help. Not everyone who buys this game is going to know how to play it."

Table 23.17 Features That Users Were Indifferent about According to Delaney's Research

Story Text	Estimate
As a player, I want the system to keep track of how many games I win and lose. (By the playing strength of the computer?)	3
As a player, I'd like to add annotations to saved games.	3
Total	**6**

"So you want all of the linear features. That's another thirty-two points," said Sasha.

"I know. I want it all, right? Just like every product manager in the world."

"I don't mind; I just know you want the product out in four months. We're up to 120 story points now."

"Will that take more than four months?" Frank asked, a bit concerned.

"I have no idea yet. Let's figure out what you want, and then we can see how long it will take," Sasha said.

"Fair enough," Frank said. "Of the exciters, I think we need hints, and I'd like the tutorial. Maybe we could drop it or the online help, but I want to plan on both. I like the idea of telling the user when she's made a bad move right after she makes it."

"Remember, that's an eight-point story," Allan reminded everyone. "I'm programming the move engine to find good moves. I can enhance it to find really bad moves, but it's not trivial."

"That's what I'm looking at. Let's plan on going without that for now. But let's include the story about warning the player that she's about to lose unless she plays in a particular hexagon to block the computer."

"That's twelve points from the exciters list. Do you want anything from the indifferent list?" Sasha asked.

"Not really," Frank said. "What's our total now?"

"You've got eighty-eight story points from the mandatory lists, thirty-two from the linear list, and twelve from the exciters. That's a total of 132," Sasha said.

"And you'll do all that in two iterations, right?" Frank asked with a smile.

"If we could, we would."

"Seriously, how do we know how long that will take?"

"The best thing would be to wait three iterations and answer you then," Carlos explained. "After each iteration, we can add up the story points for the stories that are finished. We call that velocity. Velocity will change from iteration to iteration, but its average is relatively stable over time."

"Yes," Allan jumped in, "our estimates may have been off. Or we may get lucky, or unlucky, on a story."

"After three iterations, we should have a good measure of how fast the team is progressing. We can divide the total amount of work remaining by the velocity, and that will tell us how long to expect," Carlos said.

"And that estimate will be pretty good?" Frank asked.

"It should be. After three iterations, you'll have a good feel for how many story points you can do in a two-week iteration," Carlos said.

"We do need to keep in mind that I'm going to talk to some more potential buyers and see if I can find any more exciters," Delaney said. "As we said earlier, our exciters seem weak. We may add some more features."

"Is there any way to get an expected schedule now?"

"Sure, Frank," Carlos said. "You've planned to do four stories in this first iteration. We can add up the points associated with each and call that our planned velocity. We have no idea if it will be, but it's our initial guess."

"I've already done that," Prasad said. "It's eighteen. We get eight points for *As a player, I can play against a weak engine that recognizes rings*. We get five points for *As a player, I can play against a weak engine that recognizes bridges*. Then we get two points for *As a player, I want the computer to recognize a winning shape* and three points for *As a player, I'd like to be able to use the system to play against another human on my computer*."

"How many iterations will the project take if our velocity is eighteen?"

"Just over seven iterations. We've got 132 points. Seven times eighteen is 126. We're six points over seven iterations," Prasad said.

"Can we just call it seven iterations?" Frank asked.

"We could, but we shouldn't," Carlos replied. "I'd prefer to give the estimate as a range. If we're looking at enough work to go into an eighth iteration, we should probably say the project will take six to ten iterations."

"I really don't want this project to take twenty weeks. But you're saying it might take only twelve, right?" Frank asked.

"It might. But it might take twenty." Carlos remained firm. "You can help it avoid taking twenty weeks by removing your lowest-priority features if velocity shows that we're headed toward ten iterations. Keep in mind, too, that Delaney is actively looking for more features. If she comes up with something, we'll have to extend the schedule or take the same amount of current features out."

"OK, I can explain twelve to twenty weeks to the other executives," Frank said. "Let's go with that as our initial plan."

"Frank, I need to reiterate that the best thing to do would be to wait *at least* two weeks, let the team run one iteration, and then base this initial plan off at least one observation of actual velocity," Carlos said.

"Understood. But everyone wants to know at least an idea of what the schedule looks like for this project."

"Make sure they know that we can provide better information every two weeks. Especially after these first three iterations, we should know a lot more," Prasad added.

"So do we need to plan what will be worked on in each iteration?" Frank asked.

"Not really," Carlos answered. "The most important thing is to know what is going to be worked on next. We did that when we planned the iteration. The next most important thing is to know those features at the bottom of the list that may or may not make it into the release."

"I understand why you need to know the top priorities, but why the bottom ones?" Frank said.

"It's not very important for this first meeting, but when we get close to the end of the release, it's sometimes important. For example, we wouldn't want marketing to design packaging that said 'Now with background music' if that's a feature that may get dropped at the last minute."

"OK, but why not spend some time today planning what we'll do in each iteration?"

"No point," Carlos said. "In two weeks, we'll know so much more than we do today. Why plan what we'll do in an iteration until we have to? We don't have to. On a larger project, particularly with multiple teams that need to coordinate work, we might look ahead two or three iterations. But we don't need to do that on this project."

"So are we done with release planning, then?" Frank asked.

"Yes. I'll stack up the story cards you said you really want in the release, and that's our plan," Carlos said. "Before we get together again, two weeks from today, you and Delaney should talk about the stories and identify the ones you'd most like to see in the next iteration. In the meeting, we'll talk about why you want those stories. The others may ask you to reconsider and move in one or two that they want to do because they're risky or because they'll learn a lot by doing them. But the ultimate prioritization decision will be up to you."

"Don't take this the wrong way," Frank said, "but it didn't really feel up to me today."

"It was," Carlos said, "but selecting the right things to work on next is really a whole-team effort. If the programmers were selecting a bunch of technical mumbo-jumbo or features you wouldn't be able to see, I would have stopped that and had them work on other stories. I assume you're happy with the stories that were selected?"

"Ecstatic. It will be great to see all that in two weeks."

Two Weeks Later

"I wish we could have finished everything. Still, I'm impressed with what we've got," Sasha said to the others while waiting for the meeting to begin.

"It's unfortunate that we had to drop the *As a player, I want the computer to recognize a winning shape* story. But I really needed your help on the move-engine code, Sasha. Thanks," Allan thanked the other programmer.

"Not a problem, Allan. We're all in this together, and being able to demonstrate an engine that makes rings and bridges is more important," Sasha said.

"So are we ready for the demo?" Frank asked as he walked into the room promptly at nine. He laid a box of bagels on the large table.

"Absolutely," Sasha said. "Do you know if any of the other executives or other project members are coming to watch the iteration review?"

"I know Phil and Laura said they'd be here," Frank said, referring to the chief executive officer and the chief financial officer.

"And a couple of the engineers on other teams said they'd be here as well. They're curious about our new agile development process," Allan said.

Over the course of the next half-hour, the team showed what they'd completed. They demonstrated the game engine making rings and bridges. They showed how two humans could play against each other, trading the keyboard between them to make moves. They'd even hooked the two pieces of functionality together so that a human could play against the computer. The human usually won, but that wasn't surprising against the easy move engine.

The graphics were rudimentary—just Rose's quick illustrations. But Phil, the CEO, was ecstatic to see that after only two weeks, some small part of the game had been developed and was functional. He was even more pleased when Prasad handed him the keyboard and he was able to play the game himself, barely winning the new game.

"This is fantastic, everyone," Phil announced, rising from his seat. "Every two weeks, you'll show more?"

"Absolutely. Every other week, right here at nine," Sasha said.

"I'll be back next time. I'm going to put these meetings on my schedule. This thirty minutes of seeing the actual software working is more useful than any status report I ever read. And how's your schedule? Can I ask that now?"

"You can," Frank said. "Right now, we're sticking by our estimate of twelve to twenty weeks. We're going to plan the next iteration after this meeting. We'll know more in two to four weeks. At that time, we should be able to commit to a schedule that we can tell publishers about."

"Great," Phil replied. He and Laura left the conference room. So did the half-dozen others who had come to see the project.

Planning the Second Iteration

"If I recall correctly," Frank said, "we planned a velocity of eighteen story points."

"Correct," said Delaney.

"But we couldn't finish the story about recognizing when the game had been won. So our velocity is less than eighteen. Do we give ourselves one point for doing half of that story?" Frank asked.

"No," Carlos said. "In general, we want to apply an all-or-nothing approach to the story points. It's too hard to give ourselves partial credit, because we really don't know how much work is left. Rather than guessing, we don't get any credit until we get it all."

"So our velocity was sixteen, because we originally estimated the unfinished story as two points," Rose said.

"We have to plan on the project taking longer. Right?" Frank asked.

"We're still within the twelve to twenty weeks you told the executives," Sasha said. "We started with 132 story points. We finished 16, so we have 116 left. Dividing 116 by 16, our velocity, gives us 7.25. To be safe, let's call that eight more two-week iterations. Including the two weeks we just spent, that's a total of eighteen weeks."

"That's two weeks longer than four months, Frank. Does that matter?" Prasad asked.

"Not really. The release isn't tied to any specific date. We just want it out as soon as possible," Frank said. "I haven't had a chance to tell you this yet: We still haven't finalized the contract for *Deep Black & White* with the Japanese publisher. They still want to publish the game. And we're *this close* to signing the final contract." He held his fingers millimeters apart. "But they don't want to release it until they have time to gear up a big marketing campaign, with ads in all the major magazines. That's probably four months. And the way that works, we won't see any royalties until the quarter after the game is released. We could be looking at eight months before *Deep Black & White* brings any real money in the door. Ideally, Havannah could be a quick win for us. Not on the scale of *Deep Black & White*. But because it won't need the marketing ramp-up, the revenue will be more immediate."

"And Frank, I'm sorry, but because I had to do more testing than I expected, I didn't do much product research during this iteration," Delaney said.

"OK. That's fine, but let's make that a priority this time, even if it means you test less," Frank said.

"So Frank, what would you most like to see finished in this next iteration?"

The team planned their second iteration in the same way that they'd planned their first. When they finished, they had committed to completing the user stories shown in Table 23.18.

Table 23.18 User Stories Planned for the Second Iteration

Story Text	Estimate
As a player, I want the computer to recognize a winning shape.	2
As a player, I can play against a weak engine that recognizes forks.	8
As a player, I'd like to be able to choose between a wooden board and pieces and a metal board and pieces.	8
Total	**18**

"So if our velocity was sixteen in the last iteration, why are we planning for eighteen this time?" Frank asked.

"We use velocity as a guide for measuring progress against the release plan," Carlos said. "We don't automatically plan each new iteration to have exactly the velocity of the last iteration or the average velocity of the last few iterations. We plan each iteration based on how much work we can commit to. We add up the points only after we've figured out what we can commit to. When we do, the velocity should be somewhere close to our historical average, but it will vary."

"Why?"

"Two primary reasons," Sasha began. "First, we're making more effective use of Rose this time. She's primarily an artist, not a tester. It was great that she helped with so much testing last time, but this time, she's going to draw the art for the wooden and metal boards and pieces. I'll do the coding to let a user choose between them, and Prasad will probably be the one to test that story. But other than that, most of that eight-point story comes from Rose. Second, we've got a bit of a head start on the story about recognizing a winning shape. We started it last iteration but didn't get far. I feel pretty good about the stories we selected. Even though it's eighteen points again, it added up to fifteen total hours less than the last iteration."

"I'm convinced," Frank said. "Let's do it."

Two Weeks Later

At the next iteration review, the team again demonstrated good progress. They had completed each of the stories they'd planned. And Delaney had time to complete her product research. The executives, Phil and Laura, attended again. Because the news had spread about how much had been accomplished in their first two weeks, even more people from other teams attended the second review.

"The game is coming together. I can't believe your move engine can already beat me," Phil said. "And Rose, those first two boards look fantastic. Are we still looking at the same schedule? That would be eight to sixteen weeks from now."

"Our rate of progress is right about where we expected it to be," Frank said. "So we're good there. Delaney did some more product research during this iteration, and she's found some interesting features we may need to include. I'll make the call on that, but I need to hear the team's view first. I may suggest changing the schedule. We're confident the new features will bring in more money. Now I need to weigh that against the extra development cost and the extra time."

"I like the part about bringing in more revenue," Laura, the chief financial officer, said.

"Me, too," Phil agreed. "But I'm not wild about a possible slip already."

"It wouldn't be a slip, Phil," Frank said. "If you want to deliver the product in the originally planned twelve to twenty weeks, we're feeling pretty good about that. What we're going to discuss after this meeting is how much longer it would take to create a more valuable game. And then we'll see if there are features we can drop that would get us that more valuable game in close to the same twenty weeks we gave as our upper end."

"I'm always interested in more valuable games. Let me know what you recommend," Phil said as he stood and left the conference room. The rest of the guests left as well, leaving only the project team.

Revising the Release Plan

"Frank has already told you that I found some new exciters," Delaney said. "A couple of you heard me talking on the phone with potential buyers about these. The good news is that our target audience really wants two features we haven't thought about. First, they want the computer player to have different personalities who each play the game differently. One character may be very aggressive; another, conservative. A character that a lot of people asked for is one who taunts them. It says mean things after a bad move, laughs at them when they lose...stuff like that."

"That does sound fun," Allan said. "It'll change the move engine, but probably not much. It's already configurable to allow me to tune it for more aggressive or more conservative play."

"That's the first new feature," Delaney continued. "The second is online play. People want to play this game online against other humans."

"That's huge," Sasha said. "We'd need to get space in a data center, acquire the hardware, and hire the staff."

"We could partner for all that," Frank said. "It's not out of the question, but you're right that's it's big. Delaney, do you have any sense of which feature is more important?"

"The characters. Good characters would be a big exciter. That is a feature that people really like but that they don't expect," Delaney said.

"Delaney, you just told us that we've got scope creep. And we were already at the upper end of our twelve- to twenty-week estimate," Prasad said. "Why did you say you have 'good news'? Do you have something else to tell us?"

"No, that's it, Prasad," Delaney said. "But this is good news. We just found two new features that could help us sell more units, and at a higher price. Yeah, if we do them, the schedule will change. But that's a good problem to have. We can ship the product based on today's schedule and make a certain amount of money. Or we can change the schedule and plan on making more money. Plans are always point-in-time predictions. We just found a better future to aim at. I've already written the user stories for both features. We should estimate them and decide if we want to change the plan to include either or both."

"Let's do it," said Frank. "I'm completely willing to change the date of the project if we can make enough more money and it's not a big delay. It sounds like these features could be very lucrative."

"But Delaney, why didn't the questionnaire you sent out identify these features?" Prasad said.

"Questionnaires are good for prioritizing what we already know," Delaney said. "They obviously aren't good for discovering features we don't know about. Some of the questionnaires we got back did mention characters and online play, but not enough that I thought there was a trend. I spent this past iteration talking to more likely buyers to confirm that these are good ideas and adjusting my financial models to show how much more revenue these features are likely to bring in."

"I like the sound of that," Allan said. "If the game makes more money, maybe Frank will take us somewhere more expensive than Fatburger to celebrate this release."

"I liked burgers to celebrate the release of *Deep Black & White*," Prasad said.

"Not me. After this one, I say Frank springs for sushi," Rose said.

The team estimated the new stories Delaney had written. In doing so, they split some of her original stories and combined others. When they were done, the stories for online play added to thirty story points. They estimated creating the first character as fifteen story points. Each character after that would be five additional points. The team discussed it and agreed that five characters would be a reasonable number. This meant an additional thirty-five story points for developing the characters.

Because Delaney's financial forecasts showed that characters were likely to generate more revenue than online play, everyone agreed that they should adjust their plan to include characters but not to include an online version.

"In the first two iterations we finished sixteen and then eighteen points. We just added thirty-five points. We're going backward!" Allan joked.

"You're right, Allan," Carlos said as he reached for a calculator. "We've got 133 points. With our current average velocity of 17 points per iteration, that's 7.8 more iterations."

"Eight more iterations, plus the two we've already done, and we finish in ten iterations," Frank said.

"It's cutting it awfully close, Frank," Sasha said. "Yes, it seems like we'll finish in ten iterations. It's a good thing our original schedule was a range and that we didn't just tell people 'eight iterations.' However, if anything goes wrong—if a story is bigger than we think, or if we slow down, or if someone gets sick—we could take longer than eight more iterations."

"Are you saying we should change the schedule?" Frank asked.

"Not necessarily," Carlos answered. "If we want to keep the schedule at ten iterations, though, we should make sure we're willing to drop some low-priority stories if we start to run out of time. If you're not willing to do that, we should convey the expectation that it may take longer than ten iterations."

"I can probably drop a few stories, if necessary," Frank said.

"Good. Remember how I told you it's important to know the stories at the top of your priority list and those at the bottom? This is a time when it's important to know those at the bottom. I'll feel more comfortable keeping expectations at no more than ten iterations if you can point out at least seventeen points of stories that you could live without if it meant going longer than ten iterations," Carlos said.

"Here are a couple I could live without: *As a new player, I'd like to be warned after making a horrible move and be given the chance to take it back* and *As a new player, I want to be able to view an interactive tutorial for the game*. Each of those is eight points. I've already said I could live without the six points of background-music stories."

"So you should work on those last. If you start to run out of time by the tenth iteration, drop one or more of those," Carlos said.

"And if we're on schedule and choose not to implement those stories, we could release at least an iteration sooner, right? When would we release if we left out those stories?" Frank asked.

"We've got 133 points planned. You're willing to drop twenty-two points. That gives us 111," Carlos said as he reached for the calculator. "With a velocity of seventeen, you need seven more iterations. You could be done in eighteen instead of 20 weeks."

"Let's keep those stories in the plan for now. I'll drop them if we need to, but they're probably worth two additional weeks," Frank said. "I want to go run the new plan by Phil, because he asked to hear what we decided. Does anyone want to join me?"

Delaney and Allan both said they did. It wasn't a surprise that Delaney did. As the analyst, Delaney was often involved in product and schedule decisions. Frank was surprised by Allan's interest, though. Normally, Allan, one of the most hard-core technical people in all of Bomb Shelter, wanted nothing to do with business discussions. He'd really engaged in those discussions, though, since starting this project four weeks ago. Frank appreciated that. It was leading to better product decisions all around.

"I'm going up there now," Frank said. "Let's do it."

"Shouldn't we prepare anything for Phil first?" Allan asked.

"Nope. He's got a whiteboard. We'll just draw on that."

Presenting the Revised Plan to Phil

"Hi, Phil. Do you still want to hear what we've decided about those new features in Havannah?" Frank asked.

"Absolutely. These are the features Delaney mentioned this morning?"

"Yes."

"I've got about fifteen minutes now. Will that work?"

"It should be plenty," Frank said. He then asked Delaney to explain how her research had led to the discovery of the new ideas for online play and characters.

"Phil, do you remember a few weeks ago when I told you how we are estimating in story points?"

"Sure."

"And that story points are a measure of size. We started out with 132 story points. In the first iteration, we finished sixteen. In the second, we finished eighteen. Allan, can you draw that?" Frank asked, pointing to an empty space on Phil's whiteboard. Allan went to the whiteboard and drew Figure 23.5.

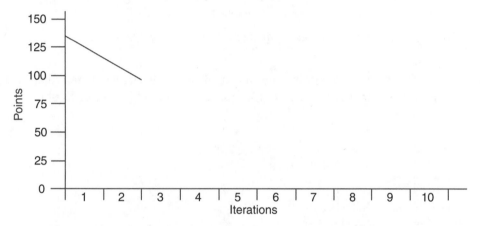

Figure 23.5   The Havannah release burndown after the first two iterations.

"What you see here," Frank continued, "is what we call a release burndown chart. From looking at it, you can see our rate of progress. After two iterations, we're down thirty-four points. If you extended a trend line from this data you'd see that we are on pace to finish during the eighth iteration. That's sixteen weeks total."

While Frank was speaking, Allan drew the trend line shown in Figure 23.6.

"The whole Havannah team thinks that adding the characters Delaney identified is a good idea."

"How long will that take?" Phil asked.

"We think we need five characters. It's a total of thirty-five points," Frank said.

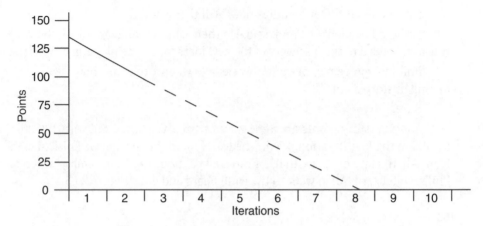

Figure 23.6 A trend line based on the burndown of the first two iterations.

"That means that our burndown actually moves back up to here," Allan said. He drew a vertical line up to 133 points on the whiteboard, as shown in Figure 23.7.

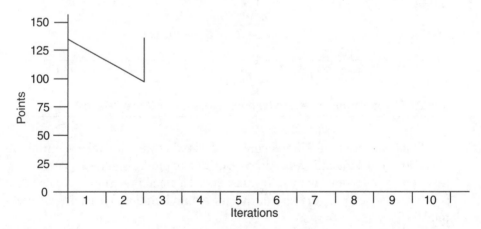

Figure 23.7 The Havannah release burndown with the character features included.

"Hmm. That doesn't look so good. After two iterations, you're no better off than where you started."

"We're actually much better off. We've made four good weeks of progress," Allan said, pointing to the progress on the chart. "We've eliminated some of the riskiest parts of the project, because I've demonstrated how I'm pursuing the move engine. I've only done the weak game engine, but I'm starting to see how we'll write the strong engine. We've also learned a lot. We learned about a new feature that Delaney says is 'exciting' to our target audience. Normally, we'd find that out much later. If I look at where we're at, yes, we still have as much work to do as we thought four weeks ago, but now I'm more confident in the plan than I was four weeks ago. And every time we put a new data point on this burndown chart, I get more confident, even if not every new point is good news. It will be news I can trust about the progress we're making." Allan paused. "We're much better off than we were four weeks ago."

"So how long will the project take if we add the characters?" Phil asked. Frank was surprised, but pleasantly, that the question had been directed at Allan.

"Probably eight more iterations, or a total of twenty weeks. We're completing seventeen points of work per iteration. We call that our velocity. If we draw a trendline showing seventeen points of progress per iteration, we finish in eight more iterations." Allan drew the trend line shown in Figure 23.8. "That cuts it pretty close, so we've identified a few low-priority pieces we could drop if we start to get behind or if we decide to release after eighteen weeks instead of twenty."

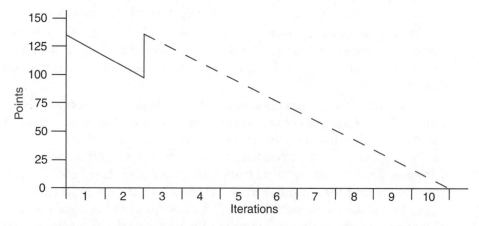

Figure 23.8   An updated burndown chart showing the predicted completion of Havannah.

"And the game would sell more or be at a higher price?" Phil asked.

"Yes, I'm certain of that," Frank said. "I want to do a bit more research and modeling to determine if we should sell more copies at the current price or if we should increase the price by $5."

"I'm sold. Thanks for showing this to me," Phil said.

Allan started to erase the chart he'd drawn.

"Don't. Leave it there," Phil said. "I want to update that every two weeks."

"Thanks for your time, Phil," Frank said as he, Delaney, and Allan left the office.

Eighteen Weeks Later

"Great job, team. The game looks wonderful," Frank said at the end of the final iteration review meeting. "I don't see anything that's missing. The engines play very well. And Rose, I love the characters. The way that each character is tied to an engine is great. Players will select a character to play against rather than a level to play at. I admit I was skeptical of cartoonish characters rather than real characters at first, but they're great. I like how the pirate taunts the player and how you hooked a friendly mermaid to the easy move engine. Her dialogue is definitely going to help new players learn the game. I think we're ready to ship."

"I admit the game is great, but I still don't like the feeling that we're late. We originally thought we'd be done in just over fourteen weeks. But we told everyone twelve to twenty. Now we've slipped two weeks past that," Prasad said.

"Yes, and here we are done in twenty-two weeks," Sasha said. "We never said we'd be done in fourteen weeks. After the first iteration planning, we told everyone twelve to twenty weeks and that a more accurate estimate would come after six weeks."

"And Prasad, keep in mind that we could have shipped two weeks ago if we'd wanted," Frank said. "We chose to take time to incorporate additional changes into the characters based on the positive responses we were getting from beta testers. They loved the characters but gave us some great suggestions we wanted to incorporate. We made the pirate taunt a little more often, based on their feedback. And we gave the rap singer more dialogue. Sure, the initial schedule was wrong, but so was the product design. That game wouldn't have made us anywhere near the return that this one will. You've played the new version. You know how much better it is now, only two weeks off our initial high-end estimate. If we could have released a version 1.0 without characters and then added characters later, I would have done that. But we can't do that in our industry. I'm ecstatic with the product. It's more than we expected and only two weeks later than an estimate given at the start of the project."

"And don't forget *Deep Black & White* was six months late, not two weeks."

"So Frank, are you buying us burgers again to celebrate this release?"

"No, this time I'm buying whatever you want."

Reference List

Abdel-Hamid, Tarek K. 1993. Adapting, Correcting, and Perfecting Software Estimates: A Maintenance Metaphor. *IEEE Computer* 26(3):20–29.

Ambler, Scott W. 2004. Less Is More. *Software Development*, November.

Anderson, David. 2004. *Agile Management for Software Engineering: Applying the Theory of Constraints for Business Results.* Prentice Hall.

Andrea, Jennitta. 2003. An Agile Request For Proposal (RFP) Process. *Agile Development Conference.*

Armour, Phillip. 2002. Ten Unmyths of Project Estimation. *Communications of the ACM* 45, no. 11:15–18.

Baker, Simon. 2004. Email to agileplanning@yahoogroups.com on November 3, 2004.

Ballard, Glenn, and Gregory A. Howell. 2003. An Update on Last Planner. *Proceedings of the 11th Annual Conference of the International Group for Lean Construction*, pp. 1–13.

Beck, Kent. 2002. *Test Driven Development: By Example.* Addison-Wesley.

Beck, Kent, and Martin Fowler. 2000. *Planning Extreme Programming.* Addison-Wesley.

Beck, Kent, et al. 2001. Manifesto for Agile Software Development, www.agilemanifesto.org.

Bentley, Jon. 1999. The Back of the Envelope. *IEEE Software* 16(5):121–125.

Bills, Mark. 2004a. ROI: Bad Practice, Poor Results. *Cutter IT Journal* 17(8):10–15.

———. 2004b. Useful Back-of-the-Envelope Calculations. *Cutter IT E-Mail Advisor*, October 27.

Boehm, Barry. 1981. *Software Engineering Economics*. Prentice Hall.

———. 2002. Get Ready for Agile Methods, with Care. *IEEE Computer*, 35(1):64–69.

Boehm, Barry, and Richard E. Fairley. 2000. Software Estimation Perspectives. *IEEE Software* 17(6):22–26.

Bossi, Piergiuliano. 2003. Using Actual Time: Learning How to Estimate. In *Extreme Programming and Agile Processes in Software Engineering: 4th International Conference*, edited by Michele Marchesi and Giancarlo Succi.

Bossi, Piergiuliano and Francesco Cirillo. 2001. Repo Margining System: Applying XP in the Financial Industry. Proceedings of the 2nd International Conference on Extreme Programming and Flexible Processes in Software Engineering (XP2001).

Brenner, Lyle A., Derek J. Koehler, and Amos Tversky. 1996. On the Evaluation of One-sided Evidence. *Journal of Behavioral Decision Making* 9:59–70.

Brooks, Fred. 1975. *The Mythical Man Month: Essays on Software Engineering*. Addison-Wesley.

Center for Quality of Management. Special Issue on Kano's Methods for Understanding Customer-defined Quality. *Center for Quality of Management Journal* 2(4).

Cirillo, Francesco. 2005. Tracking the Project with the Pomodoro. Unpublished article.

Clark, Kim B., and Steven C. Wheelwright. 1993. *Managing New Product and Process Development: Text and Cases*. The Free Press.

Cockburn, Alistair. 2002. Agile Software Development Joins the "Would-Be" Crowd. *Cutter IT Journal* 15(1).

Cohn, Mike. 2004. *User Stories Applied: For Agile Software Development*. Addison-Wesley.

Constantine, Larry L., and Lucy A. D. Lockwood. 1999. *Software for Use: A Practical Guide to the Models and Methods of Usage-Centered Design*. Addison-Wesley.

DeGrace, Peter, and Leslie Stahl. 1990. *Wicked Problems, Righteous Solutions: A Catolog of Modern Engineering Paradigms*. Prentice Hall.

DeLuca, Jeff. 2002. *FDD Implementations*. www.nebulon.com/articles/fdd/fddimplementations.html.

DeMarco, Tom, and Timothy Lister. 2003. *Waltzing with Bears: Managing Risk on Software Projects*. Artech House.

Duggan, Jim, Jason Byrne, and Gerald J. Lyons. 2004. A Task Allocation Optimizer for Software Construction. *IEEE Software* 21(3):76–82.

Ganssle, Jack. 2004. The Middle Way. *Embedded Systems Programming*, October 14.

van Genuchten, Michiel. 1991. Why Is Software Late? An Empirical Study of Reasons for Delay in Software Development. *IEEE Transactions on Software Engineering* 17(6):582–590.

Gilb, Tom. 1988. *Principles of Software Engineering Management*. Addison-Wesley.

Githens, Greg. 1998. Rolling Wave Project Planning. *Proceedings of the 29th Annual Project Management Institute 1998 Seminars and Symposium.*

Goldratt, Eliyahu M. 1990. *What Is This Thing Called Theory of Constraints and How Should It Be Implemented?* North River Press.

———. 1992. *The Goal: A Process of Ongoing Improvement,* 2nd rev. ed. North River Press.

———. 1997. *Critical Chain.* North River Press.

———. 2000. *Necessary But Not Sufficient.* North River Press.

Grenning, James. 2002. Planning Poker, www.objectmentor.com/resources/articles/PlanningPoker.zip.

Griffin, Abbie, and John R. Hauser. 1993. The Voice of the Customer. *Marketing Science* 12(1):1–27.

Hagafors, R., and B. Brehmer. 1983. Does Having to Justify One's Decisions Change the Nature of the Decision Process? *Organizational Behavior and Human Performance* 31:223–232.

Highsmith, Jim. 2004a. *Agile Project Management: Creating Innovative Products.* Addison Wesley.

Highsmith, Jim. 2004b. Email to agilemanagement@yahoogroups.com on February 16, 2004.

Hobbs, Charles. 1987. *Time Power.* Harper & Row Publishers.

Hoest, Martin, and Claes Wohlin. 1998. An Experimental Study of Individual Subjective Effort Estimations and Combinations of the Estimates. *Proceed-*

ings of the 20th International Conference on Software Engineering, pp. 332–339.

Hunt, Andrew, and David Thomas. 1999. *The Pragmatic Programmer: From Journeyman to Master*. Addison-Wesley.

Jeffries, Ron. 2004. Email to extremeprogramming@yahoogroups.com on July 1, 2004.

Jeffries, Ron, Ann Anderson, and Chet Hendrickson. 2001. *Extreme Programming Installed*. Addison-Wesley.

Johnson, Jim. 2002. Keynote speech at Third International Conference on Extreme Programming.

Johnson, Philip M., Carleton A. Moore, Joseph A. Dane, and Robert S. Brewer. 2000. Empirically Guided Software Effort Estimation. *IEEE Software* 17(6):51–56.

Jørgensen, Magne. 2004. A Review of Studies on Expert Estimation of Software Development Effort. *Journal of Systems and Software* 70(1–2):37–60.

Jørgensen, Magne, and Kjetil Moløkken. 2002. Combination of Software Development Effort Prediction Intervals: Why, When and How? *Fourteenth IEEE Conference on Software Engineering and Knowledge Engineering*.

Keen, Jack M., and Bonnie Digrius. 2003. *Making Technology Investments Profitable: ROI Roadmap to Better Business Cases*. John Wiley & Sons.

Kennedy, Michael N. 2003. *Product Development for the Lean Enterprise: Why Toyota's System Is Four Times More Productive and How You Can Implement It*. The Oaklea Press.

Kernighan, Brian, and Plauger, P. J. 1974. *The Elements of Programming Style*. McGraw-Hill.

Larson, Carl E., and Frank M. J. LaFasto. 1989. *Teamwork: What Must Go Right / What Can Go Wrong*. SAGE Publications.

Laufer, Alexander. 1996. *Simultaneous Management: Managing Projects in a Dynamic Environment*. American Management Association.

Leach, Lawrence P. 2000. *Critical Chain Project Management*. Artech House.

Lederer, Albert L., and Jayesh Prasad. 1992. Nine Management Guidelines for Better Cost Estimating. *Communications of the ACM* 35(2):51–59.

———. 1998. A Causal Model for Software Cost Estimating Error. *IEEE Transactions on Software Engineering* 24(2):137–148.

McClelland, Bill. 2004. Buffer Management. *The TOC Times*, February.

McConnell, Steve. 1998. *Software Project Survival Guide*. Microsoft Press.

Macomber, Hal. 2004. Achieving Change in Construction Is a Matter of Mental Models. *Reforming Project Management* 3(35): August 29.

Malotaux, Niels. 2004. Evolutionary Project Management Methods. www.malotaux.nl/nrm/pdf/MxEvo.pdf.

Martin, Robert C. 2004. PERT: Precursor to Agility. *Software Development*, February.

Miranda, Eduardo. 2001. Improving Subjective Estimates Using Paired Comparisons. *IEEE Software* 18(1):87–91.

Mugridge, Rick, and Ward Cunningham. 2005. *FIT for Developing Software: Framework for Integrated Tests.* Prentice Hall.

Nejmeh, Brian A., and Ian Thomas. 2002. Business-Driven Product Planning Using Feature Vectors and Increments. *IEEE Software* 34(6):34–42.

Newbold, Robert C. 1998. *Project Management in the Fast Lane: Applying the Theory of Constraints.* St. Lucie Press.

Parkinson, Cyril Northcote. 1958. *Parkinson's Law: The Pursuit of Progress.* John Murray.

Poppendieck, Mary and Tom. 2003. *Lean Software Development: An Agile Toolkit.* Addison-Wesley.

Poppendieck, Mary. 2003. Lean Development and the Predictability Paradox. *Agile Software Development and Project Management Executive Report* 4(8). Cutter Consortium.

Putnam, Lawrence H., and Ware Myers. 1997. How Solved Is the Cost Estimation Problem? *IEEE Software* 14(6):105–107.

Rakitin, Steven R. Creating Accurate Estimates and Realistic Schedules. *Software Quality Professional* 4(2):30–36.

Reinertsen, Donald. G. 1997. *Managing the Design Factory: A Product Developers's Toolkit.* Free Press.

Rising, Linda. 2002. Agile Meetings. *Software Testing and Quality Engineering* 4(3):42–46.

Saaty, Thomas. 1996. *Multicriteria Decision Making: The Analytic Hierarchy Process.* RWS Publications.

Sanders, G. S. 1984. Self Presentation and Drive in Social Facilitation. *Journal of Experimental Social Psychology* 20(4):312–322.

Sauerwein, Elmar, Franz Bailom, Kurt Matzler, and Hans H. Hinterhuber. 1996. The Kano Model: How to Delight Your Customers. *International Working Seminar on Production Economics* 313–327.

Schwaber, Ken, and Mike Beedle. 2002. *Agile Software Development with Scrum.* Prentice Hall.

Smith, Preston G., and Donald G. Reinertsen. 1997. *Developing Products in Half the Time: New Rules, New Tools,* 2nd ed. Wiley.

Standish Group International, Inc., The. 2001. *Extreme Chaos.* www.standishgroup.com/sample_research/PDFpages/extreme_chaos.pdf.

Takeuchi, Hirotaka, and Ikujiro Nonaka. 1986. The New New Product Development Game. *Harvard Business Review,* January.

Tockey, Steve. 2004. *Return on Software: Maximizing the Return on Your Software Investment.* Addison-Wesley.

Van Schooenderwoert, Nancy J. 2004. Interview with Ward Cunningham and Scott Densmore. *Agile Times* 6:61–69.

Vicinanza, S., T. Mukhopadhyay, and M. J. Prietula. 1991. Software Effort Estimation: An Exploratory Study of Expert Performance. *Information Systems Research* 2(4):243–262.

Weinberg, Gerald M., and E. L. Schulman. 1974. Goals and Performance in Computer Programming. *Human Factors* 16(1):70–77.

Wiegers, Karl. 1999. First Things First: Prioritizing Requirements. *Software Development,* September.

Index